Policy Making in an Independent Judiciary

The Norwegian Supreme Court

Gunnar Grendstad, William R. Shaffer
and Eric N. Waltenburg

First published by the ECPR Press in 2015

The ECPR Press is the publishing imprint of the European Consortium for Political Research (ECPR), a scholarly association, which supports and encourages the training, research and cross-national co-operation of political scientists in institutions throughout Europe and beyond.

ECPR Press
Harbour House
Hythe Quay
Colchester
CO2 8JF
United Kingdom

Typeset by Lapiz Digital Services

Printed and bound by Lightning Source

British Library Cataloguing in Publication Data

A catalogue record for this book is available from the British Library

ISBN: 978-1-785-521-30-0
PDF ISBN: 978-1-785-521-43-0
EPUB ISBN: 978-1-785-521-44-7
KINDLE ISBN: 978-1-785-521-45-4

www.ecpr.eu/ecprpress

For my parents – offering precedents, encouraging dissent
GG

For Sydney, a most judicious partner
WRS

For my parents
ENW

Contents

List of Figures and Tables

Tables

Acknowledgements

Since 2007 we have been able to present our research on judicial behaviour on the Norwegian Supreme Court at a number of venues. These venues range from large international conferences to informal meetings and lunch seminars. We are grateful for both the constructive comments and challenging questions that we have received. Our research is better for the comments and challenges from: Jørgen Aall, Henriette Sinding Aasen, Frank Aarebrot, Michael Alvarez, Svein Tore Andersen, Iwar Arnstad, Sunniva Bragdø-Ellenes, Jan Oskar Engene, Johan Giertsen, Mark Gibney, Chris Hanretty; Eirik Holmøyvik, Benedikte Moltumyr Høgberg, Bjørn Høyland, Elisabeth Ivarsflaten, Rune Karlsen, Terje Knutsen, Åge Lind, Sam Lopeman, Anne-Mette Magnussen, Linda Sangolt, Eivind Smith, Rorie Solberg, Kristin Strømsnes, Jørn Øyrehagen Sunde, Andreas Tjernshaugen, Vibeke Wøien Hansen, and Bjarne Øymyr.

Our research project has received funding from several sources. This funding permitted us to improve data collection, hire research assistants, and present our research at various conferences. We are grateful to The Meltzer Foundation at the University of Bergen, the University of Bergen, The Faculty of Social Sciences, and the Department of Comparative Politics.

A number of historians, lawyers, justices and politicians have sat down with us for discussions and interviews. Following our agreement with them, none of the information that resulted from these meetings is translated into quotes or citations. The key actors from the Norwegian legal elite have offered insights and patiently explained procedural and legal niceties to us. We are extremely grateful for them taking time from their busy schedules. The book is better for their insights and criticism. We thank them all: Berit Reiss-Andersen, Jon Gunnar Arntzen, Kirsti Coward, Odd Einar Dørum, Sven Ole Fagernæs, Grete Faremo, Kari Gjesteby, Ketil Lund, Magnus Matningsdal, Nicolay Nyland, Erling Sandmo, Carsten Smith, Ingse Stabel, and Kåre Willoch.

A special thanks to Supreme Court justice Bård Tønder who generously commented on our paper – 'Policy making by appointment. The composition of the Norwegian Supreme Court, 1945–2009' – at a seminar at the University of Oslo Law School 12 May 2011. We are also indebted to Beate Kronen at Lovdata who gave generously of her time in teaching us how to use the rich Lovdata database on judicial decisions effectively. We are also grateful to Svein Tore Andersen at the Supreme Court of Norway's information services at The Norwegian Supreme Court for providing us with helpful information in a timely manner.

In addition we received helpful assistance when we sought information at The National Court Administration, the Norwegian Supreme Court Administration, The National Archives of Norway, The Attorney General of Civil Affairs (The Government Advocate), The Higher Prosecution Authorities (Director General of

Public Prosecutions), and The Ministry of Justice and the Police (as of 1 January 2012, renamed The Ministry of Justice and Public Security).

Gunnar Grendstad is grateful to the nearly two-dozen students who participated in his judicial behaviour classes at the Department of Comparative Politics in the spring of 2010 and 2011.

A number of students have worked as research assistants on our project, ranging from digging deep into remote library shelves and government archives to coding and punching data. Special thanks goes to Arild Een, Are Fuglehaug, Eirik Meling, Ola Randa and Anders Sondrup who contributed much to our early research efforts and thus helped our project to pick up speed. We also appreciate the research assistance of Henrik Litleré Bentsen, Kurt-Rune Bergset, Heidi Ann Bruknapp, Nesli Cin, Terje Mikal Espedal, Terje Kolbu Jacobsen, Marius Svendsen, Jon Kåre Skiple, Turid Vaage and Kristina Vikesund. We are especially grateful to five students who made an extra effort to stress test one of our earlier analyses on judicial behaviour on public economic interests versus private economic rights: Henrik Litleré Bentsen, Terje Mikal Espedal, Johan Lie Hammerstrøm, Jon Kåre Skiple and Øivind Skjervheim.

The database (*Doranoh*) we have developed as an integrated part of our research project on judicial behaviour has been approved by the The Data Protection Official for Research at the Norwegian Social Science Data Services (NSD), #23648.

Finally, we owe a debt of gratitude to Kurt-Rune Bergset and Morten Nadim for reading the whole book. They offered a number of suggestions for improvement and detected errors and mistakes. In a similar vein we also greatly appreciate the constructive comments from the publisher's anonymous referee. As elsewhere, but even more important when political scientists veer into the legal world, any errors and mistakes in the book are our responsibility.

Gunnar Grendstad, William R. Shaffer and Eric N. Waltenburg
Bergen, Santa Cruz, West Lafayette, May 2015

Preface

This research project has its genesis in a comment made during a panel on judicial decision making at the International Political Science Association's 2003 meetings in Durban, South Africa. Eric Waltenburg and Sam Lopeman, Eric's friend from their graduate school days, presented a paper and served as panel discussants at the IPSA convention. While discussing a paper on the decisional outputs of the Norwegian Supreme Court, Sam suggested that the author consider the justices' preferences and values as a possible systematic explanation for the behaviour uncovered in the paper. The notion that a justice's attitudes might bear upon his or her decisions was hardly novel to Sam and Eric. The role of attitudes in judicial behaviour has been an accepted paradigm in American political science for a very long time, so when Sam's suggestion was met by some scepticism, they were somewhat taken aback. Both being a bit bull-headed, however, they were convinced the effect of attitudes on the decisional outputs of Norwegian Supreme Court justices was an empirical puzzle worthy of analysis. And although the panel's participants told them in no uncertain terms that Norway's justices decided cases according to the law, that politics (ideology) had no place in their rulings, Sam and Eric decided to explore the role of attitudes on the votes of Norway's justices.

That empirical exploration, however, would be daunting. The problem was that neither Sam nor Eric knew much about Norwegian law and politics. Luckily, Bill Shaffer, Eric's colleague at Purdue University, had long nurtured a deep and abiding interest in all things Norwegian (he may even like lutefisk!). Upon returning to the United States, Eric related to Bill the reaction that Sam's comment had engendered. Having listened to Eric's recounting of how the Norwegian Supreme Court allegedly did not venture into the 'political thicket', Bill agreed that he should follow up while on sabbatical leave at the University of Bergen in 2006–2007. Specifically, he would investigate the proposition that politics, not simply legal reasoning, plays a key role in Norwegian judicial behaviour. He discovered immediately that (1) the Supreme Court received almost no coverage in the Norwegian press; (2) among the multitude of political scientists – faculty and graduate students alike – only one person even knew the name of the Chief Justice of the Norwegian Supreme Court; and (3) very little behavioural political science research on the Court had been published. From there, Bill asked Gunnar Grendstad from the University of Bergen if he would kindly join in the research effort. Fortunately, Gunnar acceded to his request and as a result the research flourished, culminating in this book.

Gunnar and his research assistants built the data set that is used in the analyses presented here. Its breadth and level of detail are striking. At the individual justice level, they have gathered data on almost all the decisions the Norwegian Court has handed down from the end of World War II through the first decade of the twenty-first century. To these case data and judicial outputs, they have added data concerning key attributes of the individual justices (e.g. age at the time of appointment, the partisan colour of the appointing government, place of birth, and prior occupational experience). To our knowledge, no comparable data set on judicial behaviour exists for any other court in Scandinavia. Indeed, it is not too great an exaggeration to assert that the data set used here is comparable to the better-known U.S. Supreme Court Database[1] for its richness of detail and scope of coverage.

Several additional notes on the data used here and our discussion are in order. First, for most of the statistical analyses presented in the book, we employ data that run from 1945 to 2009. Chapter Eight systematically examines the Court's judicial review decisions. Thus, the justices' votes occur in plenary sessions. These decisions do not occur with great frequency, and as a result we expand the time period of cases and votes we analyse. Accordingly, Chapter Eight concerns judicial review rulings that were handed down between 1926 and 2010. Furthermore, there are aspects in several chapters where we draw on developments, events, and data after 2009 for documentation and/or to explore further trends that had developed in the 1945 to 2009 time period. Second, this is, after all, an analysis of the behaviour of *Norwegian* Supreme Court justices. As a result, we draw heavily upon Norwegian texts. The authors are responsible for all translations from Norwegian to English. Finally, throughout the book, we note and cite Norwegian Supreme Court decisions by their official reference – e.g. Rt-2010–143 – which refers to the decision's official publication in *Norsk Retstidende* by year and first page.

---

1. Online. Available http://www.supremecourtdatabase.org (last accessed 21 November 2014).

Chapter One

Introduction: Politics and the Norwegian Supreme Court

This is a book about the Norwegian Supreme Court as an important governmental institution that plays a vital role in the political life of a country on the northern periphery of the European continent. As central as the Court is to adjudicating constitutional and significant policy questions, until very recently it has received surprisingly little popular or scholarly attention. Working largely out of public view, the justices seek to make the best legal judgments while deciding cases. The Court operates within the confines of a putatively consensual political system, and there is no evidence that the citizenry views it as anything other than a highly legitimate legal institution, simply applying the law to civil and criminal cases. Few, if any, perceive the Court as politically divisive, or even as a political institution for that matter. It simply reflects values that inform and underlie Norway's political consensus. Against this backdrop, even political scientists have paid almost no attention to the Supreme Court. There is more here than meets the eye, however. Consider, for example, a recent Court decision that reveals anything but legal consensus.

On 12 February 2010 the Court handed down its plenary decision (Rt-2010–143) in the *Ship Owner's Taxation* case. Here, the Court ruled 6–5 against the government's claim that it had the constitutional authority to levy *ex post facto* taxes to the amount of twenty-one billion kroner ($3.547 billion[1]) on the nation's ship owners. Now, this highly divided Court was not the product of pure chance. Rather, there is an ideological dimension that appears to explain the justices' decisional behaviour. Conventional wisdom tells us that on economic issues pitting public versus private interests, non-socialists are more sympathetic to private economic interests, while socialists lean towards the public position. It is therefore unlikely that mere happenstance divided the Court so that five of the seven justices appointed by socialist governments sided with the government, while all four of the justices appointed by non-socialist governments backed the ship owners. To put it bluntly, on sheer political grounds it appears that the ideological orientation of the government appointing a justice matters. But why? Did justices appointed by socialist governments receive a different legal education than those elevated to the High Court by non-socialist governments? Or were their legal interpretations informed by some ideological value preferences? However one chooses to answer these questions, the disposition of the Court was clearly

---

1. Based on the average exchange rate of 5.92 NOK/USD in February 2010. Online. Available http://www.norges-bank.no/Statistikk/Valutakurser/valuta/USD/ (last accessed 15 November 2014).

political in rendering a constitutional interpretation on an important matter of public policy.[2]

In the context of judicial behaviour, suggesting that decision making is 'political' may invite strenuous, and sometimes strained, denials. To clarify our position on this matter we allude to Hodder-Williams's (1992) six-fold nomenclature, in which a court is political in that (1) it involves 'the authoritative allocation of values' (Easton 1965); (2) it is used by people to achieve political results; (3) it is a setting in which justices try to convince colleagues to adopt their view in cases; (4) decisions often take into account likely consequences; (5) judges often stake out positions grounded in policy preferences or ideology; and (6) judicial actions can have an effect on other actors in the political system.

We contend that (1) value allocation, (2) litigants seeking outcomes, and (6) impacts on other system players are virtually given, pretty much no matter how justices behave. After all they are relevant actors in the political system. Justices move more closely to overt political behaviour when (3) they try to draw other justices to their position and (4) when they consider consequences for the broader system. However, such persuasion and assessment of impact, while political, can be rationalised in legal, rather than political, terms. In this work, we explicitly embrace (5) the notion that justices behave politically in that they act on policy preferences and ideology.

The transportability of an American model?

To assess the political behaviour of justices, we start by observing that extensive study of high courts as political institutions has been a common approach among American political scientists for decades. The *Attitudinal Model* (along with its various permutations and corrections) is one outgrowth of this analytical focus. The principal feature of this model is the empirical relationship between the ideology and policy preferences of the justices and their votes on cases heard by the Supreme Court. The notion that attitudes, rather than purely legalistic reasoning, account for much of judicial voting behaviour has found American adherents for over half a century and is arguably the current paradigm of choice *(see,* for example, Pritchett 1948; Schubert 1965; Segal and Spaeth 2002; Segal and Cover 1989; Bailey *et al.* 2005; Wahlbeck *et al.* 1998; Rohde and Spaeth 1976).[3]

The American perspective, which historically has placed a premium on ideology and partisanship in explaining judicial behaviour, is grounded not only in twentieth century research but, we contend, can be intellectually traced back to the beginnings of the Republic. Federalists and Anti-Federalists struggled mightily to define the new nation, with the former successfully reshaping government from a weak, decentralised system to a dramatically more centralised one. Anti-Federalists gave a good account of themselves, nearly thwarting this effort at nation building.

---

2. In this policy-making context we are reminded of Lasswell's definition of politics as '[w]ho gets what, when, how' (Lasswell 1936).

3. But *see* Epstein and Knight (2013).

The intense political conflict did not subside, owing to the deep division over the structure and proper role of government. Profoundly important constitutional issues continued to divide the young nation's political elite, so that by the time Thomas Jefferson won the presidential election of 1800, the 'Federalists, seeing themselves about to lose control of the Executive and Congress, proceeded to take steps to convert the Judiciary into an avowedly partisan stronghold' (Corwin 1919: 220). Or, as Gouverneur Morris, one of the framers of the American Constitution, more poetically put it: 'They are about to experience a heavy gale of adverse winds; can they be blamed for casting many anchors to hold their ship through the storm?' (Sparks 1832: 153–514; quoted in LaCroix 2010: 285). Very little has changed since then. Throughout American history, political strife over the control of the courts, with its attendant ideological ramifications, quite naturally leads many American political scientists to view judicial behaviour as largely driven by the policy preferences held by justices.

European experience with the study of courts has been very different. For the most part, social scientists expended little effort analysing the judiciary, which explains the dearth of literature on the subject. As one scholar noted recently, 'political scientists did study and compare legislative and executive bodies, but they ignored the courts' (Dyevre 2010: 298). And this makes some practical sense, inasmuch as conventional wisdom holds that 'courts and judges were outside politics' (Dyevre 2010: 298). The legal community also sought to maintain the myth of political neutrality and tended to think that the effort to account for judicial decisions 'in terms of strategic decision making and preference maximization appeared subversive'. For their part, legal academics thought it was an effort to 'undermine judicial review' (Dyevre 2010: 298). Little wonder that European courts have been the orphans of political science.[4] And yet there are good, conceptual reasons to study the Continent's high courts as political, policy-making institutions.[5]

To put the matter simply, the institutions of the American Supreme Court and its European counterparts are not completely distinct. There are a number of features of the American Supreme Court that facilitate its policy-making ability and its members' pursuit of their policy goals. These features reduce to elements of means, motives, and opportunities; and, importantly, they are present among Europe's high courts as well. To begin, the U.S. Supreme Court's powers to interpret the law and of judicial review afford it the capacity to act as a policy-making institution in the nation's political system. In other words, the institution presents its members with the means to act in pursuit of their policy preferences. With the power of interpretation, the justices can bend the law's implementation in a specific policy direction, and the exercise of the judicial veto enables the Court to act as a counter-majoritarian check. Various political interests recognise

---

4.   But *see* an early European effort to analyse judicial policy making (Volcansek 1993).

5.   Much of the discussion that follows is the product of conversations among the authors and other participants at the Judicial Politics Workshop held at the University of Bergen, June 3–5 2014. We are especially indebted to Professor Rorie Solberg.

this and can strategically locate their energies in the judicial arena either to pursue objectives frustrated in Congress, and/or to consolidate or overturn policies enacted by national law-making majorities. The litigation saga of the *Affordable Care Act* ('Obamacare') is but one recent example of this process.

To say that the U.S. Supreme Court is not the only national court with the power of interpretation is to state the obvious. Indeed, to one degree or another, it is intrinsic to the judiciary to say what the law is. Consequently, the justices of courts of other nations can bend policy as well. Neither is the power of the judicial veto unique to the U.S. Supreme Court. Many European judiciaries possess it, although its exercise is most often restricted to specialised constitutional courts (de Andrade 2001: 981). Importantly, the authority of judicial review in Europe can be more sweeping than in the United States. The German Federal Constitutional Court, for example, has the power 'to rule on the constitutionality of [all] legislative acts and executive decrees' (Rios-Figueroa and Staton 2014: 116; *see also* Gunlicks 2011: 225) *regardless of whether an actual constitutional injury occurred.* In other words, Germany's constitutional court may strike down a law 'before it has been applied' (Gunlicks 2011: 225); it has abstract and concrete judicial review authority. The U.S. Supreme Court, on the other hand, has only the latter. And one final point that is particularly relevant to European courts as political, policy-making institutions: these constitutional courts often direct the legislature how to write the legislation so that it passes constitutional muster (de Andrade 2001: 982).[6]

Along with the Supreme Court's power to 'say what the law is' (*Marbury v. Madison* 5 U.S. 137 [1803]), the Court's deep reservoir of diffuse support or institutional credibility acts as the foundation for its policy-making role. That the Court is perceived as highly legitimate helps to ensure that its policy pronouncements are accepted or at least tolerated (Clawson *et al.* 2003; Clawson and Waltenburg 2009). In other words, its legitimacy gives its interpretations and its vetoes bite.

Legitimacy is crucial to governing institutions, and courts of other nations enjoy high levels of diffuse support as well. Indeed, Gibson, Caldeira, and Baird present data reporting that five European nations' high courts possess greater average levels of diffuse support than does the U.S. Supreme Court. Moreover, Bulgaria – the nation with the lowest supreme court diffuse support score – is only 13.4 index points below the United States (Gibson *et al.* 1998: Table 5).

When it comes to motivations, a variety of explanations have been offered for a justice's decisional behaviour. Students of courts, for example, have considered a justice's role conceptions, concerns over the regard of salient audiences, the institution's reputation, and even something as banal as carving out sufficient leisure time as reasons for a justice's actions[7] (Baum 1997; Posner 2008; Epstein *et al.* 2013). Attitudinal preferences certainly must be added to this list. Indeed, it is perhaps axiomatic that individuals want to see their preferences enshrined in policy. This is

---

6. According to de Andrade, the German Constitutional Court not only has the power to veto laws that run contrary to the German Constitution; it has also declared that it can 'compel the legislature to make laws'. The Hungarian Court possesses a similar authority (de Andrade 2001: 983).

7. We discuss several of these in greater detail below.

the basic assumption of the attitudinal model, and as a motivation for the decisional behaviour of Supreme Court justices, preferences assume a certain primacy.

First, everything we know about the formation of political attitudes militates against the likelihood that these mature, highly educated members of the elite public are without preferences on the full range of social, political, and economic issues that are argued before them. Second, an awareness of these likely preferences among the relevant actors engaged in the selection process bear upon the individual's elevation to the Court.

Here again, U.S. Supreme Court justices, while perhaps an extraordinary example, are not a distinct and isolated species of judge – i.e. they are not *sui generis*. The Supreme Court justices of other nations are also drawn from the upper strata of society. They too come to the bench with lived experiences under their belts and are products of advanced legal education. And it is not unusual for them to be known to actors responsible for the selection process. In Sweden, for example, there is some indication that 'being known in government circles [...] is relevant to promotion' (Bell 2006: 249). Thus, it is quite likely that the attitudinal preferences of Europe's justices bear upon their behaviour on the bench. And if so, the attitudinal model could guide empirical research in European judicial systems as well. For instance, in Spain there is a clear political and ideological connection in the composition of the Constitutional Court, such that 'the magistrates [nominated by the legislature] are identified immediately with the party that supported them. Consequently, the Court is divided along clear political lines, leaving any contested decision by the Court open to political attack' (Lopez 2008).

At this point, we hasten to note that the attitudinal model does not assume a specific set of attitudes invariant across time and space. Partisanship, for example, may matter a great deal in the United States but may have little or no direct application to Norway and other European countries. A variety of political, economic, and social values may hold sway over the decisional behaviour of justices, even though these principles may vary from nation to nation. The point is that these values are *extra-legal*, implying that judges do not simply hold the facts up against the law and ensure that the former squares with the latter, as the 'legal model' demands.

With respect to opportunity, the U.S. Supreme Court as an institution offers its members sufficient independence to pursue their policy preferences *sincerely*. The justices are unelected and serve for terms of good behaviour. Consequently, concerns over maintaining their seat on the High Bench matter little in their decisional calculus. The Court is a highly respected co-equal constitutional institution and sits at the apex of the judiciary. Thus, there is little consideration given to career advancement. There is a very limited likelihood of the Court's articulation of policy being challenged and overturned.[8] As a result, there is little need for the justices to behave strategically vis-à-vis the other policy-making institutions (*see* Baum 1997: Table 2.1, for a list of the institutional features and their expected effects on a justice's goals and behaviour.)

---

8.   Baum notes, however, that not all scholars agree on this point (1997: 36).

It also bears mentioning that the mix of cases before the Court presents the justices with a favourable climate of circumstances to act according to their policy preferences. The Court's sweeping constitutional jurisdiction, coupled with its nearly total power to select which cases it wants to hear, results in it devoting the lion's share of its energies to those 'hard' cases where the chance to make social, economic, or political policy is most likely (*see* Baum 1997: 66 on the opportunity 'hard' cases present for justices to pursue their individual policy preferences; *see also* Stone Sweet 2000: 29).

The features of independence and jurisdiction that facilitate policy-making opportunities for U.S. justices are present for the justices of other nations' courts as well (but *see* Rios-Figueroa and Staton 2014 for a cautionary note on the degree to which institutional features yield the expected behavioural incentives). What is more, the U.S. Supreme Court does not 'set the bar' for the world's judiciaries with respect to either *de jure* (i.e. the legal or constitutional foundation for a court's independence) or *de facto* (i.e. the practical autonomy of judicial behaviour) independence (*see* Rios-Figueroa and Staton 2014; Feld and Voigt 2003). Indeed, Feld and Voigt report indices of *de jure* and *de facto* independence on which the U.S. Supreme Court ranks thirtieth out of seventy-one countries and thirty-fifth out of eighty-two countries respectively (2003: 523–6). Obviously, then, the justices of other countries have the opportunity to pursue their policy preferences.

The preceding discussion of the appropriateness of the attitudinal model to European judiciaries is, quite clearly, deliberately sketchy and not the least bit exhaustive. Our point is that grounding empirical research on other European systems in the attitudinal model should contribute to a fuller understanding of judicial behaviour than we currently enjoy. Such a research agenda requires an intensive study of each judicial system, much as we have undertaken here on the Norwegian Supreme Court. In doing so, future analyses need to be sensitive to the unique legal cultures in any given country, much as we have done in the present analysis (Nylund 2010; Sunde 2014).

The case for Norway

Having made the case that the means, motives, and opportunities are present for European justices to act according to their policy preferences, the reader may still wonder why we would study the Norwegian Supreme Court, but be too polite to ask. So we will pose the questions ourselves. What is the value of examining the Norwegian judicial process? What exactly does this particular case study bring to the table? We contend that that these traits of European courts in general are true of Norway in particular. When, in the middle of the twentieth century, Norwegian historian Jens Arup Seip (1964) proclaimed that the Norwegian Supreme Court was a 'political organ', he seemed to gain little traction among his fellow scholars. Certainly, Norwegian political scientists appear not to have taken this characterisation to heart, at least not if one goes on the basis of most of the extant literature and university textbooks, neither of which provide a thorough understanding of the place of the judiciary in the broader political system. Yet, contemporary European social scientists seem to have at least waded into the conceptual Rubicon and (re)discovered courts as political institutions. Undoubtedly, a systematic study of the decisional behaviour of the Norwegian Supreme Court should be included as part of this larger movement.[9]

Norway is also an example of a region at the northern European periphery, which is connected in its politics, culture and history (Einhorn and Logue 2003). Each Scandinavian country can be labelled a 'consensual democracy', a type of democracy that 'emphasizes consensus instead of opposition, that includes rather than excludes, and that tries to maximize the size of the ruling majority instead of being satisfied with a bare majority' (Lijphart 1984: 23). Without question, we can say that Scandinavia has been governed in a fashion that has been consensual. To be sure, other European nations could be placed in that category as well. Two factors, however, distinguish Scandinavian consensual democracy from other European democracies: '(1) the political success of the Social Democrats and (2) the policies pursued by Social Democratic governments since the Great Depression' (Einhorn and Logue 2003: 173).

For approximately a quarter of a century after World War II, the northern periphery was home to consensual welfare states. The governing style that evolved – often referred to as a 'Middle Way', incorporating both socialist and free market principles – received broad support across all sectors of society. Scandinavian governance reflected the notion that the 'more consensual the democracy, the more it tends towards depoliticization; the more dissensual, the more towards destabilization' (Elder *et al.* 1988: 9). Concentration of policy making seemed to be a sure-fire way to 'depoliticise' the system.

In Norway, little conflict or 'dissensus' was in evidence until the early 1970s, after which time Labour Party dominance was on the wane. The post-1970 years have witnessed increased division on a number of vital issues, not the least of which was the narrow defeat of two hotly contested referenda on European Union membership. Even when the EU was off the front burner, though, other salient issues such as taxation, environmental protection, and immigration divided both voters and elected officials.

In summary, the Norwegian Supreme Court suffers (or benefits) from the same kind of inattention extended to judicial systems across Europe. At the same time, as a previously consensual Scandinavian country, Norway has seen the collapse of a post-World War II political consensus that is characterised by increased conflict. As an example of both Europe in general and Scandinavia in particular, our intensive case study should help fill a sizeable gap in our knowledge of judicial decision making, and suggest lines of research on other courts, especially those in the other Scandinavian nations.

---

9. A discussion that will surface several times in this book is the degree to which theories developed on the basis of the U.S. legal system and U.S. Supreme Court can be transferred and applied to a Norwegian context. Johs. Andenæs once stated that American experience is instructive because in its enlarged form it illustrates problems that in Norway are more hidden (in Smith 1975: 301). *See also* the debate between Jørn Øyrehagen Sunde and the authors (Grendstad *et al.* 2012b; Sunde 2012).

Theoretical foundation

As the *Ship Owner's Taxation* case indicates, the Court addresses important constitutional and policy questions, and its rulings seem to be grounded, at least in part, in the ideological values of the justices. In this book we shall claim, as others have done before us, that justices have preferences about public policy, and that their behaviour on the bench to a significant degree reflects those dispositions. Indeed, we could go so far as to assume that justices actively pursue policy goals. Yet, we recognise that the value preferences of justices do not account for the totality of judicial decision-making behaviour. As James Gibson puts it, justices' 'decisions are a function of what they prefer to do, tempered by what they think they ought to do, but constrained by what they perceive is feasible to do' (Gibson 1983: 9). In other words, judicial behaviour is a complex brew of individual preferences, role expectations, and institutional constraints.

In any event, conventional wisdom regarding the judicial decision-making process in Norway places substantial emphasis upon only one of these ingredients – the institutional constraints that courts, as legal institutions steeped in 'the law' and precedent, impose upon the decisional behaviour of the justices. For the most part, the Norwegian legal community embraces the image of the justice rising above personal prejudice in order to decide a case purely on its legal merits (Mathiesen 1997). Doctrine and precedent, legislative intent, textualism, and the intent of the framers of the Constitution guide the justices' decisions, not their individual value preferences. In short, justices are *initially* taken to be objective, impartial umpires who simply hold up the facts against the law and render just decisions to resolve the cases they have decided to hear.

Embracing this perspective denotes an acceptance of the 'legal model', which asserts that justices arrive at decisions by relying upon the 'plain meaning' of the law (Segal and Spaeth 1993; Richards and Kritzer 2002; Kritzer and Richards 2005). Presumably, such a decision-making orientation immunises a justice from yielding to any personal biases he or she internalised in a previous existence. Freed from the influence that personal policy preferences may exert in the deliberative process, the justice can focus all of his or her energies on the plain meaning of the law.

A number of established legal principles ostensibly lift the justice above base attitudinal preferences when deciding a case. Reliance upon precedent, for instance, is thought to foster a measure of objectivity, inasmuch as the ruling is grounded in settled law, which may have been established before any or all of the Court's incumbents were elevated to the bench (*see* Segal and Spaeth 2002: 49,76). Simply put, if a court decides to adjudicate a dispute, the facts of which are fundamentally the same as those in the case establishing a precedent, all the justices have to do is determine whether the facts are indeed the same, and then invoke the pre-existing legal principle of *stare decisis* – stand by the decided law. Arguably, justices can leave their value preferences at the courtroom door, and mechanically invoke precedent to impartially decide the outcome of a case.

Another method of adjudication, which could enable the justice to behave as a neutral arbiter, focuses upon the *intent of legislators* who crafted the law in question. Rather than impose their personal biases upon the litigants, a judge would defer to the language of the relevant statute and its accompanying preparatory works to render a legally sound decision. Surely there is a wealth of information both in the law and material pertinent to the formulation of the final statute passed by the legislature, and justices could predicate their decision on statutory material and legislative intent. Taken a bit further, Alexander Hamilton, contemplating the yet to be installed American judiciary, made it quite plain that courts should not 'substitute their own pleasure to that of the legislative body' (Wills 1988: 396).

By extension, justices can, and arguably should, rely upon the meaning of the country's constitution and the intent of its framers when reviewing a law. After all, a nation's constitution is fundamental law, and as such it must always trump a law or act that is in violation of it. Thus, the role of the judicial agent is simply 'to lay the article of the Constitution which is invoked beside the statute which is challenged and decide whether the latter squares with the former' (*U.S. v. Butler* 297 U.S. 1, 62 [1935]). Certainly, there is no paucity of historical documentation, scholarship and expert commentary offered up by the jurisprudential intelligentsia to assist in sorting out constitutional principles. There is neither room nor need for the influence of personal preferences in the adjudicative process.

To sum up, the long-standing *legal model* of judicial decision making provides the tools of conventional legal analysis to render judgments that do not degenerate into contentious political battles. To explicate the plain meaning of the law, justices have at their disposal precedent, legislative intent, the text of the Constitution, and the intentions of its framers as means to arrive at an objective, dispassionate legal ruling. By all indications, whether through literature and legal texts, Norwegian Supreme Court justices, indeed the bulk of the Norwegian legal community, embrace this model of the judicial process. Indeed, until the 1960s the law and practice were the primary, indeed only, formalised elements of the Norwegian legal method (Michalsen 1994). While not disputing the value of this form of legal reasoning, we wish to analyse the behaviour of Norwegian Supreme Court justices from a rather different perspective, namely through a modified *attitudinal model* (or 'motivational model', *see* Epstein and Knight 2013) of judicial decision making.

In simple, unambiguous terms, the attitudinal model assumes the decisions justices make are largely explained by their fundamental political attitudes. This especially would be the case when focusing attention upon the highest court in the land, which deals with the most important legal issues in a country. Consider with whom we are dealing. Supreme Court justices are intelligent, highly educated, politically informed legal experts and practitioners. They are not blank slates; they know who they are and what they stand for. We contend that their political preferences inform their behaviour on the bench. Some go so far as to portray judges as 'single-minded seekers of legal policy' (George and Epstein 1992).

If the attitudinal model is at the core of our explanation, how do we square its theoretical perspective with the key features of the legal model? For example, settled law can shape judicial decision making for significant periods of time through the precedents enshrined in any given legal regime (Kritzer and

Richards 2005; Richards and Kritzer 2002). By relying on principles established in prior cases, justices appear to be grounding their decisions on principles they may not have even had a role in formulating. However, the apparent objectivity may only serve to mask the value preferences upon which a court case is decided. Presumably, precedent is invoked when a case is similar to one in which the precedent was established. Of course, similarity of case circumstances is not always an easy call to make. Moreover, justices may have quite a number of precedents from which to select.[10] We contend that deciding which precedent to apply and whether or not that precedent fits the case under review is predicated upon a justice's political preferences (Segal and Spaeth 1996a; Segal and Spaeth 1996b; Segal and Spaeth 2002).

Eschewing personal bias by shifting the basis for a court decision to the intention of the framers of the constitution is something of a legal sleight of hand. Presumably, one can infer intention from records created at the time of a constitutional convention, but these are incomplete at best, and piecing together bits and pieces of evidence may not produce a clear picture of just exactly what was the collective intent of the founding fathers (Segal and Spaeth 2002). So, we imagine that the justices can choose the intent of the constitutional delegate that supports his or her preferred interpretation. Clearly, pretty much the same thing can be said of the intent of legislators who push a bill through the parliament. After all, MPs may support a piece of legislation for a number of different reasons. Whose intent is the salient one, and what can we say about the collective intention of the body as a whole? Regarding the applicability of the legal model, we would simply say that the 'plain meaning' of the law, whether rationalised on the basis of such principles as precedent or intent, is the 'plain *political* meaning' of the law.

Moreover, the legal model leaves plenty of room for a variety of extra-legal forces to enter into the decisional process.

Ideology and partisanship

Of the extra-legal forces we would include under the aegis of the attitudinal model, perhaps the most important is the set of core values comprised in one's world view, i.e. ideology. If, for example, justices harbour socialist values regarding the proper role of government, then surely they would either actively pursue leftist policy goals, or be predisposed to see the world through a socialist lens. On the other hand, conservative justices would lend support to more right-of-centre policies, or again, see cases through conservative eyes. It does not require a stroll along the road to Damascus to have one's eyes opened to the role of ideology in judicial deliberations.

There is a dearth of information available on the party identification and ideology of the justices sitting on Norway's highest bench, but a bit of

---

10. A recent development on the court is the practice of the parties' advocates submitting their briefs to the justices before the oral hearings. The briefs bring relevant legal sources to the justices' attention, including precedents (Schei 2008).

anecdotal evidence is at least suggestive. Consider, for example, Ingse Stabel. Analyses of non-unanimous plenary decisions handed down between 2000 and 2007 showed that Associate Justice Stabel was among those who tended to support what is defined as the 'public', rather than private economic interests (Grendstad *et al.* 2010). A follow-up analysis of the Court's purely economic decisions showed that she also had the most pro-public economic sector voting record (Grendstad *et al.* 2011). If Stabel's location in ideological space as inferred from the 2000–2007 non-unanimous plenary session votes indicates a pro-public ideology on a left-right economic dimension, we would assume that she sided with the government in the *Ship Owner's Taxation* case. And she did.

While there is little information about a justice's party affiliation or ideology, Stabel's votes on Supreme Court cases appear to be understandable, given some aspects of her background. She was appointed to the Supreme Court by a government headed by Jens Stoltenberg, and it was Stoltenberg's red-green coalition government that was the government party in the *Ship Owner's Taxation* case. Looking back four decades, Stabel was an activist in the new feminist movement (Bjerck 2006), which is surely an indicator of early leftist sentiments. Fast forwarding to the new millennium, she headed the 'Stabel Committee', which was charged with reviewing collective bargaining practices. Among the Committee's recommendations were proposals to strengthen the government's role in the negotiating process (Eurofound 2001). Finally, she is an Oslo native, and findings suggest that this predisposes a justice to support the government in cases that regard public versus private economics (Grendstad *et al.* 2010, 2011).

Employing these (not so) unobtrusive measures of ideology, we would be a bit surprised if she were to discern the same 'plain meaning' of the Constitution in the *Ship Owner's Taxation* case as Justice Jens Edvin A. Skoghøy. Skoghøy was the most supportive of private economic interests in the analysis of rulings involving economic disputes during the 2000–2007 period (Grendstad *et al.* 2011). Skoghøy is from the periphery of the country. He was born in Tromsø, and after earning a Cand. Jur. Degree at the University of Oslo, he returned to the periphery to practice law. Eventually, he received a Dr. Juris. Deg. from the University of Tromsø, after which he served on the Tromsø law faculty until he was appointed to the Supreme Court in 1998. Again, if – as earlier votes suggest – Skoghøy is right-of-centre on public–private economic disputes through 2007, we would expect him to side with the ship owners. And he did. Thus, scant anecdotal evidence suggests that Stabel and Skoghøy may interpret the Constitution differently, at least in part because they are located at different points along an ideological spectrum.[11] To modify and apply a pithy conceptual explanation of the attitudinal model (*see* Segal and Spaeth 1993: 65) to the Norwegian Supreme Court, 'Skoghøy votes the way he does because he is conservative; Stabel votes the way she does because she is liberal'.

---

11. Indeed, that is what we found when we in 2011 asked a sample of 163 Norwegian Supreme Court lawyers to place the twenty-four justices and two interim justices on a left–right scale (Grendstad *et al.* 2012a). *See* the Appendices.

Background

While by no means distinct from ideological proclivities, as we intimate above, the socioeconomic backgrounds of justices shape their views on political conflict. For example, occasional differences among Norwegian Supreme Court justices can be observed for those with Oslo residence and those ascending to the Bench from other parts of the country (Grendstad *et al.* 2010; 2011). In the Norwegian context, this would not be at all surprising in light of Stein Rokkan's (1967) seminal work on political divisions observed along a centre-periphery dimension. Moreover, an empirical case can be made that the jurisprudential community huddled together in and around a nation's capital may be a tight-knit elite (McGuire 1993), and by extension, one that could share professional values.

Another background factor that might influence the adjudication of a case is the gender of the justice. Norway, like other nations, placed women in its High Court rather belatedly. Arguably, the experiences of women and men may be sufficiently different to instil somewhat different perspectives that may be salient for some disputes. Such an extra-legal force would be attitudinal in nature, and not an extension of purely legal reasoning.

And then there are other professional backgrounds and the concomitant life experiences that might predispose justices to decide cases differently (Tate 1981; Tate and Sittiwong 1989; Tate and Handberg 1991; Lazarsfeld *et al.* 1944). A non-trivial number of justices have ascended to the High Bench (either as interim or permanent appointees) after toiling in the Legislative Department of the Government's Ministry of Justice (*Lovadelingen*). And since the 1970s, more justices have been drawn from the ranks of academia, particularly the nation's law schools.

Audience

An intriguing extra-legal force modifying or reinforcing a justice's attitudinal predispositions are the audiences most salient to them, a theoretical perspective nicely explicated by Baum (2008). This framework assumes that people want to be 'liked and respected' – an impulse that applies to judges and that influences their behaviour. Justices do not expect universal adoration, focusing instead on a number of personally relevant audiences. They may seek approval from specific segments of society, perhaps an interest group, other lawyers and judges, certain partisans and ideologues, or they may be influenced by the political milieu of the nation's capital.

One way to approach the impact of audiences is to think in terms of judges' social networks, both in terms of their connections in the context of face-to-face interaction with valued individuals, and in terms of reference groups whose favour they seek to curry. An example of such activity may reinforce the core-periphery effect referred to above. Justices from Oslo might have been socialised by virtue of growing up in the nation's capital, but they also may be part of a socio-political network that includes audiences by whom they seek to be 'liked and respected'.

They may desire the approval of like-minded lawyers and judges, government officials, university law professors, or for that matter the general public. In the last instance, justices may seek to act in such a way as to foster the trust of the citizenry, the basis for a court's legitimacy (Clawson and Waltenburg 2009; Skiple *et al.* 2013).

Public opinion

When the focus of attention is on a court about which few people have much factual knowledge, the impact of public opinion upon judicial attitudes and behaviour is murky at best. As appointed officials, Norwegian Supreme Court justices serve without ever having to face the voters. Thus, there is little incentive for them to actively consider the sentiments of the voting public. Elected officials may be motivated to sift meticulously through public opinion surveys in an effort to divine whether or not they are in the good graces of the masses, and then scurry about appealing to likely voters. Norway's justices are spared this potential ignominy. They serve until the age of seventy without ever having to face the spectre of the public in a re-election campaign. Other than the Baum hypothesis that judges – along with Aretha Franklin, Rodney Dangerfield, and humans in general – just want a little respect, there may not be reason for them to court public opinion.

However, to say that public opinion, especially as mediated through the electoral process, is of no consequence is wide of the mark. Consider the simple diagram depicted in Figure 1.1, on which the public has an indirect effect upon Court behaviour. Few would quibble with the immediate and direct impact voters have on the subsequent government (path a), and we contend that the sitting government, in turn, appoints justices who tend to be more compatible with the party (or parties) controlling government than the opposition parties (path b). Indeed, as we show in Chapters Two and Four, the type of appointing government partially determines the ideological composition of the Court on some important questions of public policy (Grendstad *et al.* 2010; 2011).

Figure 1.1: Effect of Public Mood on Decisional Behaviour

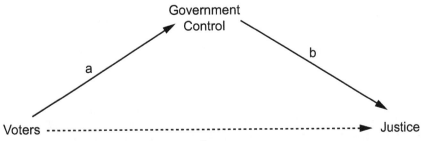

Regarding path c, we expect a fairly weak direct effect of the public on judicial behaviour, as indicated by the dotted line. We leave open the possibility that Norwegian justices may be affected by mass preference when deciding on cases. For example, justices may choose to view the general public as one of their audiences (Baum 2008). Certainly in the American context, there is evidence that Supreme Court justices respond directly to public opinion, even though they are not dependent upon voters to keep them on the bench (Mishler and Sheehan 1993; Flemming and Wood 1997; McGuire and Stimson 2004; but *see* Norpoth and Segal 1994). In any case, we hypothesise that public opinion will directly influence, at least modestly, Court behaviour, even when justices realise that they operate in virtual secrecy.[12]

Equitable consideration

Although the Norwegian legal community, by and large, appears to embrace the legal model as the operative paradigm (Magnussen 2005; Doublet and Bernt 1992), there is ample evidence that the attitudinal model is more helpful in explaining the decision-making behaviour of Supreme Court justices. We have already suggested how the attitudinal model can account for the 'plain meaning' of the law. However, we would also note that some decisions in the Norwegian Supreme Court are justified already on the basis of 'equitable consideration' (Magnussen 2005; Doublet and Bernt 1992; Eckhoff and Helgesen 2001), a doctrine of 'fairness' that enables justices to base rulings on changing political and social conditions (Eckhoff 1971). The student of judicial behaviour might ask: How do judges determine what is fair and equitable without basing their conclusions on political or ideological values?

Norwegian adherents of the Legal Model view with some alarm the potential for politicising the Court, with 'equitable considerations' being the camel's nose under the tent. Some have argued that this doctrine enables bad behaviour in that judges can substitute their own value preferences for sound legal reasoning (Askeland 2003). Indeed, if the Court becomes more politicised through an increased reliance upon equitable considerations, outcomes may be far less predictable than one can expect from more formal legal reasoning (Kinander 2002). Moreover, there is concern that the doctrine binds the Court to conventional politics in a way that produces a 'politically correct and unsophisticated form of armchair speculation' (Bergo 2002: 953, quoted in Askeland 2003: 20).

Our take is that separating fairness in light of the political and social context from judicial decisions is a Sisyphean task, inasmuch as some Norwegian Supreme Court justices allow that personal opinions do come into play in their deliberations. Included in that group of jurists are ex-justice Georg Fredrik

---

12. This, of course, is not to suggest that the Court's actions always occur out of the public's eye. Consider, for example, the media attention given to the plenary *Kløfta* case (Rt-1976–1), *Ship Owner's Taxation* case (Rt-2010–143), and the *Verona* and *Shabazi* cases (Rt-2012–2039 and Rt-2012–1985).

Rieber-Mohn (Kristjánsson 2010), Justice Wilhelm Matheson (Rønning 2009), Chief Justice Tore Schei (2009), and Justice Kirsti Coward (Gjerstad 2010). Some careful observers of Norwegian jurisprudence have expressed alarm at the prospect of what in their view would be an undue emphasis on 'equitable considerations'.

> If equitable considerations were allowed to pre-empt more formal legal reasoning, this would mean *demolishing the legal system* as such. If a judge emphasizes equitable considerations, it means that he or she no longer bases his or her judgments on established legal rules and interpretations of law, but on the consideration of complex questions of rationality, justice and expediency (Magnussen 2005: 71, italics added).

But alas, justices can cherry-pick 'established legal rules', and 'interpretations of the law' are not always shared across justices, but are subject to the judges' value preferences.

In the final analysis, then, even a near religious commitment to the legal model would not keep the attitudinal genie in the bottle. After all, justices are appointed, not elected, and serve as long as their behaviour does not create visions of impeachment in the heads of those who would seek their removal.[13] What is to prevent justices from voting their preferences cloaked in legalese (Hall 1987, 1992, 1995; Staats and Percival 2010)? These independent political actors, serving on the court of last resort, have the final say over major public policy questions and constitutional principles, and they have great discretion over whether to even hear a case. All this creates opportunities to infuse their own value preferences into the deliberative process. That ideological predispositions are in play is reflected in the non-trivial number of non-unanimous rulings emanating from the Supreme Court.

Embellishments

While there is a consensus among political scientists that judicial decisions are made on the basis of justices' policy preferences, we hasten to point out that the pursuit of policy preferences by judges is neither automatic nor mechanical, any more than the behaviour the rudimentary Legal Model of judicial decision making envisions. As political actors, judges may on occasion appear to behave in a manner that is inconsistent with their ideological proclivities. For example, they may behave strategically rather than 'sincerely', if they cannot achieve their policy ideal. Such behaviour is consistent with the Attitudinal Model, providing a richer and more complete explication of the process.

---

13. In 2013, in the case of the *Government v. Judge Tor Bertelsen*, the Oslo District Court ruled that Bertelsen of Bergen District Court should be dismissed because he was unfit to be a judge (TOSLO-2012-144087). This was the first dismissal of a judge in Norway since 1945. In September 2013, Judge Bertelsen appealed the decision, but in July 2014, the Borgarting Appeals Court upheld the Oslo District Court decision (LB-2013-171610-2). In November 2014, the Supreme Court rejected Bertelsen's appeal (HR-2014-2174-U).

Judicial behaviouralists do not share a dominant paradigm, and their differing tastes seem to lead us in a number of different directions simultaneously. One disciplinary sect favours a rational choice framework, which ostensibly provides an integrated, comprehensive, and more scientific model of political behaviour – of which judicial decision making is a type. In the most thorough rational choice theory explication of U.S. Supreme Court actions, the attitudinal model is deemed less than satisfying, in part due to a lack of conceptual clarity. Simply put, is the Attitudinal Model based upon a stimulus response psychological metaphor, or a rational choice one (Hammond *et al.* 2005)? That conceptual confusion prompts Hammond and his co-authors to develop a classical rational choice model that pays attention to strategic behaviour among justices at five basic stages of Supreme Court action – docketing, the initial vote taken in conference, the majority opinion assignment, coalition building, and the final vote on a case's merits (Hammond *et al.* 2005).

In another – less formal but equally impressive – treatment of strategic behaviour, Epstein and Knight (1998) assert that justices 'are unconstrained actors who make decisions based only on their own ideological attitudes' (Epstein and Knight 1998: 10). They too incorporate a variety of strategic actions that can move a justice away from his or her favoured position on a case. Strategic maneuvers can include such actions as adopting a somewhat less attractive stance in order to gain support of other justices, and taking into account other institutional actors, such as Congress and the president (Epstein *et al.* 2013). The Epstein-Knight treatment of strategic behaviour does not adopt the normally restrictive rational choice assumption that judges are 'single-minded seekers of policy'. Instead, they prefer a more nuanced assumption, namely that 'a major goal of all justices is to see the law reflect their preferred policy positions, and they will take actions to advance this objective' (Epstein and Knight 1998: 11).

For some critical observers, the Attitudinal Model myopically presumes that judges 'cast votes and write opinions that perfectly reflect their own views, regardless of what their court colleagues and other policymakers might do in response' (Baum 2008: 7). As stated above, we argue here for a 'modified' Attitudinal Model in which a justice's ideological or policy preference is the central feature (*see also* Epstein and Knight 2013). In our estimation, a strategic or rational choice component is merely a refinement of the most rudimentary assumption that judges act in a manner consistent with their ideology or policy preferences. The idea that justices need to take into account the positions of other political actors is hardly grounds for setting aside the basic attitudinal model. Instead, we see it as a valuable elaboration of the basic tenets of the attitudinal model.

Another fairly recent theoretical embellishment (re)introduces legal reasoning into the decision-making process, but not in any kind of mechanistic fashion. Specifically, a 'jurisprudential regime' may enshrine a legal precedent that 'structures the way in which the Supreme Court justices evaluate key elements of cases in arriving at decisions in a particular legal area' (Richards and Kritzer 2002: 1308). In an effort to move beyond the earlier legal model elements of 'plain meaning, precedent, or intent of the drafters' (Kritzer and Richards 2005: 134), jurisprudential regimes include precedents, while reflecting the policy preferences of those justices creating a precedent, affect the deliberations of other justices, as well as those who enunciated the principle in the first place (Richards and Kritzer 2002). Richards and Kritzer have reported findings that demonstrate a significant impact made by jurisprudential regimes.

We take this as a valuable corrective to the Attitudinal Model. To be sure, lawyers, judges, and legal scholars have cause to be sceptical of a claim that legal reasoning is of no meaningful consequence. They were trained in the law and spend entire careers applying legal principles to emergent cases. From their perspective the point of their profession is to apply the law to legal disputes in a reasoned fashion. Members of the jurisprudential community understandably cringe at the thought that court behaviour can be reduced to crass political preference. In our view the concept of jurisprudential regimes accommodates the potential of a predominantly legal factor to affect a case, even though ideological values may influence decision-making behaviour as well.

As with rational choice theory and strategic behaviour, jurisprudential regimes were not brought down from Mount Sinai on stone tablets. On the contrary, they were determined by the value preferences of an earlier court, or at least by a majority of justices serving on an earlier court. To be sure, the value preferences of judges may exhibit the most important impact on judicial decision making, but incorporating strategic behaviour and legal regimes into our model adds to our ability to account for Supreme Court decisions. In the final analysis, rational choice modelling, strategic behaviour, and legal regimes simply provide us with a more nuanced and fully developed Attitudinal Model.

A dangerous branch?

If justices decide cases on the basis of ideology, as the Attitudinal Model envisions, will the judiciary forfeit its status as the 'least dangerous' branch of government? Observing U.S. Senate Judiciary Committee confirmation hearings in the post-Bork period would suggest that whether the nominee was an 'activist' or a 'strict constructionist' (code phrases for liberal or conservative) judge would determine the course of public policy for years to come. Senate members of the minority party can become nearly apoplectic, especially if the ideological balance on the Supreme Court would shift in their least favoured direction. Many hope that any such transformation would lead to favoured policy outcomes in a variety of areas, including abortion, civil rights, regulation of the financial sector, campaign finance, religion, and the death penalty. For many, 'legislating' from the bench is an onerous usurpation of power.

Although the High Court could privilege some policy interests at the expense of others, we must be mindful of the limits within which 'political' decision making must operate. We could point to any number of landmark cases in the U.S. that smacked of Supreme Court 'activist' policy making. *Brown v. Board of Education* (347 U.S. 483 [1954]) and *Roe v. Wade* (410 U.S. 113 [1973]) would seem prototypical, but even these cases are not 'slam dunks'. While newly discovered constitutional interpretations appear to craft public policy – undoubtedly a plausible inference – there are sceptics. For example, one such denier of courts as policymakers boldly states that

> Even when major cases are won, the achievement is often more symbolic than real. Thus, courts may serve an ideological function of luring movements for social reform to an institution that is structurally constrained from serving their needs, providing only an illusion of change (Rosenberg 2008: 427).

By this account, activists would be wise not to waste scarce resources on litigation and direct them to political action instead (Rosenberg 2008). Civil rights and women's rights were advanced most fundamentally by political action, not by Supreme Court proclamation. After all, the High Court lacks the ability to administer a policy (Rosenberg 2008).

A historically powerful case in point is the *Cherokee Nation v. State Of Georgia* (30 U.S. 1 [1831]) Supreme Court ruling. The Cherokee Nation sought to prevent the state of Georgia from removing them from their lands. John Marshall's Supreme Court supported the Indians' claim. When expected to follow the Court's ruling, however, President Andrew Jackson, upset with the Court's decision, supposedly said, 'John Marshall has made his decision, now let him enforce it' (Curry *et al.* 2008: 228). Extreme as Jackson's response may have been, it nicely underscores the Court's limits, and careful observers know full well that the Court needs to pay attention to other political institutions when handing down rulings (Epstein and Knight 1998; Epstein and Segal 2007).

With respect to the Norwegian Supreme Court, we may not expect quite the same flair in a culture given to collective humility. In the Court's decision in the *Medical Record* case (Rt-1977–1035), for instance, there were no statutes that governed a patient's right to gain access to her own records. The Court's decision could go either way. But writing for the unanimous Court, Justice Elisabeth Schweigaard Selmer – although she did not use this term explicitly – emphasised equitable considerations and ruled in favour of the plaintiff's rights (Eckhoff and Helgesen 2001: 390f). It was an unprecedented decision. But the outcome correlated with legislative bills on patients' rights that were percolating through the two other branches of government.

Nevertheless, the proper distribution of power among the institutions of government is a legitimate concern in any democratic nation. If, as we theorise, judicial decision making is primarily driven by ideology and policy preferences, then does the Norwegian Supreme Court legislate from the bench? If it aggressively pursues policy goals, has the Supreme Court, as a non-elective body, overstepped its bounds? We would counsel against the view that the Court is a *politically unconstrained* player. At the same time, however, it is at least a participant in handing down decisions that identify winners and losers. We take the position, then, that the Norwegian Supreme Court is a 'political organ', but not a 'dangerous' one.

The invisible hand of justice

Notwithstanding any debate over the real power of a high court, given that a number of attitudes and extra-legal background factors inform judicial decisions on vitally important constitutional and policy questions (*see*, for example, George and Epstein 1992; Tate 1981; Tate and Sittiwong 1989; Tate and Handberg 1991; Ulmer 1962, 1970, 1973; Goldman 1966, 1975; Gryski and Main 1986; Nagel 1961; Lloyd 1995), we are perplexed by the extent to which the Norwegian Supreme Court operates in a political shadow. The citizenry appears almost oblivious to the vital political role played by the Court and, in fact, possesses very little knowledge of the Court.[14] While people have an awareness of the *Storting* (the Parliament) and the prime minister, there is something of an informational black hole when it comes to judicial policy making.

That Supreme Court justices render important judgments out of the limelight may be a result of a lack of focus on judicial behaviour on the part of political scientists and journalists. The popular press column inches devoted to the decisions of the Court have been spare, and social scientists have not produced a surfeit of scholarly work on the topic. Indeed, the Court does not register with the scholarly community to any great extent. Not long ago, the authors asked a sizeable number of Norwegian political scientists who was the Chief Justice of the Norwegian Supreme Court. Only one correctly identified Tore Schei as the incumbent of that role, and virtually all others could not even venture a guess. While this may appear to the reader as a benign parlour game, there are some potentially important ramifications of the invisibility of the hand of justice.

Although important policy and constitutional issues may hinge on the composition of the Court, one could not tell this from the media coverage of the appointment process. The recruitment of Norwegian Supreme Court justices appears to prompt a collective yawn from the media. A clear example occurred during the late spring of 2010, when four candidates applied for the two recent openings on the Court, while President Barack Obama nominated a justice to the U.S. Supreme Court. The media's attention was on the latter, and not the former.

Since members of the Norwegian Supreme Court are prohibited from serving past the age of seventy, there is no real reason that the media would be caught unawares of impending vacancies. Anyone paying attention would have known that Justices Kirsti Coward and Karin Bruzelius would be turning seventy in late 2010 and early 2011, respectively. So, the Court Administration announced the two openings on the Court in the national media on 31 March and again on 4 April 2010, stipulating a 3 May application deadline. Even a casual observer would know from previous practice that the list of applicants would be announced on the Court Administration's website within a week or so after the deadline. Although this stage of the recruitment process was very public, the media – perhaps reflecting the general indifference toward the Court – saw little reason to spill much ink on the selection of two new Supreme Court justices.

---

14. Admittedly, the American mass public knows very little about its far more visible Court.

Oddly enough, whereas there were no references in the Norwegian media to the fact that there would be changes on the *Norwegian* court, Norwegian newspapers ran five stories about an opening on the *U.S.* Supreme Court, this at a time when the two recruitment processes were taking place almost simultaneously. Then, on Friday 7 May, the Norwegian Court Administration posted on its website the names of the four applicants to the two openings on the court. Listed in the order given by the Court Administration and with a brief rundown of their professional backgrounds, the applicants were Henrik Bull, Morten Holmboe, Ragnhild Noer, and Knut M. Kallerud. Three days later President Obama announced that he was nominating U.S. Solicitor General, Elana Kagan, one of a handful of candidates that the American media had already speculated would be on the president's shortlist, as the next Supreme Court associate justice. In the wake of these announcements, there was one article in *Dagens Næringsliv* on the Norwegian applicants three days after they were identified, while the very day after the Kagan nomination was announced, there were six (!) articles in Norwegian newspapers.

It bears noting that the elevation of Kristin Normann and Aage Thor Falkanger to the Supreme Court by the King in Council on the very day the landmark *Ship Owner's Taxation* case was publicised – while perhaps nothing more than a curiosity to be included in the Norwegian edition of Trivial Pursuit – juxtaposes the selection of judicial elites and a constitutional ruling freighted with ideological substance. Why did neither the media, legal scholars, nor political scientists make the connection? There is one to be made. By way of contrast, no one seems to miss the association when the president of the United States announces a U.S. Supreme Court nominee. Much is at stake. Will the new appointee alter the ideological balance of the Court? If so, the long knives may be drawn during the Senate Judiciary Committee confirmation hearings. Even when the new justice to be does not affect the Court's ideological majority, given the level of political polarisation in American politics, nominees these days feel the need to be circumspect before the Judiciary Committee, if not downright evasive. One slip could cost them the opportunity of a lifetime. While Kagan was cautious in answering Judiciary Committee questions, she was fairly candid when asked by Senator Klobuchar (D-MN) if she thought that Supreme Court justices should act as 'umpires'. Kagan did not fully embrace this baseball metaphor, indicating that she did not think that the 'law is a kind of robotic enterprise' with an 'automatic quality to it'. She went on to say that 'not every case is decided 9–0', and that many of these cases 'frequently [involved] clashes of constitutional values'.[15]

Ignoring for a moment the fact that baseball is a strange, foreign sport rarely played in the Scandinavian periphery, we are not persuaded that Norwegian Supreme Court justices are any more 'robotic' than their American counterparts. Furthermore, an increasing number of cases are not unanimous, and those can and do reflect 'clashes of constitutional values'. For whatever reasons, the Norwegian

---

15. The Kagan quotations were recorded in the transcript of the third day of her hearings before the Senate Judiciary Committee.

judiciary is a blind spot both for political scientists, who do not cover it in government textbooks, and journalists, who energetically cover an array of other political events, which are occasionally of less importance than Court actions. When Georg Fredrik Rieber-Mohn, former Director General of The Higher Prosecution authorities as well as Supreme Court justice, stepped down as justice in 2007 due to health problems, he reminisced that the media that had trailed him as Director General would disappear when he entered the Supreme Court: 'No journalist seems to pay attention to the Supreme Court in any systematic way', Rieber-Mohn said (Rønning 2007).

We are not intimating that Norway should adopt the three-ring circus antics of the American judicial appointment process. Notwithstanding senatorial theatrics, U.S. Supreme Court appointments *are* an extremely serious matter, and much is at stake politically. The American system is one of separation of powers (or, separated institutions sharing powers), with explicit checks and balances among the branches of government. The fact that legislative confirmation hearings are an integral part of the judicial recruitment process merely reflects a type of oversight in the spirit of the American constitutional system. In a sense, this keeps the president – as nominator-in-chief – honest and may limit the extent to which unqualified individuals are given lifetime appointments to the highest court in the land. In addition, in the current climate, Senate confirmation ties appointment to the politics of the moment, and in doing so, assures a measure of accountability to court appointments by holding nominees up for public scrutiny (Epstein and Segal 2007).

Like their American counterparts, Norwegian Supreme Court justices enjoy a high degree of independence and are not subject to periodic review.[16] Unlike in the United States, however, the Norwegian appointment process is not transparent, in part by design and in part by the studied inattention of academics, the media and other political actors. While striking a balance between independence and accountability is no simple matter (Epstein and Segal 2007), the latter is in very short supply in Norway, a fact that may have implications for democratic governance.

The Supreme Court needs independence to adjudicate without undue external political pressures. However, to the extent that some or all of the Court's activities are shrouded in secrecy, Norway operates with a democratic deficit. Democratic philosophers prescribe an electorate that is informed and participatory, and it is fair to say that Norway generally meets that standard in most respects. Levels of voter turnout in elections are very high, much higher than those observed in American elections. Surely, the near 90 per cent turnout in the 1994 Norwegian European Union referendum speaks eloquently to the democratic spirit so pervasive throughout Scandinavia. In such an environment, the invisible hand of justice – aka the Supreme Court of Norway – stands as a perplexing anomaly in

---

16. Indeed, at the Norwegian Association of Judges' 100 year anniversary in 2012, the book celebrating their first 100 years was dedicated to the independence of the judges (Engstad *et al.* 2012).

an otherwise highly democratic system. At a minimum one expects that in such a culture the high court is found to be open and transparent, although empowered to decide in an independent fashion the cases it chooses to hear.

Research question

Returning to where we began this chapter, we find a Norwegian Supreme Court dealing with policy-relevant constitutional issues freighted with ideological ramifications. Given that a modified or expanded attitudinal model is our theory of choice, we would ask legal model devotees some pointed questions: (1) In deciding the *Ship Owner's Taxation* case, what precedent could the six justices in the majority embrace that the five justices in the minority could not? (2) Likewise, what different readings of constitutional or legislative intent could these two blocs of justices invoke? (3) Why would those justices appointed by socialist and non-socialist governments evince such markedly different understandings of the plain meaning of the law?

Our tentative answer to these related questions is that independent Supreme Court justices not infrequently adjudicate cases involving very important policy and constitutional matters and, given their ideological orientations, they are not indifferent to the outcome in the rulings handed down by the Court.

Plan of the book

In the remainder of this monograph, we build the case for this interpretation of judicial behaviour. In Chapter Two we review the basic institutional structure of the Norwegian Supreme Court and its post-World War II history. After all, Norway's Supreme Court justices are members of a reactive policy-making institution, and their ability to achieve their policy preferences is constrained by the design of the institution in which they act. The Supreme Court's jurisdiction, its place in the judiciary, the judiciary's place in Norway's constitutional design, as well as the tenure and independence of the justices themselves affect the justices' policy-making capacity. To understand what the justices perceive as feasible in the pursuit of their policy goals, it is necessary to understand the institutional design of the Court itself because that design constrains the justices' policy outputs.

The discussion in Chapter Three continues in this vein. The Court's institutional design constrains the justices' policy preferences, but so too do the decisional processes that the justices follow. Some cases present crystalline legal or constitutional questions that only allow for a certain answer. These cases do not afford the justices much opportunity to pursue their policy preferences. Other cases are more complex or ambiguous. They allow for the justices' attitudinal preferences to play a role. Indeed, preferences might be required in order to weigh and select from competing legal resolutions. In this chapter, we discuss the decisional procedures operating in the Court, paying particular attention to the Court's docketing decisions. This is the step in the decision-making process where complex cases are separated from easy ones.

Throughout this monograph, we rely upon the nature of the appointing government as a proxy for the individual justice's attitudinal preferences. This suggests that the appointment process affects the outputs of the Court. In Chapter Four, we explore this possibility in some detail. There, we provide a discussion of the composition of the Supreme Court, accompanied by an analysis of the potential political implications (policy making by appointment) of the Court's changing membership over time.

Chapters Five through Seven provide more systematic assessment of the links between judicial preferences, the appointment process, and judicial outputs. Chapter Five explores the relationship between a justice's preferences and his or her votes in cases dealing with economic rights. We find that justices appointed by socialist governments are significantly more supportive of public economic interests than are their non-socialist appointed counterparts. In Chapter Six we turn our attention to an examination of the effect of the Norwegian state's concerted effort to bring about greater representation of women on the High Bench. We show that this has paid numerical dividends, at least when it comes to descriptive representation. However, there is no evidence that women bring a distinctive voice to the Bench; nor do they appear to have a leavening effect on the decisional behaviour of male justices. Finally, in Chapter Seven we show that the appointment process tends to seat justices who are more likely to find for the government in cases where it is a litigant.

In the preceding analytical chapters we focused on the decisional behaviour of the individual justice in five-member panels, the most common mode of Supreme Court decision making. In Chapter Eight we turn our attention to votes in plenary and Grand Chamber sessions of the Court. Specifically, we focus on a special subset of cases involving issues the Court has identified as particularly consequential and salient – *viz.*, Sections 97 and 105 of the Constitution – which address the principle of a prohibition of *ex post facto* laws and expropriation without full compensation, respectively. These cases are heard and decided in plenary session in order to ensure that the maximum number of justices has a hand in determining the Court's final output. With respect to both constitutional articles, the Court is engaging in the power of judicial review – that is, determining whether an act of government comports with the Constitution. Thus, these are the instances where the justices exercise the greatest policy-making authority. Accordingly, to better understand the systematic forces affecting these decisional outputs is of no mean consequence.

Finally, Chapter Nine offers a summary of the Norwegian judicial picture as we have painted it. Here, we also discuss how this project informs studies of other judicial systems, starting with other Scandinavian polities, followed by some theorising about the broader European legal context.

References

Askeland, B. (2003) 'Rettskildelærens Utvikling i Rettsteoretisk Belysning', *Jussens Venner* 38 (1): 8–23.

Bailey, M. A., Kamoie, B. and Maltman, F. (2005) 'Signals from the Tenth Justice: The Political Role of the Solicitor General in Supreme Court Decision Making', *American Journal of Political Science* 49 (1): 72–85.

Baum, L. (1997) *The Puzzle of Judicial Behavior,* Ann Arbor: The University of Michigan Press.

—   (2008) *Judges and Their Audiences: A Perspective on Judicial Behavior,* Princeton: Princeton University Press.

Bell, J. (2006) *Judiciaries within Europe: A Comparative Review,* Cambridge: Cambridge University Press.

Bergo, K. (2002) *Høyesteretts Forarbeidsbruk,* Oslo: Cappelen.

Bjerck, B. (2006) 'Kampen for selvbestemt abort på 1970-tallet med særlig vekt på kvinnebevegelsen', Oslo: Forskningsrådet.

Clawson, R. A., Kegler, E. R. and Waltenburg, E. N. (2003) 'Supreme Court Legitimacy and Group-Centric Forces: Black Support for Capital Punishment and Affirmative Action', *Political Behavior* 25 (4): 289–311.

Clawson, R. A. and Waltenburg, E. N. (2009) *Legacy and Legitimacy: Black Americans and the Supreme Court,* Philadelphia: Temple University Press.

Corwin, E. S. (1919) *John Marshall and the Constitution: A Chronicle of the Supreme Court,* New Haven: Yale University Press.

Curry, B. W., Pacelle Jr., R. L. and Marshall, B. W. (2008) '"An Informal and Limited Alliance"': The President and the Supreme Court', *Presidential Studies Quarterly* 38 (2): 223–247.

de Andrade, G. F. (2001) 'Comparative Constitutional Law: Judicial Review', *Journal of Constitutional Law* 3 (3): 977–989.

Doublet, D. and Bernt, J. F. (1992) *Retten og Vitenskapen: En Introduksjon til Rettsvitenskapens Vitenskapsfilosofi,* Bergen: Alma Mater.

Dyevre, A. (2010) 'Unifying the Field of Comparative Judicial Politics: Towards a General Theory of Judicial Behaviour', *European Political Science Review* 2 (2): 297–227.

Easton, D. (1965) *A Framework for Political Analysis,* Englewood Cliffs: Prentice-Hall.

Eckhoff, T. (1971) *Rettskildelære,* Oslo: Tanum.

Eckhoff, T. and Helgesen, J. (2001) *Rettskildelære,* Oslo: Universitetsforlaget.

Einhorn, E. S. and Logue, J. (2003) *Modern Welfare States: Scandanavian Politics and Policy in the Global Age,* Westport: Praeger.

Elder, N., Thomas, A. H. and Arter, D. (1988) *The Consensual Democracies?: The Government and Politics of the Scandinavian States,* Oxford: Basil Blackwell.

Engstad, N. A., Frøseth, A. L. and Tønder, B. (eds) (2012) *Dommernes Uavhengighe: Den Norske Dommerforening 100 år,* Bergen: Fagbokforlaget.

Epstein, L. and Knight, J. (1998) *The Choices Justices Make,* Washington DC: CQ Press.

— (2013) 'Reconsidering Judicial Preferences', *Annual Review of Political Science* 16: 11–31.

Epstein, L., Landes, W. M. and Posner, R. A. (2013) *The Behavior of Federal Judges: A Theoretical and Empirical Study of Rational Choice,* Cambridge, Mass.: Harvard University Press.

Epstein, L. and Segal, J. A. (2007) *Advice and Consent: The Politics of Judicial Appointments,* New York: Oxford University Press.

Eurofound (2001) 'Public Committee Proposes Changes to Rules on Mediation and Strikes'. Online. Available http://www.eurofound.europa.eu/eiro/2001/04/feature/no0104129f.htm (last accessed 22 January 2013).

Feld, L. P. and Voigt, S. (2003) 'Economic Growth and Judicial Independence: Cross-Country Evidence Using a New Set of Indicators', *European Journal of Political Economy* 19 (3): 497–527.

Flemming, R. B. and Wood, B. D. (1997) 'The Public and the Supreme Court: Individual Justice Responsiveness to American Policy Moods', *American Journal of Political Science* 41 (2): 468–488.

George, T. E. and Epstein, L. (1992) 'On the Nature of Supreme Court Decision Making', *American Political Science Review* 86 (2): 323–337.

Gibson, J. L. (1983) 'From Simplicity to Complexity: The Development of Theory in the Study of Judicial Behavior', *Political Behavior* 5 (1): 7–49.

Gibson, J. L., Caldeira, G. A. and Baird, V. A. (1998) 'On the Legitimacy of National High Courts', *The American Political Science Review* 92 (2): 343–358.

Gjerstad, L. (2010) 'Frikjenner pressen - under tvil', *Journalisten,* 30 April.

Goldman, S. (1966) 'Voting Behavior on the United States Court of Appeals, 1961–1964', *American Political Science Review* 60 (2): 374–383.

— (1975) 'Voting Behavior on the United States Court of Appeals Revisited', *American Political Science Review* 69 (2): 491–506.

Grendstad, G., Shaffer, W. R. and Waltenburg, E. N. (2010) 'Revealed Preferences of Norwegian Supreme Court Justices', *Tidsskrift for Rettsvitenskap* 123 (1): 73–101.

— (2011) 'When Justices Disagree: The Influence of Ideology and Geography on Economic Voting on the Norwegian Supreme Court', *Retfærd* 34 (2): 3–22.

— (2012a) 'Ideologi og Grunnholdninger hos Dommerne i Norges Høyesterett', *Lov og Rett* 51 (4): 240–253.

— (2012b) 'Mellom Nøytralitet og Aktivisme: Lovene Tolker Ikke Seg Selv', *Tidsskrift for Rettsvitenskap* 125 (4): 521–534.

Gryski, G. S. and Main, E. C. (1986) 'Social Backgrounds as Predictors of Votes on State Courts of Last Resort: The Case of Sex Discrimination', *The Western Political Quarterly* 39 (3): 528–537.

Gunlicks, A. B. (2011) *Comparing Liberal Democracies: The United States, United Kingdom, France, Germany, and the European Union*, Bloomington: iUniverse, Inc.

Hall, M. G. (1987) 'Constituent Influence in State Supreme Courts: Conceptual Notes and a Case Study', *Journal of Politics* 49 (4): 1117–1124.

— (1992) 'Electoral Politics and Strategic Voting in State Supreme Courts', *Journal of Politics* 54 (2): 427–46.

— (1995) 'Justices as Representatives: Elections and Judicial Politics in the American States', *American Politics Quarterly* 23 (4): 485–503.

Hammond, T., Bonneau, C. and Sheehan, R. (2005) *Strategic Behavior and Policy Choices on the U.S. Supreme Court,* Palo Alto: Stanford University Press.

Hodder-Williams, R. (1992) 'Six Notions of "Political" and the United States Supreme Court', *British Journal of Political Science* 22 (1): 1–20.

Kinander, M. (2002) 'Trenger man Egentlig Reelle Hensyn?', *Lov og Rett* 41 (4): 224–241.

Kristjánsson, M. (2010) 'Splittet om økonomi', *Klassekampen*, 25 February.

Kritzer, H. and Richards, M. J. (2005) 'The Influence of Law in the Supreme Court's Search and Seizure Jurisprudence', *American Politics Research* 33 (1): 33–55.

LaCroix, A. L. (2010) *The Ideological Origins of American Federalism*, Cambridge, Mass.: Harvard University Press.

Lasswell, H. D. (1936) *Politics: Who Gets What, When and How,* New York: Whittlesey House.

Lazarsfeld, P. F., Berelson, B. R. and Gaudet, H. (1944) *The People's Choice,* New York: Duell, Sloan and Pierce.

Lijphart, A. (1984) *Democracies: Patterns of Majoritarian and Consensus Government in Twenty-One Countries,* New Haven: Yale University Press.

Lloyd, R. D. (1995) 'Separating Partisanship from Party in Judicial Research: Reapportionment in the U.S. District Courts', *American Political Science Review* 89 (2): 413–420.

Lopez, E. G. (2008) 'Judicial Review in Spain: The Constitutional Court', *Loyola of Los Angeles Law Review,* 41 (2). Online. Available http://www.digitalcommons.lmu.edu/llr/vol41/iss2/3.

Magnussen, A.-M. (2005) 'The Norwegian Supreme Court and Equitable Considerations. Problematic Aspects of Legal Reasoning', *Scandinavian Political Studies* 28 (1): 69–89.

Mathiesen, T. (1997) 'Høyesterett - superstruktur med skjør autoritet', *Aftenposten,* 25 November.

McGuire, K. T. (1993) 'Lawyers and the U.S. Supreme Court: The Washington Community and Legal Elites', *American Journal of Political Science* 37 (2): 365–390.

McGuire, K. T. and Stimson, J. A. (2004) 'The Least Dangerous Branch Revisited: New Evidence on Supreme Court Responsiveness to Public Preferences', *The Journal of Politics* 66 (4): 1018–1035.

Michalsen, D. (1994) 'Ny og Gammel Rettskildelære: Refleksjoner ved Lesning av Lars Björnes Bok om Nordisk Rettskildelære på 1800-tallet', *Tidsskrift for Rettsvitenskap* 107: 192–239.

Mishler, W. and Sheehan, R. S. (1993) 'The Supreme Court as a Countermajoritarian Institution? The Impact of Public Opinion on Supreme Court Decisions', *American Political Science Review* 87 (1): 87–101.

Nagel, S. (1961) 'Political Party Affiliation and Judges' Decisions', *American Political Science Review* 55 (4): 843–850.

Norpoth, H. and Segal, J. A. (1994) 'Comment: Popular Influence on Supreme Court Decisions', *American Political Science Review* 88 (3): 711–716.

Nylund, A. (2010) 'Mixing Past and Future: The Making of a Nordic Legal Culture 1850–2050', in Sunde, J. Ø. and Skodvin, K. E. (eds) *Rendezvous of European Legal Cultures*, Bergen: Fagbokforlaget, pp. 167–181.

Posner, R. A. (2008) *How Judges Think*, Cambridge, Mass.: Harvard University Press.

Pritchett, C. H. (1948) *The Roosevelt Court: A Study in Judicial Politics and Values 1937–1947*, New York: Macmillan Co.

Richards, M. J. and Kritzer, H. (2002) 'Jurisprudential Regimes in Supreme Court Decision Making', *American Political Science Review* 96 (2): 305–320.

Rios-Figueroa, J. and Staton, J. K. (2014) 'An Evaluation of Cross-National Measures of Judicial Independence', *Journal of Law, Economics, and Organization,* 30 (1): 104–137.

Rohde, D. W. and Spaeth, H. J. (1976) *Supreme Court Decision Making*, New York: W.H. Freeman.

Rokkan, S. (1967) 'Geography, Religion, and Social Class: Crosscutting Cleavages in Norwegian Politics', in Lipset, S. M. and Rokkan, S. (eds) *Party Systems and Voter Alignments: Cross-National Perspective.* New York: Free Press, pp. 367–444.

Rosenberg, G. N. (2008) *The Hollow Hope: Can Courts Bring About Social Change?*, Chicago: The University of Chicago Press.

Rønning, A. J. (2007) 'Profilen Georg Fr. Rieber-Mohn Fortsatt skuddklar', *Advokatbladet* 87 (11): 36–40.

—   (2009) 'Får være med på å skape rett', *Advokatbladet* 11: 24–28.

Schei, T. (2008) 'Disposisjoner til prosedyrer i Høyesterett', *Advokatbladet* 88 (4): 52–54.

—   (2009) 'God sammensetning', *Aftenposten,* 7 October

Schubert, G. (1965) *The Judicial Mind: The Attitudes and Ideologies of Supreme Court Justices, 1946–1963*, Evanston: Northwestern University Press.

Segal, J. A. and Cover, A. D. (1989) 'Ideological Values and the Votes of U.S. Supreme Court Justices', *American Political Science Review* 83 (2): 557–565.

Segal, J. A. and Spaeth, H. J. (1993) *The Supreme Court and the Attitudinal Model,* New York: Oxford University Press.

— (1996a) 'The Influence of Stare Decisis on the Votes of United States Supreme Court Justices', *American Journal of Political Science* 40 (4): 971–1030.

— (1996b) 'Norms, Dragons, and Stare Decisis: A Response', *American Journal of Political Science* 40 (4): 1063–1082.

— (2002) *The Supreme Court and the Attitudinal Model Revisited,* New York: Cambridge University Press.

Seip, J. A. (1964) 'Den norske høyesterett som politisk organ', *Historisk Tidsskrift* 43: 103–135.

Skiple, J. K., Gudbrandsen, F. and Grendstad, G. (2013) '.som speiler det samfunnet vi har. Høyesterett, asylbarn og den alminnelige rettsoppfatning', *Lov og Rett* 52 (9): 609–629.

Smith, C. (1975) 'Domstolene og rettsutviklingen', *Lov og Rett* 14: 292–319.

Sparks, J. (1832) *The Life of Gouverneur Morris: With Selections from His Correspondence and Miscellaneous Papers Detailing Events in the American Revolution, the French Revolution, and in the Political History of the United States,* Boston: Gray and Bowen.

Staats, J. and Percival, G. (2010) 'The Influence of Constituency Preferences on Elected State Trial Court Judges', Prepared for delivery at the Annual Meeting of the Western Political Science Association, San Francisco, CA, 1–3 April.

Stone Sweet, A. (2000) *Governing with Judges: Constitutional Politics in Europe,* Oxford: Oxford University Press.

Sunde, J. Ø. (2012) 'Andre premiss og anna resultat - refleksjonar kring politikk, Høgsterett og dissensar', *Tidsskrift for Rettsvitenskap* 125 (1–2): 168–204.

— (2014) 'Live and Let Die: An Essay Concerning Legal-Cultural Understanding', in Adams, M. and Heirbaut, D. (eds) *The Method and Culture of Comparative Law,* Oxford: Hart Publishing, pp. 221–234.

Tate, C. N. (1981) 'Personal Attribute Models of the Voting Behavior of U.S. Supreme Court Justices: Liberalism in Civil Liberties and Economics Cases, 1946–1978', *American Political Science Review* 75 (2): 355–367.

Tate, C. N. and Handberg, R. (1991) 'Time Binding and Theory Building in Personal Attribute Models of Supreme Court Voting Behavior, 1916–1988', *American Journal of Political Science* 35 (2): 460–480.

Tate, C. N. and Sittiwong, P. (1989) 'Decision Making in the Canadian Supreme Court: Extending the Personal Attributes Model Across Nations', *Journal of Politics* 51 (4): 900–916.

Ulmer, S. S. (1962) 'The Political Party Variable in the Michigan Supreme Court', *Journal of Politics* 11 (2): 352–363.

— (1970) 'Dissent Behavior and the Social Backgrounds of Supreme Court Justices', *Journal of Politics* 32 (3): 580–598.

— (1973) 'Social Backgrounds as an Indicator to the Votes of Supreme Court Justices in Criminal Cases, 1947–1956 Terms', *American Journal of Political Science* 17 (3): 622–630.

Volcansek, M. L. (ed.) (1993) *Judicial Politics and Policy-Making in Western Europe*, London: Frank Cass.

Wahlbeck, P. J., Spriggs, J. F. and Maltzman, F. (1998) 'Marshalling the Court: Bargaining and Accommodation on the United States Supreme Court', *American Journal of Political Science* 42 (1): 294–315.

Wills, G. (ed.) (1988) *The Federalist Papers by Alexander Hamilton, James Madison, and John Jay*, New York: Bantam Books.

Chapter Two

Institutional Structure and Process

Norwegian judicial policy making does not occur in a vacuum, but in a well-defined institutional milieu. While our focus is upon the decisional behaviour of justices as a function of political values, we understand that actions predicated on such preferences take place within an institution, which in turn can help shape the judicial policy outcomes. Typically, the initial organisational structure of a court system is specified in a nation's constitution, and Norway is no exception.

Not an international player, and thus relatively weak, Norway fell under Danish rule for nearly four centuries. Denmark was forced to relinquish control of Norway as a result of its unfortunate choice of allies during the Napoleonic Wars. The victorious English and Swedish forces handed Norway over to Sweden on 14 January 1814, in the Treaty of Kiel. Danish Prince Christian Frederick, in an effort to minimise Sweden's control over Norway, worked to stimulate interest at a meeting in Eidsvoll which convened on 10 April 1814 (Larsen 1950; Midgaard, 1986). A fairly representative contingent of '47 officials, 37 peasants, 16 town representatives, and 12 from the services' attended (Derry 1968: 132). Wasting little time, just over one month later – on 17 May 1814 to be precise – this assembly had produced a national constitution.

The convention at Eidsvoll rewarded Christian Frederick by choosing him as King of Norway. Sweden eventually got its act together, and in August 1814 it defeated Norway in a brief skirmish, removing Christian Frederick from the throne and creating a Norwegian union with Sweden that lasted until 1905. Notwithstanding Norway's transfer to Sweden, the Norwegian Constitution was retained – albeit with some slight changes to accommodate the union with Sweden – and it is this document that established the original institutional structure of the Norwegian court system. From that point on, any additions and modifications to that system have been undertaken in response, at least in part, to demands placed upon the judiciary.

In the remainder of this chapter, we shall discuss (1) the constitutional foundation of the judiciary, (2) the basic structure of the judicial system, (3) the administration of the judicial system, paying particular attention to the appointment process, and (4) political appointments. We begin by describing the initial form of the judicial institutions established in the 1814 Constitution.

Constitutional provisions

Articles 86–91 of the Norwegian Constitution make explicit reference to two courts: (1) the Constitutional Court of the Realm (Impeachment) and (2) the Supreme Court (*Høyesterett*). The impeachment court is not part of the ordinary court system, so we shall come back to it momentarily.

As depicted in Figure 2.1, the Supreme Court sits at the pinnacle of the Norwegian judicial system and as such is the court of last instance.[1] Fully consistent with its role as the highest court in the land, the Supreme Court, under Article 90 of the Constitution, may not have any of its decisions appealed. Article 88 is also

Figure 2.1: Norwegian Ordinary Courts

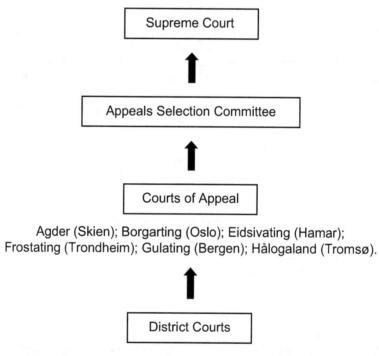

Supreme Court

Appeals Selection Committee

Courts of Appeal

Agder (Skien); Borgarting (Oslo); Eidsivating (Hamar);
Frostating (Trondheim); Gulating (Bergen); Hålogaland (Tromsø).

District Courts

Alstahaug, Alta, Asker og Bærum, Aust Agder, Aust Telemark, Bergen,
Brønnøy, Dalane, Drammen, Eiker Modum og Sigdal, Fjordane, Follo,
Fosen, Fredrikstad, Gjøvik, Glåmdal, Halden, Hallingdal, Hammerfest,
Hardanger, Haugaland, Hedmarken,Heggen og Frøland, Inntrøndelag,
Jæren, Kongsberg, Kristiansand, Larvik, Lister, Lofoten, Moss, Namdal,
Nedre Romerike, Nedre Telemark, Nord-Gudbrandsdal, Nord-Troms,
Nord-Østerdal, Nordhordland, Nordmøre, Nordre Vestfold, Ofoten, Oslo,
Oslo byfogdembete, Rana, Ringerike, Romsdal, Salten, Sandefjord,
Sarpsborg, Senja, Indre Finnmark (Sis-Finnmárkku diggegoddi), Sogn,
Stavanger, Sunnhordland, Sunnmøre, Sør-Gudbrandsdal, Sør-
Trøndelag, Sør-Østerdal, Søre Sunnmøre, Trondenes, Tønsberg,
Valdres, Vest-Telemark, Vesterålen, Øst-Finnmark, Øvre Romerike

---

1. In 1995, Borgarting was established – with its headquarters in Oslo – by a separation from Eidsivating.

interpreted to require the Supreme Court to make decisions within a hierarchical structure of courts. Statutory law, rather than the Constitution, generally specifies any membership requirements for the Court, with the exception that Article 91 requires an appointee to be at least thirty years old and with an exceptional record. In 2010, the requirement of exceptionalism was dropped. Today, a nominee for a Supreme Court seat must meet the minimum educational requirements of being a lawyer and the requirement of being a Norwegian citizen. A justice must retire by his or her seventieth birthday.

While placed under the heading of 'legislative', rather than 'judicial' powers, Article 83 permits the *Storting* to request advisory opinions of the Supreme Court on various points of law. We find this a most intriguing enumerated power, in that the *Høyesterett* might have a somewhat more immediate effect upon public policy by virtue of this constitutional provision. To the extent that Parliament solicits such legal opinions the Court's political preferences may shape legislation at the front end of the process.[2] Thus, the Court is not necessarily limited to a purely reactive role. Rather than waiting for litigation concerning legislation before speaking on a policy, the Court might be given the opportunity to offer its views during the law-making process itself.

The Constitution is silent on the other courts included in Figure 2.1, but it does devote two sections (86 and 87) to the Constitutional Court of the Realm, a more specialised adjudicative panel created to handle cases involving the impeachment of public officials (*see* Figure 2.2). Under Article 86, Parliament can impeach government officials for crimes and misconduct violating constitutional responsibility. While the *Storting* creates the rules for indictment, there is a minimum statute of limitation of fifteen years. Under the 1814 Constitution, five Supreme Court justices and ten members of the *Lagting* (something of an 'upper chamber' of the *Storting*) composed the Impeachment Court. The *Odelsting* (the other parliamentary division) prosecuted the case. As of 2009, the *Storting* became unicameral. Consequently, five Supreme Court justices and six 'lay judges' (Brattestå 2008) constitute the Impeachment Court, with the *Storting* acting as prosecutor. Statutory law prescribes the composition of this court.

As important as impeachment cases are, only eight have been prosecuted, and none since 1927. Of those cases, three led to convictions. In 1821, Thomas Fasting was impeached for a conflict of interest. In 1836 Severin Løvenskiold, Governor General of Norway under Swedish King Karl Johan, was convicted and fined for not counselling the king against dissolving the *Storting*. His impeachment and conviction, however, were not politically fatal. Løvenskiold continued to serve as Swedish prime minister (Regjering.no 2011). Finally, Prime Minister Christian August Selmer was impeached in 1884 when he supported King Oskar II's claim of absolute veto power. The impeachment crisis

---

2.   This procedure has not been sought since 1945. The Norwegian Progress Party states in its party program of 2009 that the Supreme Court is to be required to offer its opinion on the constitutionality of statues when at least a third of the members of the *Storting* requests it.

Figure 2.2: Norwegian Specialised Adjudicative Bodies

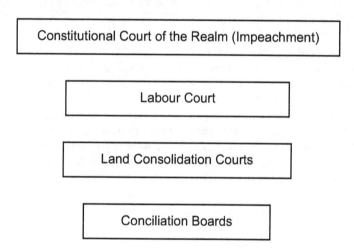

was triggered when the king vetoed a statute requiring his ministers to attend parliamentary meetings. That Prime Minister Selmer did succeed in securing 'the unanimous opinion from the law faculty of the university that the veto was absolute' (Derry 1968: 178), might offer some support for the role of personal attitudes in rendering legal decisions.

Notwithstanding its infrequent use, a well-designed and efficient impeachment system is an essential check on official abuse of power, for the absence of such a process 'would in fact mean that our most powerful leaders were granted immunity for their offences' (Brattestå 2008: 4).

Court structure

As depicted in Figure 2.1, the Norwegian judicial system is hierarchically structured. At its base are the sixty-six district courts, sitting in both urban and rural areas of the country. The district courts have original jurisdiction in civil cases, criminal cases, administrative cases, and constitutional cases. If a party is not satisfied with a ruling at this level, the case can be appealed to the next tier in the structural hierarchy – the courts of appeal. Professional judges (sometimes supplemented by assistant judges, i.e. law school graduates who have been appointed by the King in Council) preside over the district courts. They are supplemented by 'lay' judges.[3] Lay judges are citizens. They are not required

---

3. During their terms, lay judges sit in 'pools' from which an individual can be drawn to participate in cases before the district courts (Domstoladministrasjonen, nd). Lay judges are typically included on panels that hear criminal cases; they participate in civil cases only upon the request of at least one of the parties (Norges Domstoler 2013).

to have a law degree, but lawyers are not excluded as lay judges. Municipal councils select them to serve terms of four years, and their presence ostensibly helps to ensure that ordinary citizens have a hand in determining judicial outcomes. It bears mentioning that lay judges are not necessarily representative of Norway's mass public. Some occupations are excluded (e.g. employees of the Ministry of Justice and police officers); there are age restrictions; and the lion's share are political party appointees (Domstoladministrasjonen, nd; Malsch 2009: 47–48).

In the larger context of this study, we find the inclusion of non-professional, and non-law school trained judges intriguing. With little in the way of legal socialisation, what sorts of predispositions do these judges bring to a court? In the absence of formal indoctrination in the norms of the legal system, it is unlikely that their decisional behaviour is significantly constrained by formal judicial role expectations. The notion that pure legal reasoning informs court rulings may thus be considerably weakened. In any case, the issue is worthy of future investigation particularly in light of the fact that lay judges serve on the Appeal Courts as well.

The six courts of appeal compose the second level of the nation's judicial system. They take criminal, civil, administrative and constitutional cases on appeal, principally from the district courts (*see* Figure 2.1).[4] These courts help manage an ever increasing caseload, underscored by the fact that up until the mid-1990s the Supreme Court had a burdensome number of criminal cases. Prior to 1995, serious criminal offenses were originally tried in the appeal courts, and appeals of those decisions were directed to the Supreme Court. In 1995 the district courts assumed original jurisdiction in these cases, and any initial round of appeals of the district court decisions were made to the courts of appeal (Matningsdal 1996). A consequence of this court reform was a substantial reduction in the Supreme Court's mandatory appellate jurisdiction. In short, since the Court was no longer the first court of appeal in serious criminal cases, it was able to reserve its docket for more consequential cases[5] – cases that would allow it to bore with a more consequential policy-making auger.

Perched at the top of Norway's judicial system is the Supreme Court and its gatekeeping entity, the Appeals Selection Committee. The Supreme Court has jurisdiction over all cases involving social security, civil, criminal, administrative, and constitutional law (*see* Figure 2.1). As the nation's highest court, it has independent and final authority to pass on the constitutionality of the decisions of the government and legislation enacted by the Norwegian parliament. (Certain decisions can also be appealed to the European Court of Human Rights.) At the Supreme Court, all cases are argued orally. The Court only hears cases arriving on

---

4. The courts of appeal also take social security cases on appeal.

5. A point made by law Professor Carsten Smith twenty years earlier (Smith 1975).

appeal, and, as we noted above, a limited number of those at that. In other words, the Norwegian Supreme Court has discretionary jurisdiction, but since it is an appellate court only, it has no original jurisdiction.[6]

According to Article 88 of the Norwegian Constitution, the Supreme Court shall consist of a Chief Justice and six 'associate' justices.[7] The total number of justices on the Court has never been fixed by statute or convention, but since 1945 the number of sitting justices has generally varied from 18 to 20. In 2009 the Court requested and was granted – with neither public nor parliamentary debate – an additional justice. Therefore, as of 2015, the Norwegian Supreme Court consists of a Chief Justice and 19 'associate' justices.

Before the Court hears a case on its merits, the case must first have been passed on by a majority of the Appeals Selection Committee (*see* Chapter Three for a more detailed description of the Court's decisional processes). Although historically classified as a separate court, the Appeals Selection Committee is itself composed of three sitting Supreme Court justices.[8] The three justices are drawn from a rotating group of five temporarily designated justices. Two justices serve as back-ups in demanding cases or due to lawful absence. Basically, the Committee acts as a gatekeeper for the Supreme Court.

The Supreme Court typically divides into two parallel randomly assigned five-justice panels that hear its docketed cases.[9] Cases raising a constitutional issue or when two justices signal that they intend to deviate from precedent, however, are heard *en banc* – i.e. in the full plenary session, twenty-member court.[10] As the national court of last resort, the Supreme Court's rulings cannot be appealed.

As depicted in Figure 2.2, the Norwegian judicial system also comprises a number of 'special' courts. We have already discussed one of these – the Constitutional Court of the Realm (with jurisdiction over impeachments). In addition, there are special adjudicative bodies, two of which deal with particular areas of the law. First, the Labour Court considers disagreements over collective agreements and any damages that may be awarded in such labour cases (Arbeidsretten 2011). This tribunal is composed of seven members – 'three judicial judges and four judges nominated by the labour

---

6. The combination of having no specialised courts and that all cases are argued orally makes Norway pretty distinct.

7. This section has been changed four times. *See* http://www.grunnloven.lovdata.no (last accessed 15 November 2014).

8. *The Court Act* of 2001 no longer defines the Appeals Selection Committee as a separate court. The Appeals Selection Committee was named *Høyesteretts kjæremålsutvalg*, but changed its name to *Høyesteretts ankeutvalg* as of 1 January 2008.

9. *See* Smith (2000) on the possibility that the three-justice Appeals Selection Committee and the two parallel five-justice panels do not represent the view of the whole Court. *See* Chapter Three for a more detailed description of the Court's decisional processes.

10. An intermediate function of a 'Grand Chamber', in which eleven justices meet and are chaired by the Chief Justice, was initiated in 2008. In instances where an even number of justices are eligible to serve on a plenary case, the most junior justice steps down.

market parties' (Arbeidsretten 2011). The Labour Court has sole jurisdiction on contractual matters and as a general rule, its rulings are final and not subject to appeal (Arbeidsretten 2011).

Another highly specialised court is the Land Consolidation Court, whose jurisdiction 'includes both land consolidation and planning and the solving of boundary disputes' (Rognes and Sky 2004: 59). There are forty-one Land Consolidation Court districts from which cases may be appealed to the Land Consolidation Appeal Courts. Sitting on these adjudicative bodies are two lay judges and a 'land consolidation judge', who 'must have a Masters Degree from the Agricultural University of Norway' (Rognes and Sky 2004: 60). Although the Land Consolidation Courts exercise both original and appellate jurisdiction, their decisions may be appealed to the Courts of Appeal in the ordinary court system.

Finally, Conciliation Boards hear the great majority of minor civil cases. Consisting of three lay judges, Conciliation Boards try to mediate disputes, with most minor civil cases ending in a negotiated settlement (Justice and Police Department 2001). If no agreement can be reached, however, the Board may render a decision or send it to the district court system for adjudication (Olsen 2005: 8).

Once again, given our abiding interest in the extent to which political values are infused into the judicial process, we note that there is at least the potential to tie civil legal decisions to local politics. Consider one observer's description of the recruitment of lay judges who serve on local Conciliation Boards:

> [The lay judges] are nominated by their political party in caucus and their names are submitted to the town council which elects the slate. This allows for *proper political balance* from the municipality's point of view. In Oslo Vestre (West) Forliksråd there was one conservative party member and two labor party members, one of whom was chairman. In Oslo Ostre (East) Forliksråd, the numbers are reversed. They serve for a period of four years, i.e. as long as the municipal government is in office. A new election may bring a new town council and hence new 'forliksmannen' (Shaughnessy 1992: 27, authors' italics).

Presumably, maintaining the 'proper political balance' amounts to more than mere window dressing. Awarding judgeships on the basis of local election outcomes certainly suggests that political values matter not only in executive and legislative bodies, but in judicial ones as well.

The administration of the judicial system

Mapping the overall judicial system places the Norwegian Supreme Court in its general institutional context. Also relevant to the Supreme Court's decision-making process are the key administrative mechanisms associated with its functions. It is to a discussion of these agencies that we now turn.

The Ministry of Justice and Police

The Ministry of Justice and Police (hereafter, The Ministry of Justice) is among the oldest ministries in the nation, dating back to Norway's emergence as a state in 1814.[11] (Norway did not secure full, formal independence from Sweden until 1905.) The administration of the Norwegian courts and judges was firmly located within the Ministry of Justice.[12] Although the consensus was – and is – that the judges of the third branch of government should be independent and judge impartially, nothing prevented the organisation of the courts to be located within the second branch of government.

Section 21 of the Constitution states that '[t]he King selects and appoints, after having listened to his Council, all civilian, clergy, and military officials.' Only the King in Council, therefore, has the authority to appoint judges, and a constitutional amendment would be required for other institutions to take on this constitutional prerogative. In addition, the only way to receive the status of 'high civil servant' (embetsmann), with the concomitant job security, standing, and benefits, is through appointment by the King in Council. The Constitution itself, however, does not in any way prescribe the procedures by which judges are appointed.[13] According to Sections 91 and 92 of the Constitution, to be eligible for appointment to the Supreme Court one must be at least thirty years old and a Norwegian citizen. These are the only formal constitutional requirements.[14] Beyond the Constitution itself, later statutes and administrative regulations prescribe that judges must have a law degree (until 2012: of highest standard) and be on a sound economic footing.[15] Lower court judges must be at least twenty-five years old.

Until the reorganisation in 2002, the Ministry of Justice administered the courts and the judges. The appointment process included the possibility of the Ministry seeking informal advice from an advisory council. Regardless of the statutes and regulations that emerged over time dealing with judicial appointments, the complete administrative and evaluative processes were solely the responsibility of the Ministry of Justice. It handled judicial appointments by simply passing its recommendation to the King in Council (NOU 1999: 230).

---

11. Effective as of January 2012, the official name is the Ministry of Justice and Public Security.

12. Two separate ministries originally were responsible for the administration of the courts and the judges. These functions were merged in the Ministry of Justice in 1818.

13. Statutes (Tjenestemansloven) prescribe the manner in which the government announces openings, publicises lists of applicants, and provides information on the appointment process to the public. Until changes in the appointment processes of judges took effect in 2002, the use of an advisory council did not apply to judges as high civil servants (NOU 1999: 229–230).

14. Being taciturn with respect to eligibility requirements for a seat on the nation's highest bench is not unique to Norway. The U.S. Constitution lists no formal requirements whatsoever.

15. Determining sound economic footing (økonomisk vederheftig) is, of course, left to the Ministry's discretion. The criterion dates back to King Christian V's Norwegian Law of 1687, which specified that the judge's debt was not to surpass his income. In modern days, the criterion has been interpreted as the judge being solvent.

There were no disruptions in the business and proceedings of the Supreme Court until World War II. When the Germans invaded, on 9 April 1940, the Norwegian King and government fled the country. The Supreme Court, however, continued to operate. By 21 December 1940, the justices were no longer able to accept the German conditions, and they resigned collectively (Hem 2012). The German occupation appointed new justices. They were referred to as the Commissary Supreme Court (*kommissarisk høyesterett*).

The increasing politicisation of the Ministry of Justice

The pre-war justices of the Supreme Court officially resumed their work during a solemn ceremony on 14 May 1945. Five of the pre-World War II justices had passed away. It was evident that the Court was understaffed, particularly in light of the daunting challenges promised by the war trial cases. Towards the end of the war, the exiled Nygaardsvold government in London had already suspended the mandatory retirement age for the justices of the pre-war Court. On 21 September 1945, the interim maximum-size multiparty coalition government – with Einar Gerhardsen of the Labour Party sitting as prime minister – appointed five new justices and one interim justice.[16] The parliamentary election in October 1945 renewed Einar Gerhardsen's mandate as prime minister, this time with a majority government consisting solely of the Labour Party, and on 11 April 1946, the Labour Party government appointed seven more justices to the Supreme Court. Clearly, by 1952, Norway's highest court was a 'Labour Party' court. Oscar Christian Gundersen, who served as Minister of Justice during Gerhardsen's 1945–1951 Labour Party government, implied as much when he later boasted that he had appointed virtually all the justices, including two Chief Justices, to the High Court (Smith 1996a; Solstad 1996).[17]

By the early 1950s, the war trial cases had been processed and the Supreme Court was, in a sense, back to its normal routine. The Second World War did not substantially disrupt the Ministry of Justice's organisation of the courts nor did it remove the long shadow of the Minister of Justice over the appointment processes of Supreme Court justices. To be sure, there were occasional public debates concerning judicial appointments, and attempts were made to remove the responsibility for court administration from the Ministry of Justice. These attempts first began in the 1960s, but they went nowhere and faded quickly. The effort resurfaced in the 1990s, becoming highly contentious and polarised as the

---

16. The Minister of Justice during these post-war months was Johan Cappelen of the Conservative Party (*Høyre*).

17. Later, after he had stepped down as Chief Justice, Terje Wold rebuked O.C. Gundersen's statement on his dominance over appointments of justices. 'It cannot be right', he wrote in an unpublished memo, 'that one Minister of Justice can sit for so long and [...] have the sole authority' for appointments (quoted in Smith 1996a: 193). As Minister of Justice in exile during World War II, Terje Wold never occupied a position permitting the appointment of justices to the High Court. In May 1958, when Wold was elevated to Chief Justice, O.C. Gundersen – appointed to the Court in 1953, after having stepped down as Minister of Justice for the Labour Party government – left the Supreme Court to become ambassador to Moscow.

parliament and the judiciary itself pushed for a reduced administrative role for the Ministry.[18] At stake was the organisation of the administration of the third estate. The emphasis lay on the subsequent principle of organisation – by democratic procedures or by the rule of law – and on location – either continued location within the Ministry of Justice or as a separate entity outside of the Ministry. The courts' autonomy to judge was uncontroversial and not at issue. Rather, the concern was the potential for politicians and the government administration to interfere with judicial appointments, and thereby unduly influencing the organisational operations of the courts. The *Storting* resolved these essentially political questions in May 2001, when it established the independent and external National Court's Administration that would also handle the application processes. The Judicial Appointments Board (*Innstillingsrådet for dommere*) does not solicit applicants, but merely administers the application process and, in the end, sends a list of ranked candidates to the Ministry of Justice. To showcase the independence of the National Court's Administration, the *Storting* decided to locate it in Trondheim, 500 kilometres away from Oslo and Norway's largest city without a law school.

The 1960s

Discussions of the political influence on judicial appointments occasionally surfaced throughout the second half of the twentieth century. One notable period was in the 1950s and 1960s and involved Terje Wold. In 1939 Wold became Minister of Justice for the Labour Party government of Johan Nygaardsvold and served most of his term during World War II, when the government was located in London. In September 1945, Prime Minister Einar Gerhardsen's interim post-war government appointed Wold (and four other men) to the Supreme Court. In October of that same year, however, a complication arose when Wold was also elected to serve a four-year term as the Labour Party representative in the *Storting* for Finnmark County. Wold resolved the complication by letting his Supreme Court appointment sit in abeyance until he had served his four-year *Storting* term. (Exercising superb economic rationality, Wold did collect his Supreme Court check rather than his legislative wages during his four-year stint in parliament.)[19] When Sverre Grette left the Chief Justiceship in 1958, the third Gerhardsen Labour Party government – with Jens Haugland as Minister of Justice – elevated Terje Wold to Chief Justice. Wold would hold that position until 1969.

Terje Wold addressed the annual meetings of the Norwegian Association of Judges in 1954, 1960, and 1964.[20] In each of his speeches, he addressed the relationship between the organisation of the courts within the Ministry of Justice

---

18. Subsequent sections rely heavily on Veland (2008), Grønlie and Flo (2009: 353–363), NOU 1999:19 (1999) and Ot.Prop.nr.44 (2000–2001).

19. During this time period, the average, default annual salary for an MP was 10,250 NOK, while the average annual salary for a Supreme Court justice was about 18,700 NOK (Norges Statskalender, various years: 6–7). (The National Archives of Norway, Supreme Court justices, various files).

20. The addresses were also published; *see* Wold (1954; 1960; 1964).

and the possible political influence that might thereby be exerted. In 1960 he argued for greater independence of the courts from the government and lamented that Norway was one of only very few countries in which the government was the sole player in the appointment of justices. In his 1954 speech Wold said that even the traditional practice of the Supreme Court opining on the appointment of justices was effectively non-existent. One is left with the impression, he claimed, that the Ministry of Justice considers the courts inferior to the second branch of government. In his 1964 address, he more than hinted at the potential for political appointments of justices, especially when the same party remained in office for years on end (1964: 395). However, Wold's criticisms and concerns seemed to fall on deaf ears.[21]

In 1965 a non-socialist government ousted Labour from power. Within two years the new government established a commission whose task it was, *inter alia*, to report on recruitment to the courts and on the education of lawyers. The commission consisted of three lawyers: Erling Sandene (county governor and later Chief Justice); Supreme Court advocate Eiliv Fougner (who would later become father-in-law of later Minister of Justice Else Bugge Fougner); and Andreas Schei (father of the current Chief Justice Tore Schei). Andreas Schei had been appointed to the Supreme Court in 1946 and was on leave from the Court as Parliamentary Ombudsman when he was asked to head the commission. In the conclusion of its 1970 report, the commission suggested that an independent council for the appointment of justices be established. Greater court independence, however, was still limited because the Minister of Justice – the politician in charge of the courts and judges – remained accountable to the *Storting*. In the subsequent round of hearings, the Supreme Court justices themselves were unanimously cool to the idea of an external council for the appointment of justices, since judicial appointments would remain the constitutional prerogative of the King in Council. Over the next two decades, no governments acted on this recommendation of the Schei commission.

The 1990s

Between 1945 and the end of the 1980s, the process for appointing judges remained unchanged. The Ministry of Justice announced all judgeship openings, apart from those to the Supreme Court. The Ministry also received the applications and took care of the administration of the application process. The deadline for applications was not absolute; it was up to the Ministry to decide whether applications that missed the deadline could still be considered (NOU 1999: 230).[22] In 1990, there

---

21. Jens Haugland, Minister of Justice for Gerhardsen's third Labour Party government and in charge of the Ministry when Terje Wold was elevated to Chief, did not think highly of Wold. In 1959 Haugland (1986: 81) writes in his diaries that he observed Wold taking part in a discussion in the *Storting* on a bill concerning conscientious objectors, where Wold disagreed with the position taken by the Ministry of Justice. Haugland states that '[i]t becomes more and more clear that Terje Wold is unable to fill the position as chief on the Supreme Court. It is a pity that Gerhardsen and I failed to get O.C. Gundersen to take that job'.

22. In 1929 Paal Berg's application for the position of Chief Justice was submitted after the deadline. He was still appointed (Hem 2012).

was a first sign of an institutional change in the appointment process. A cooperative entity between the Ministry of Justice and the Norwegian Association of Judges was established – the Advisory Committee on the Appointment of Judges (*Rådgivende organ for dommerutnevnelser*). This committee was not created by statute, and the Ministry of Justice determined its mandate. The Committee had three members, all of whom were nominated by the Norwegian Associations of Judges and appointed by the Ministry of Justice. The members of the Committee were not to interview the applicants. Rather, the Committee's task was to secure references and undertake an oral assessment of the applicants from the senior judge on the court at which there was an opening. Presumably, the Committee members would use their personal networks – social capital – to provide the best possible assessments of the applicants. The Committee was not expected to hold any meetings or offer any written documents or justifications for its views. Rather, the Committee was simply to communicate to the Ministry the name of the one person it considered most qualified for the opening. Informal and non-written communications could take place after the Committee's recommendation had been passed to the Ministry. The advice was not to be publicised nor be made available to the applicants (NOU 1999: 230–231).[23]

Significantly, the Advisory Committee would not convene for vacancies on the Supreme Court. The appointment process to the High Bench remained the near exclusive prerogative of the Ministry of Justice. The only external input in this process was the view on the applicants from the Supreme Court, as conveyed by the Chief Justice. The views of the Chief and the Court were shared in private communications with the Minister of Justice and would therefore not be publicised.

Winds of change

A variety of developments outside Norway focused attention on the large shadow cast by the executive branch over judicial appointments. At the end of the 1980s the fall of the communist states in Eastern Europe laid bare examples of unprincipled intermingling between the executive and judicial branches of government. The events were a reminder of the 1985 UN report, *Basic Principles on the Independence of the Judiciary*, which Chief Justice Carsten Smith (1996a: 188) referred to as 'the courts' Magna Carta'. In the 1990s, the drive for expansion of the European Union called for greater awareness of the role of courts and judges. The UN report was complemented by documents like the 1994 Council of Europe's 'Recommendations on Independence, Efficiency and Role of Judges', and the 1997 European Association of Judges' 'Judges Charter in Europe'. The development of an 'executive bias' as well as the 'presidentialisation' of the executive branches of several countries (Poguntke and Webb 2005) was a further reminder that the third branch was losing its relative position in a theoretical system of co-equal branches of government. Sweden, Denmark, and Iceland – perennial countries of comparison – had already completed, or were in the process of completing, court

---

23. The Advisory Committee was made permanent in 1993.

reforms that would achieve greater independence of the courts (Ot.prp. no. 44, 2000–2001: 7). It was evident that Norway, with its system of exclusive executive branch authority in judicial appointments, was an international outlier.

In February 1995, the Norwegian Association of Judges organised a seminar on the administration of the courts, focusing on the courts' administrative superstructure, the appointment of judges, and disciplinary procedures against judges. Funded by the Ministry of Justice, invitations were extended to judges from all court levels, as well as lawyers, law and political science professors at the University of Oslo, and undersecretaries and high civil servants at the Ministry of Justice. Later, in a unanimous decision at their 1995 annual meeting, the judges themselves stated that they wanted to increase the independence of the courts. The newly elected head of the Norwegian Judges' Association – senior judge of the Hålogaland Court of Appeal, Arild O. Eidesen – wrote that the Ministry of Justice was no longer competently staffed to administer the courts, since the Ministry had hired too many non-lawyers who made unsound decisions (Eidesen 1995). Also the judges disapproved of the management-by-objectives system that had taken hold in the Ministry.[24] The Ministry of Justice had grown substantially over the years, and courts and judges were administered from the hard-pressed Civil Affairs Department. The judges also grumbled that it was unprincipled that the third branch of government should be administered from within the Ministry of Justice – an entity of the second branch of government (Øystå 1995). Eidesen made it the Association's top priority to 'liberate the judges from the administrative grip of the Ministry of Justice' (Pedersen and Larsen 1995a). The immediate response of the Minister of Justice – Grete Faremo of the Labour Party – was to establish a separate Court Department within the Ministry. It was to take effect on 1 January 1996.

During these discussions, several judges voiced their discontent. For example, Øyvind Smukkestad – the chief judge at the Trondheim Urban Municipal Court – averred that the *Storting*, as 'our most representative democratic body', should establish an independent advisory council for the appointment of judges. He argued that the Ministry of Justice was unfit to appoint judges and he was concerned that the government who appointed the judges was often one of the parties in cases before the courts.[25] He suggested that the *Storting* should appoint a council to handle the application process, publicise its ranking of the three top applicants, and send its recommendation to the Minister of Justice. Smukkestad showed special disdain for the practice of secret telephone calls in the application process (Smukkestad 1995).

---

24. Management by objectives (MBO) aims to streamline an organisation by setting goals, choosing courses and making decisions in a participatory manner by management and employees (Drucker 1954). MBO has been criticised for putting too much emphasis on quantitative and monitorable results, leading to instrumentalism. MBO was more likely to fail when its framework was rigidly applied to public organisations or to organisations where goals could not be meaningfully quantified (Christensen *et al.* 2007).

25. The government was the most frequent party in Court cases. For the 1992–1995 period, the government as prosecutor was necessarily a party in every criminal case, and the government was a party in 20 per cent of the civil cases before the Supreme Court (Smith 1996a: 192).

Chief Justice Carsten Smith, who addressed the judges' meeting in June 1995, lamented that the present system of appointments administered by the Ministry of Justice did not give the courts the 'appearance of independence'. From a principled perspective, Smith said, for the person who was not familiar with it, the present system 'does not look very pretty'. He added that we know too little about the long-term effects of this close intermingling (1996a: 192). Smith, who had sensed the political parties' disagreements on the issue, initially suggested that members of the Supreme Court refrain from participation in a government-appointed commission on the matter. However, broad political agreement on the necessity of a commission eventually developed and, upon reflection, the political differences turned out to be too great. Therefore, Smith concluded, it would be 'correct of the Supreme Court to be represented' on the commission (1996a: 196).[26] In 1996 the Judges' Association sent a letter to the Minister of Justice and to the Standing Committee on Justice in the *Storting* requesting the establishment of a commission to make a report on the administration of the courts. Grete Faremo promptly responded and promised to establish such a commission.

Faremo's response snatched the initiative from the *Storting*, where preparations for establishing such a committee were already underway (Pedersen and Larsen 1995b). The vice president of the *Storting* – Edvard Grimstad of the Centre Party – had composed a private proposition (*Dokument 8-forslag*) where the *Storting* itself would appoint a commission to draft a report on the relationship between judges, courts, and the Ministry of Justice. Grimstad's concern focused on whether there had been improper intermingling between the courts and the Ministry of Justice that undermined the separation of powers and the rule of law. Grimstad was also concerned with what he considered to be a geographically biased recruitment to the Supreme Court, inasmuch as most of the justices were drawn from the southern part of Norway (in Veland 2008). In October 1995, Grete Faremo briefed the Standing Committee on Justice in the *Storting* that she had started to outline the commission's mandate. Carsten Smith, Chief Justice of the Supreme Court, had already agreed to chair the commission. In December 1995, unable to iron out all of the partisan differences, the *Storting* formally and finally asked the government to establish a court commission.[27] The commission could (and ultimately did) have significant consequences. Upon its recommendation, the responsibility for administering the courts was removed from the Ministry of Justice, discontinuing a practice that had been in effect since 1814.

---

26. The vice president of the *Storting* – Edvard Grimstad of the Centre Party – was interviewed in 2007 on the establishment of the commission. Grimstad stated that 'Carsten [Smith] was extremely careful not to interfere in the political process, but if you asked him a question, you would get an answer' (Veland 2008: 35).

27. The majority behind the request from the *Storting* consisted of members from the Conservative Party (*Høyre*) and the Labour Party (*Arbeiderpartiet*). They held that, historically, the Court's independence related to its judging and not to its administration. That the government appointed the commissions was therefore unproblematic. The minority consisted of the smaller parties who were far more sceptical of the larger parties' traditional sway over the Ministry of Justice. They preferred that the *Storting* appoint the commission.

The Court Commission

The King in Council appointed the Court Commission on 8 March 1996. It was to report on options for the organisation of the courts, the appointment processes of judges, and the procedures to be used when dealing with complaints concerning the discipline of judges. Three factors, however, hampered the Commission's abilities to meet these mandates.

First, there was significant reaction against the Commission's membership, which consisted of ten lawyers and one political scientist. Although newspapers, politicians, and law professors underscored the competence of the Commission members, critics argued that the legal profession so dominated the Commission that its recommendations would be biased in favour of the legal community. Law professor Eivind Smith (1996b) accused the government of deferring too much to judges' calls for the independence of the courts. Rhetorically, he asked whether the government would have considered appointing only teachers to a commission addressing school reforms. Even Lisbeth Holand, the chair of the Standing Committee on Justice in the *Storting*, and representing the Socialist Left Party, demanded that non-lawyers be added to the Commission (Øystå and Letvik 1996).

Second, there was growing public interest in the disclosures that many judges had supplementary income and incidental earnings in addition to their judges' salaries. At issue was whether such income would bias the judges or lead to conflicts of interest. Newspapers ran stories listing the income and wealth of Supreme Court justices, noting that some had incomes far greater than their annual government salary (Letvik 1996). Lisbeth Holand argued that courts as institutions could only be as independent as the individual judges who presided over them and requested that the Commission's mandate be expanded to include a report on the extent of supplementary income and how this might affect the judges' decisional behaviour (Øystå and Letvik 1996).

Finally, there was the explosive Lund Commission report, published on 8 May 1996. The Lund Commission – named after Supreme Court Justice Ketil Lund, who took a leave of absence from the Court to chair it – had been appointed by the *Storting* in 1994 to investigate claims of illegal surveillance of Norwegian citizens. In its report, the Lund Commission concluded that illegal surveillance had in fact taken place and that it had primarily targeted socialists and communists.[28] One of the Lund Commission's conclusions was that lower courts had failed to do their job of upholding the rule of law. According to the report, judges had been too compliant and submissive to police requests for illegal wiretapping. Chief Justice Carsten Smith publicly apologised for the failure of the courts and judges (Bonde 1996b).

---

28. Ironically, the Special Branch of the Police (*overvåkningspolitiet*) had in fact surveilled Berge Furre – one of the members of the Commission, a historian and high profile member of the Socialist Left Party – while he was taking part in the Lund Commission's investigations (Bonde 1996a). Grete Faremo, who was Minister of Justice during the time of the Lund Commission's investigations, had to resign from the cabinet when the surveillance of Berge Furre became public. Also, it was in the discussions in the aftermath of the Lund Commission's report that animosity between the Supreme Court justices Jens Bugge and Ketil Lund became so intense that for over a year – when Chief Justice Carsten Smith finally intervened – Bugge refused to sit on the same panel as Ketil Lund (Hansen 1997).

On 11 October 1996, the government expanded the mandate of the Court Commission to include both the practice of appointing interim judges and the extent and impact of the non-court earnings of judges. The government also appointed five non-lawyers to the Commission as a counterbalance to the legal community's perceived dominance in its original membership. The Commission's secretariat became based in the Supreme Court building and held all but two of its thirty-one meetings in the Court of Chief Justice Carsten Smith.

On the issue of court organisation, positions within the Commission quickly hardened into two factions and became so polarised that the factions occasionally held separate meetings. Ex-law professor, Chief Justice, and the Commission's chair, Carsten Smith, led the larger of the two factions. Emphasising the principle of an independent judiciary, the Smith faction argued for a court administration to be firmly established outside of and separate from the Ministry of Justice, so as to limit the Ministry's political influence over the courts and judges. Symbolically, it was important for Smith to sever the ties between the courts and the Ministry of Justice, thereby establishing a new type of relationship between the two. The minority faction, led by political science professor Johan P. Olsen, did not accept Smith's arguments. Perceiving the positions of the Smith faction as unrealistic, and emphasising the importance of democratic accountability, the Olsen faction averred that the administration of the courts should continue to be based in the Ministry of Justice. According to this faction, key features of a well-functioning democracy (such as its courts of law) should remain under democratic control.

Ironically, the views of lawyers and non-lawyers on the Commission did not go in their predicted directions. In terms of the intentions behind the expansion of the Commission, the plan backfired. In fact, had the Commission not been expanded to include five non-lawyers, Olsen's faction advocating the principle of democratic accountability would have carried the day. As it turned out, the non-lawyers on the Commission primarily lined up behind Smith. Most lawyers, on the other hand, declared that they had full faith in the Ministry of Justice's administration of the courts, and they did not find any reason to curb the Minister of Justice's authority in this matter. Although the minority disagreed with Carsten Smith, they acknowledged his efforts and the amount of prestige that he invested in the Commission's report.[29]

The Ministry of Justice reworked the Commission's report and in late spring 2001 sent it to the *Storting* for a vote.[30] Despite the divisions that had characterised the labours of the Commission, the *Storting* passed *The Court Act* unanimously. A new court administration was created. Not only was it removed from the Ministry of Justice, it was located in Trondheim in order to – in the words of the Ministry – fulfil the government's policy of bringing more government jobs to areas outside the Oslo region. In essence, the *Storting* vote in 2001 advanced the

---

29. The Commission's majority also suggested an amendment to the Constitution concerning the independence of the courts. The suggested amendment failed to materialise.

30. Ot.prp. no. 44. 2000–2001. Om lov om endringer i domstolloven m.m. (den sentrale domstoladministrasjon og dommernes arbeidsrettslige stilling) 2 March 2001.

processes of judicialisation, depoliticisation, and judicial independence that had so influenced the judiciaries in new democracies during the last decade (Tate and Vallinder 1997; Østerud and Selle 2006). As to the process of appointing justices to the Supreme Court, a new regime took effect in 2002.

The Norwegian Courts Administration, 2002

The Norwegian Courts Administration (NCA) was established in 2002 and added a layer of bureaucracy to promote the independence of the courts, including the Supreme Court, from the Ministry of Justice (Ot.prp. nr. 44, 2000–2001). The NCA has primary responsibility for administering the judicial system, including the sixty-six district courts and the six courts of appeal. Housed in Trondheim, the NCA plays the role of a 'support and service agency for the courts', performing a variety of administrative functions, including training, personnel matters, finances, and information technology.

With nine members, the Norwegian Courts Administration is ultimately controlled by its Board of Governors, which appoints the NCA director to a six-year term (NCA, nd). The King in Council appoints seven members of the Board (four judges, a court employees representative, and two lawyers), and the *Storting* appoints two members to represent the citizenry.[31] While this institutional structure reflects the general desire to optimise the separation of government powers, the NCA's Department of Legal Affairs 'cannot review courts' judgments but will upon request answer general questions related to the courts' work' (NCA, nd).

In addition to relieving the Ministry of Justice of its erstwhile judicial administrative responsibilities, the 2002 reform added a step to the judicial appointment process. Within the NCA, the Judicial Appointments Board (*Innstillingsrådet for dommere*) was created to accept applications for judicial vacancies, including those on the Supreme Court (*see* Figure 2.3). The King in Council appoints members of the Appointments Board as well as its chair. The seven members consist of three judges, one lawyer, one lawyer in public service, and two non-lawyers.[32] The NCA may participate in the meetings of the Judicial Appointments Board and is represented either by its Director or the Director's designate.[33] *The Court Act* Section 55 states that judges ought to be recruited – to all courts – among lawyers of a varied work background.

Upon the announcement of a Supreme Court vacancy, applications are sent to the NCA, which publishes a list of applicants and their vitas on its web page.[34]

---

31. *The Court Act*, 1915/2005: Section 33a.

32. When the council handles applications to the Land Consolidation Courts, the membership has a slightly different distribution.

33. *The Court Act*, 1915/2005: Section 55a.

34. Contrary to the practice of applicants to the lower courts, applicants to the Supreme Court cannot demand that their names be withheld from the public. This practice reduces the number of applicants for Supreme Court vacancies (Helsingeng 2013).

Eventually, the applications are forwarded to the Judicial Appointments Board, which appoints members to a group responsible for interviewing the applicants. The Chief Justice and the most senior associate justice are members of this group. The interviews themselves take place in the Chief Justice's chambers within the Supreme Court building (Aschehoug 2010). Following the interview stage, the members of the Judicial Appointments Board meet to assess and rank the applicants. A list of (typically) the top three candidates is forwarded to the Ministry of Justice. At this point, the Chief Justice – in an informal personal meeting with the Minister of Justice – communicates the Court's sense of the applicants on the shortlist.[35] After the Minister of Justice and the Ministry's high civil servants have reviewed the ranked list, they submit the Ministry's recommendation to the King in Council. The Ministry of Justice is not required to follow the ranked list of the Appointments Board, but to date no alterations have taken place. The final stage of the process between the Ministry and the King in Council is largely perfunctory, indicating that the decisive choice lies with the Ministry of Justice.[36]

Since the creation of the Judicial Appointments Board in 2002 – and starting with the appointment of Justice Toril Marie Øie in 2004 through 1 January 2015, there have been sixteen permanent justices appointed to the Supreme Court through this process.[37] During this time, neither the Minister of Justice nor the King in Council has overturned the Appointments Board's recommendation. Moreover, in all but one case the Judicial Appointments Board's ranking of candidates has been unanimous. The exception occurred in 2006 when four Council members ranked Hilde Indreberg first and Arnfinn Bårdsen second; meanwhile, three members ranked Arnfinn Bårdsen first, dropping Hilde Indreberg to fourth. The Minister of Justice and the King in Council deferred to the Council's four-vote majority (The Judicial Appointments Board 2006).[38] The sting of being denied a seat on the High Bench did not register for long with Bårdsen. In 2007 another seat opened on the Court, and he filled it.

In June 2010, Chief Justice Tore Schei broke with the tradition of the Chief's (and the Court's) assessment of the shortlist of applicants to fill a Court vacancy being privately communicated to the Minister of Justice. In that year, the Judicial Appointments Board sent a shortlist of four candidates – Henrik Bull, Ragnhild Noer, Knut Kallerud, and Morten Holmboe, ranked in that order – to the Justice Ministry. Regarding that ranking, the Court publicly announced, 'The ranking

---

35. It is important to note that although there is some potential for the Court to influence the appointment choice, the Court plays a secondary role. It does not have a hand in the appointment agenda.

36. After their appointments, the judges are bound by Section 60 of *The Court Act* and have to ensure in writing that they will execute their duties conscientiously. The Norwegian Courts Administration keeps the signed documents.

37. *See* Appendix A.

38. In this appointment process, both the majority and the minority of the Judicial Appointments Board deviated from the statute prescribing only three ranked candidates (*The Court Act*, section 55b: third clause).

Figure 2.3: Supreme Court Appointment Process Since 2002

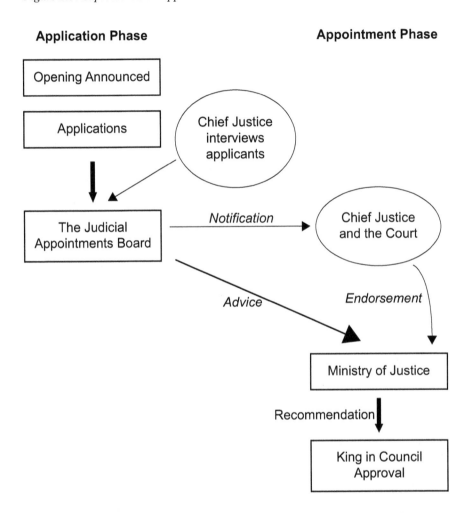

of number two and number three is not evident. Both are very good lawyers. They have different backgrounds, but both backgrounds would be important for the Supreme Court' (Gjerde 2010).[39] That message was obviously sufficient to inform applicants in the next round of judicial appointments of the Supreme Court's preference. Accordingly, in 2011, when there were two openings on

---

39. Chief Justice Tore Schei added that 'the Supreme Court has the right to voice its opinion' on which applicants are qualified and which are not (in Gjerde 2010). At the Court's annual press briefing in January 2013, Schei also claimed that when it came to the appointment of justices the political colour of the government did not matter. Schei concluded that during the last fifteen years the government has appointed the justices preferred by the Supreme Court (Valestrand 2013).

the Court, only Kallerud – the Deputy Director General of the Norwegian Prosecuting Authority – and one other applicant presented themselves. Perhaps responding to the Court's revealed preferences, the Judicial Appointments Board found only Kallerud qualified. The unfilled position was re-announced later that same year.

Finally, *The Court Act* also prescribes the appointment of interim justices, an interesting feature of the Norwegian Supreme Court. Interim appointments are made when vacancies occur because of conflicts of interest, caseload pressures, or Court reorganisation. Interim justices have all the prerogatives and responsibilities of their regular justice counterparts. However, they hold their seats only for a maximum of two years. Importantly, their interim status does not render them ineligible for a seat on the High Bench as a regular justice. That tenure of interim justices on the Court might be perceived as an 'audition' has raised some questions concerning their full independence from the government (Wold 1964; Eckhoff 1964; Hylland 2009; we systematically address this point in Chapters Five and Seven). Regardless, when it comes to the appointment of an interim justice to the Court, the Chief Justice sends a request for such an appointment to the Ministry of Justice, which in turn presents the request to the King in Council. Often, the Court's request includes the identity of the individual who is to fill the interim appointment. Individuals are drawn from the courts of appeal (particularly the court sitting in Oslo) or (a more recent trend) from law schools. The high civil servants in the Ministry of Justice handle the actual appointments of interim justices, although the Minister of Justice ultimately decides whether or not to accept their recommendation.

The Supreme Court's support staff

Internally, the Supreme Court has its own support staff, which comprises about twenty law clerks. The Court also has an information officer, as well as approximately twenty employees covering administration, library, and infrastructure services.[40] Over time, this support staff has grown. For example, prior to 1995, there were only three 'secretaries' functioning as clerks. The clerks' role does bear some additional comment. While the clerks may perform occasional tasks for individual justices,[41] their primary responsibility is to assist the Appeals Selection Committee in its gatekeeping duties. In this capacity, the clerks produce a memo summarising a case's basic legal arguments, issues, and any precedents invoked. The memo also includes a recommendation as to whether the case should be docketed. A large share of those recommendations is followed. Although the Court's support staff has increased, it remains relatively small, raising questions concerning its institutional capacity. As the Court's caseload has continued to grow, is there sufficient staffing

---

40. An organisational chart and a detailed list of all personnel can be found at http://www.domstol.no/en/Enkelt-domstol/-Norges-Hoyesterett/ (last accessed 15 November 2015).

41. Unlike in the U.S. Supreme Court, where clerks are hired by and assigned to individual justices, the Norwegian Supreme Court is supported by a 'clerk pool'.

for the Court to fulfil its role as a major player in the governance of Norway? Former Chief Justice Carsten Smith is sanguine on this subject, at least with respect to the size of the pool of clerks servicing the Court. He has written that a substantial increase in the number of clerks may not be necessary since 'there is a strong personal element in judicial decisions that limits the amount of assistance that can be drawn on' (Smith 1998: 99–100).

Political appointments?

In this chapter we have covered much of historical development of the Court, the Ministry of Justice and, in part, the relationship between the two. We have often referred to the appointment process within the Ministry of Justice. Throughout this book we take the attitudinal model of judicial behaviour as our point of departure.[42] A basic tenet of this model is that the ideology of the justice influences the direction of a justice's votes. In the absence of direct measures of the justices' ideological orientation, we rely on the appointing government as an *ex ante* measure of this. This *ex ante* indicator is a measure of political preferences. A key question that needs to be discussed given the historical background presented here is whether the political leadership of the changing governments – particularly the Prime Minister and the Minister of Justice – emphasised the political ideology of the candidates above and beyond the legal and personal quality of an applicant under consideration for promotion to the Supreme Court.

The view from the principals

One way of looking at the appointment process is from the view of the principals. Initially, it is pertinent to ask whether the Prime Ministers or Ministers of Justice, as key players in the process, were in any way tied to the legal profession. As regards the Prime Ministers, the answer is negative. Of the thirteen Prime Ministers of post-World War II governments through 2009 only two – Jon Lyng and Jan P. Syse – were educated as lawyers. Combined, their premierships add up to just thirteen months.

By contrast, a total of 33 Ministers of Justice were in office while making the 225 appointments of interim justices, permanent justices and Chief Justices who served in the 1945–2009 period covered in our analysis.[43] As to the formal education of these ministers, the post-World War II era can be divided in two distinct periods. First, all Ministers of Justice, for all governments in the period up to and including the Labour government of Odvar Nordli that terminated in February 1981, had law degrees from the University of Oslo. Second, in

---

42. We also include the socio-demographic model (*see* Tate and Handberg 1991).

43. Some of the thirty-three ministers of justice served more than once in different governments. The 225 appointments include interim justices who were appointed more than once. The number of appointments also covers Chief Justices and their appointments as associate justices. Information on the Ministers of Justice draws on *Data on the Political System* by the Norwegian Social Science Data Archive. Online. Available http://www.nsd.uib.no (last accessed TBC).

the 1981–2009 period, only half of the Labour governments' eight different Ministers of Justice had a law degree. And only three out of the five non-socialist governments' Ministers of Justice had a law degree. Evidently, there has been a distinct shift away from the expectation and informal requirement that the Ministry of Justice be led by a politician educated in law.[44] This change does not mean that in the most recent period the government placed less emphasis on the legal quality of potential candidates to the Supreme Court. But it might indicate that the Ministers of Justice can be more receptive to candidate qualities beyond the purely legal ones.

Thinking about appointments

Although we know the education of the key operators in government and our database contains indicators of the justices and their background, little is known about deliberations – within the Ministry of Justice, within the government and among other politicians and the civil servants, or even among the justices of the Supreme Court – on potential candidates, nominees and on the performances of justices on the Court. In order to gather information on this elusive topic, we have scoured political biographies and conducted several interviews. With very few exceptions, political biographies contain next to no discussion on the topic of Supreme Court nominations or appointments (or even discussions on decisions or judicial performances on the Supreme Court). From the interviews we get a clear understanding that candidate qualities have been discussed, but we have been unable to elicit what types of qualities were discussed and how they were weighed. Our conclusion is that deliberations of appointments took place, but that no arsenal of smoking guns on explicit political appointments exists. To illustrate some of the deliberations and moves that emerge, we offer brief narratives from three different appointment processes.

The memoirs of Jens Haugland

Jens Haugland was a lawyer, a member of the Labour Party and Member of Parliament (1954–1973). He also served eight years (1955–1963) as a Minister of Justice for the social democratic Labour government. Some years after he withdrew from national politics, he published his political diaries. Here, Haugland is candid on his dissatisfaction with Justice Terje Wold, whom he appointed as Chief Justice in 1958 despite Supreme Court Justice Jørgen Berner Thrap's warnings against appointing Wold. Haugland later admits having regrets over appointing Per Lykke Anker rather than Knut Tvedt – a lawyer – to the Supreme Court in 1962 (Haugland 1986).

---

44. In 1995, judges also reacted to there being too many non-lawyers in the Ministry of Justice (Eidesen 1995). The group of undersecretaries that advise the Minister of Justice are more often than not educated as lawyers.

In 1968 – now as a member of parliament after the non-socialist takeover of government in the 1965 election – Haugland grumbled about not having been appointed to the Supreme Court position he had applied for. Haugland was now on better terms with Chief Justice Wold, who had encouraged him to apply for the post, telling Haugland that the Supreme Court should not consist solely of justices from Oslo.[45] But Haugland writes at the time that he also sensed that it was payback time since he, during his time as Minister of Justice, had not appointed the current non-socialist Prime Minister Per Borten to a county governorship that Borten had wanted.

As an ex-Minister of Justice, Haugland was also privy to the tug-of-war within the government and between the government and the Supreme Court on the appointment, in 1969, of the new Chief Justice. The Conservative members of government – including Minister of Justice (and later Supreme Court Justice) Elisabeth Schweigaard Selmer – wanted to elevate Justice Axel Heiberg to Chief, a choice shared by the Conservative members of the coalition government. Outgoing Chief Wold argued that Heiberg would not have the backing of the majority of the other justices on the Court and promoted the elevation of Justice Rolv Ryssdal, who in his youth had been active in the Liberal Party (*Venstre*) (Haugland 1988).[46]

The Conservative agenda

Haugland's memoirs overlap with an extraordinary episode that took place in the Borten government that succeeded the twenty years of Labour rule. On Friday 31 May 1968, Per Borten brought his non-socialist fifteen-member coalition cabinet to the weekly meeting with the King in Council at the Royal Castle. The minutes show that when the meeting came to the issue of the appointment of three new justices to the Supreme Court, the Cabinet split in two and passed a non-unanimous vote! A minority of five Cabinet members voted in favour of appointing justices Lilly Bølviken, Jens Christian Mellbye and Per Tønseth to the Court. A majority of nine Cabinet members voted in favour of justices Lilly Bølviken, Jens Christian Mellbye and Knut Blom.[47]

What was the line-up of these two factions? The minority faction, which included the Prime Minister and the Foreign Minister, was dominated by ministers representing the Liberal and the Agrarian parties. Ministers representing the Conservative and Christian People's Parties dominated the majority faction.

45. Terje Wold was born in northern Norway, and Jens Haugland came from one of the southernmost regions of the country. Two of the three justices appointed by the non-socialist government that year came from Oslo. The third, Lilly Bølviken – the first female justice on the Court – came from the same southern region as Jens Haugland.

46. The publication of Haugland's diaries was heavily criticised for being subjective and too candid. These criticisms, however, were bluntly rejected by history professor Rolf Danielsen, who praised the rare view into the corridors of power offered by the books (Danielsen 1986).

47. Royal decree 1968-05-31 nr. 0848.

Although a moderate conservative political split was evidently dividing the two factions, we do not know the justifications behind the Cabinet lining up behind differing sets of candidates.[48]

Kåre Willoch, an economist, a conservative Member of Parliament (1958–1989), twice Minister of Commerce (1963, 1965–1970), and Prime Minister (1981–1986), was a very influential politician of his time. He was in the majority at the Council when Prime Minster Per Borten's divided cabinet appointed Knut Blom to the Court over Per Tønseth (Tønseth was appointed to the Court in the summer of 1969). In one of his many memoirs, Willoch takes pleasure in observing the impact of the non-socialist government's appointees to the Supreme Court. Although Willoch is not very specific and reveals little as to how these appointments were advanced within the government, he is especially proud of the appointment of Elisabeth Schweigaard Selmer – also a member of the Cabinet majority decision in 1968 – to the Court three months before the fall of the non-socialist Borten government. In that appointment, Selmer moved almost directly from being Minister of Justice to Supreme Court justice.[49]

Furthermore, Willoch attributes the narrow conservative 9–8 victory of the landmark *Kløfta decisions* in 1976 (that ruled expropriation without full compensation to be in violation of the Constitution's Section 105) to Selmer's and other conservative justices' presence on the Court (Willoch 2002). In fact, Justice Knut Blom wrote the majority opinion of the *Kløfta decision*. And Willoch adds:

> The minimum majority behind this landmark decision nevertheless illustrates the importance that the selection process may have had on the court. The result would hardly have been the same if the Labour Party had been in power uninterruptedly, and thereby the power over appointments to the Supreme Court, until [the 1976 *Kløfta decision*]. (Willoch 2002: 124)

Carsten Smith parachutes into the Court

A final example of the will of the government, this time against the will of the Supreme Court itself, occurred late in 1990 and early 1991. In November 1990,

---

48. Nadim (2013) argues that it is difficult to track a historical voting record of these justices. Nadim uses their votes in the 1976 *Kløfta decision* for his analysis.

49. In a 1997 article, Kåre Willoch (1997) – now ex-prime minister and county governor of Oslo and Akershus – ruminated on judicial appointments and judicial independence. He writes that all judges know that the Ministry controls appointments and promotions. The government, Willoch continues, will always be tempted to install like-minded persons who can contribute to the development it prefers, or choose judges from fields it feels close to, for example ministries. Willoch also refers to Eivind Smith's (1993) observation that a flaw exists in the Norwegian system in that there are no guarantees against the possibility of the government politically and unilaterally exploiting the possibility of appointing Supreme Court justices (Willoch 1997).

the Conservative Syse government gave way to Gro Harlem Brundtland's third Labour government. The new Minister of Justice, economist Kari Gjesteby, was briefed that she needed to prepare for the appointment of a new Chief Justice. Inside the Court, the sitting Chief Justice Erling Sandene prepared to retire as he approached his seventieth birthday in April 1991. The name of one candidate was floated early – law professor Carsten Smith. Smith's name was offered by another member of the cabinet – Secretary of State Thorvald Stoltenberg. Stoltenberg, Smith, and their wives had been close family friends since the 1950s.

Appointing Smith as the new Chief would be surprising on two counts: he would be the first law professor since World War II to migrate to the Court from the ivory tower; and he would be the first Chief parachuted into the Court without having served an 'apprenticeship' as an associate justice. The idea of serving on the Court could not be unfamiliar to Smith – he had already had three short stints as an interim justice. However, applying for the job of Chief would be different altogether: Smith was very concerned over the possibility of applying for the job and not getting it. If that were to happen, the law professor and former dean of the University of Oslo law school would appear a bit presumptuous.

He was rightly worried because the Supreme Court justices had their own internal candidate, Arne Christiansen. Although Christiansen had the backing of the Court, his disadvantage was that he was sixty-five years old and could only have five more years of service before retiring. (His law school grades were also lower than Smith's). When Erling Sandene presented Christiansen as the Court's own candidate to Kari Gjesteby, his hopes were dashed and he returned empty handed. The government had already made up its mind. Smith had the full backing of the Prime Minister and the Cabinet. Smith was assured that if he applied for the job, he would get it.

Lawyers and historians are quick to criticise analysis of the appointing-government-voting-on-the-Supreme-Court correspondence. They do so in part on the merit of causal mechanisms and in part by offering examples of justices with a political affiliation that differ from that of the appointing government. We welcome challenges of causal mechanisms. However, to the best of our knowledge, there is no conclusive evidence that clinches either the mechanism of partisan appointment or the mechanism of non-partisan appointment. While our critics conclude that appointing practices and procedures do not allow partisan appointments, we contend that appointment practices and procedures allow for targeted appointments (*see* Smith 1993; Willoch 1997). True, we have not discovered an arsenal of smoking guns. And we have not unearthed a purely legal-technocratic appointment process in which a blindfolded Lady Justice puts the Supreme Court justice applicants on the scale. We accept anecdotal evidence that the government has appointed justices who obviously did not match the government's political views. But we prefer to work systematically on the hypothesis of appointment as an *ex ante* measure of ideology, and in the analysis of justices' votes we let the chips fall where they may.

Seasoned politicians?

Since 1945 only four justices have migrated from political positions in the first and second branches of government to the Supreme Court (which is two less than the six justices that migrated from the ivory tower to the Supreme Court, all of which have done so after 1991).[50]

Terje Wold represented the Labour Party (*Arbeiderpartiet*) as Minister of Justice (1939–1945), was a member of the *Storting* (1945–1949) and was appointed to the Supreme Court effective as of 1949. He was elevated to Chief Justice by his own party government in 1958 and stepped down in 1969 at the age of seventy. Oscar Christian Gundersen represented the Labour Party (*Arbeiderpartiet*) as Minister of Justice (1945–1952 and 1963–1965) and Minister of Trade (1962–1963), and was appointed to the Supreme Court in 1953 by his own party government. He stepped down in 1958, but was appointed to the Supreme Court again in 1967 – this time by the non-socialist Borten government. He retired from the Court for a second time in 1977. Elisabeth Schweigaard Selmer represented the Conservative Party (*Høyre*) as Minister of Justice (1965–1970) and was appointed to the Supreme Court in 1970 by her own non-socialist Borten government; she stepped down in 1990. Finally, Egil Endresen represented the Conservative Party (*Høyre*) as a member of the *Storting* (1965–1973) and as Minister of Justice (1970–1971) and was appointed to the Supreme Court in 1977 by the socialist Nordli government, and stepped down in 1988.

One question is whether these four former politicians reveal a type of judicial behaviour on the Supreme Court that corresponds to the political ideology of their pre-Court years? Ostensibly, if we follow the *ex ante* measure of political ideology through appointing government we find a mismatch between their original party affiliation and the appointing party for Gundersen's second appointment and for Endresen's appointment.[51] We have, however, been unable to track the individual votes of these four ex-politicians at a level necessary for determining the degree of their ideological voting, while controlling for other likely factors.[52] Fascinating as such a detailed follow-up study of ex-politicians-turned-Supreme-Court-justices would be, in the present analyses we are still committed to the larger study of all justices on the Court.

---

50. Here we exclude Paal Berg (1873–1968) from the Liberal Party (*Venstre*), Minister of Health and Social Affairs (1919–1920) and Minister of Justice (1924–1926), since he was appointed to the Supreme Court before World War II in 1918, was elevated to Chief in 1929, and stepped down in 1946; and Emil Stang (1882–1964) from the Labour Party (*Arbeiderpartiet*), substitute representative to the *Storting* (1922–1924), since he was appointed to the Supreme Court before World War II in 1937, was elevated to Chief in 1946, and stepped down in 1952. Former professors of law turned Supreme Court justices include Carsten Smith (1991–2002), Magnus Aarbakke (1994–2002), Magnus Matningsdal (1997–), Jens Edvin A. Skoghøy (1998–), Kristin Normann (2010–), and Aage Thor Falkanger (2010–).

51. *See also* Nadim (2013).

52. But *see* our analysis of the justices' votes in plenary judicial review cases in Chapter Eight.

Conclusion

In the post-World War II era, there has been only one major formal change in the organisation of the appointment process to the Norwegian Supreme Court – *The Court Act* of 2001. Its aim was to reduce the executive's role in and influence over Norway's judicial system. And in some respects this happened. The administrative responsibility of the courts was removed from the Ministry of Justice, and a new actor in the appointment process was imposed on the Ministry. Instead of recommendations to the King in Council as to who should fill a Court vacancy occurring only within the Ministry of Justice, an added separate entity – the Judicial Appointments Board – was given a voice in the process. Yet, the executive's potential for influence over the Court is still real. To be sure, a separate institution vets and ranks applicants for vacancies on the Court, but it remains the prerogative of the Ministry of Justice to select an applicant from that ranked list and make the recommendation to the King in Council. From a ranked list of three of four names, it does not require too great a suspension of disbelief to recognise that the Minister of Justice will find an applicant whose anticipated policy preferences are consonant with his or her own. And although the Ministry has never deviated from the Appointments Board's ranking, this does not mean it cannot happen. Moreover, there is always the possibility that the Judicial Appointments Board takes the Minister's policy preferences into account and compiles a strategically ranked list. The potential applicants may also self-select, choosing to present themselves for possible appointment in light of their perceived chances of success given the nature of the Minister – not to speak of signs that may emanate from the Court itself.

Finally, we note that although efforts have been made to erect institutions to insulate the composition of the Supreme Court from political forces, other appointment considerations have come to bear since the 1980s that have indirect political implications for the appointment process. Chief among these may be the effort to broaden the Court's representational base, both in terms of gender and geography. Emphasising these characteristics constrains the pool of potential appointees which, in turn, may reduce the range of ideological preferences and other background attributes. We will address this point in greater detail in Chapters Four and Six.

Of course, while the institutional context in which the Norwegian Supreme Court operates has changed over time, so too has the nature of its decisional outputs. There have been periods of both unanimity and dissensus. In the next chapter we discuss the attributes of the Court's processing of cases, and take up, in some detail, the variation in voting agreement among the justices.

References

Arbeidsretten (2011) 'The Labour Court of Norway'. Online. Available http://www.arbeidsretten.no/index.php?module=Pagesetterandfunc=viewpubandtid=4andpid=15 (last accessed 5 February 2013).

Aschehoug, M. (2010) 'Rekordmange nye dommere i Scheis periode', *Advokatbladet* 90 (10): 26–27.

Bonde, A. (1996a) 'Berge Furre overvåket som kommisjonsmedlem', *Aftenposten*, 13 December.

— (1996b) 'Carsten Smiths råd til domstolene etter Lundrapporten: - Større vilje og dristighet', *Aftenposten*, 9 June.

Brattestå, H. (2008) 'Impeachment: Still a Relevant Institution? Recent Changes in Norway', Association of Secretaries General of Parliaments. Online. Available http://www.asgp.co/node/30134 (last accessed 6 May 2015).

Christensen, T., Lægreid, P., Roness, P. G. and Røvik, K. A. (2007) *Organization Theory and the Public Sector: Instrument, Culture and Myth*, London: Routledge.

Danielsen, R. (1986) 'Reaksjonens røst?', *Bergens Tidende*, 2 September.

Derry, T. K. (1968) *A Short History Of Norway*, Westport: Greenwood Press.

Domstoladministrasjonen (nd) Norwegian Courts Administration. Online. Available http://www.domstol.no/ (last accessed 26 November 2014).

Drucker, P. F. (1954) *The Practice of Management*, New York: Harper.

Eckhoff, T. (1964) 'Noen refleksjoner om domstolens uavhengighet' in *Festskrift tillägnad professor, juris doktor Karl Olivecrona vid hans avgång från professorämbetet den 30 juni 1964 av kollegor, lärjungar och vänner*, Stockholm: Norstedt, pp. 109–147.

Eidesen, A. (1995) 'Domstolenes administrative overbygning', *Juristkontakt* 30 (3): 2–4.

Gjerde, R. (2010) 'Vil ha full åpenhet om nye dommere', *Aftenposten*, 10 June.

Grønlie, T. and Flo, Y. (2009) *Sentraladministrasjonens Historie Etter 1945: Den Nye Staten? Tiden Etter 1980*, Bergen: Fagbokforlaget.

Hansen, K. M. (1997) 'Isfront mellom Jens Bugge og Ketil Lund', *Aftenposten*, 5 November.

Haugland, J. (1986) *Dagbok frå Kongens Råd*, Oslo: Det Norske Samlaget.

— (1988) *Dagbok frå Løvebakken: Fragment av eit Politisk Liv*, Oslo: Det Norske Samlaget.

Helsingeng, T. (2013) 'Redde for å bli vraket: Jurister dropper dommer-jobber', *VG*. 4 February.

Hem, P. E. (2012) *Megleren: Paal Berg 1873–1968*, Oslo: Aschehoug.

Hylland, A. (2009) 'Hva Bør Gjøres Når Svært Mange Høyesterettsdommere er Inhabile?', *Lov og Rett* 48 (2): 112–118.

The Judicial Appointments Board (2006) 'Minutes', 19 December 2006.

Justice and Police Department (2001) 'Hva er forliksrådet?'. Online. Available http://www.regjeringen.no/nb/dep/jd/dok/Veiledninger_brosjyrer/2001/hva-er-forliksradet.html?id=87684 (last accessed 5 February 2013).

Larsen, K. (1950) *A History of Norway*, Princeton: Princeton University Press.

Letvik, H. (1996) 'Høyesterett har mye på si', *Aftenposten*, 17 August.

Malsch, M. (2009) *Democracy in the Courts: Lay Participation in European Criminal Justice Systems*, Burlington: Ashgate Publishing Co.

Matningsdal, M. (1996) *To-instansreformen*, Oslo: Universitetsforlaget.

Midgaard, J. (1986) *A Brief History Of Norway*, Oslo: Tano.

Nadim, M. (2013) 'Er Høyesterettsdommere politisk farget? En undersøkelse av 17 dommeres votum i dissenssaker', *Lov og Rett* 52 (10): 655–671.

NCA (nd) Norwegian Courts Administration. Online. Available http://www. domstol.no/ (last accessed 26 November 2014).

Norges Domstoler (2013) 'Sivil sak'. Online. Available http://www.domstol.no/ DAtemplates/Article____3095.aspx?epslanguage=NO (last accessed 5 February 2013).

Norges Statskalender (various years) *Norges Statskalender: Fortegnelse over Konstitusjonelle Organer og Statsforvaltning*, Oslo: Aschehoug.

NOU (1999) 'Domstolene i samfunnet. Administrativ styring av domstolene. Utnevnelser, sidegjøremål, disiplinærtiltak. Midlertidige dommere', Oslo: Department of Justice. Online. Available http://www.regjeringen. no/nb/dep/jd/dok/NOUer/1999/NOU-1999-19.html?id=141812 (last accessed 25 November 2014).

Olsen, L. -J. K. (2005) 'The Conciliation Boards in Norway – A Brief Overview and Assessment of Pros and Cons', Unpublished manuscript.

Ot.prp. nr. 44 (2000–2001) 'Om lov om endringer i domstolloven m.m. (den sentrale domstoladministrasjon og dommernes arbeidsrettslige stilling)', Oslo: Department of Justice. Online. Available http://www.regjeringen. no/nb/dep/jd/dok/regpubl/otprp/20002001/otprp-nr-44-2000-2001-. html?id=164074 (last accessed 25 November 2014).

Pedersen, D. and Larsen, G. T. (1995a) 'Dommere vil ha sitt eget styre', *Aftenposten*, 30 June.

—— (1995b) 'Dommerne ber om å få sin fremtid utredet: Vil administrere seg selv', *Aftenposten*, 5 July.

Poguntke, T. and Webb, P. (eds) (2005) *The Presidentialization of Politics: A Comparative Study of Modern Democracies*, Oxford: Oxford University Press.

Regjering.no (2011) Severin Løvenskiold. Online. Available https://www. regjeringen.no/nb/om_regjeringa/tidligere/departementer_embeter/ embeter/statsminister-1814-/severin-lovenskiold/id439287/ (last accessed 6 May 2015).

Rognes, J. and Sky, P. K. (2004) 'Mediation in Land Consolidation and in Boundary Disputes' in Deakin, M., Dixon-Gough, R. and Mansberger, R. (eds) *Instruments for Rural and Urban Land Management*, Aldershot: Ashgate Publishing Limited, pp. 59–74.

Shaughnessy, E. J. (1992) *Conflict Management in Norway: Practical Dispute Resolution*, Lanham: University Press of America.

Smith, C. (1975) 'Domstolene og rettsutviklingen', *Lov og Rett* 14: 292–319.

— (1996a) 'Regjeringens justisforvaltning og domstolenes uavhengighet', *Lov og Ret* 35: 186–196.

— (1998) 'The Supreme Court in Present-day Society' in Tschudi-Madsen, S. (ed.) *The Supreme Court of Norway,* Oslo: Aschehoug, pp. 95–143.

— (2000) 'Domstolenes og dommernes rolle i fremtiden', *Juristkontakt* 35 (6): 8–15.

Smith, E. (1993) *Høyesterett og folkestyret. Prøvingsretten overfor lover,* Oslo: Universitetsforlaget.

— (1996b) 'Domstolene, demokratiet og rettsstaten', *Aftenposten,* 1 July.

Smukkestad, Ø. (1995) 'Utnevnelse av dommere', *Juristkontak,* 30 (3): 5–6.

Solstad, A. (1996) 'Notater om det aller helligste', *Dagbladet,* 1 December.

Tate, C. N. and Handberg, R. (1991) 'Time Binding and Theory Building in Personal Attribute Models of Supreme Court Voting Behavior, 1916–1988', *American Journal of Political Science* 35 (2): 460–480.

Tate, C. N. and Vallinder, T. (eds) (1997) *The Global Expansion of Judicial Power,* New York: New York University Press.

Valestrand, T. (2013) 'Får dem de ber om', *Bergens Tidende,* 15 January.

Veland, S. (2008) 'En styrket rettstat - et svekket demokrati? Etableringen av en uavhengig Domstoladministrasjon 1995–2001', Unpublished Master's thesis. Department of History. University of Bergen.

Willoch, K. (1997) 'Refleksjoner over dommernes uavhengighet og habilitet', *Lov og Rett* 36: 146–154.

— (2002) *Myter og Virkelighet: Om Begivenheter frem til Våre Dager med Utgangspunkt i Perioden 1965–1981,* Oslo: Cappelen.

Wold, T. (1954) 'Rettspleie og forvaltning', *Dommerforeningens Medlemsblad,* pp. 1340 ff.

— (1960) 'Domstolene og ombudsmannen', *Dommerforeningens Medlemsblad,* pp. 80 ff.

— (1964) 'Domstolenes deltakelse i justisforvaltningen', *Lov og Rett* 3: 385–400.

Østerud, Ø. and Selle, P. (2006) 'Power and Democracy in Norway: The Transformation of Norwegian Politics', *Scandinavian Political Studies* 29 (1): 25–46.

Øystå, A. (1995) 'Egen avdeling for domstolene', *Aftenposten,* 31 March.

Øystå, A. and Letvik, H. (1996) 'Ikke-jurister kan bli med', *Aftenposten,* 20 August.

Chapter Three

The Decisional Processes of the Norwegian Supreme Court

Consider the two following passages:

> Simply put, Rehnquist votes the way he does because he is extremely conservative; Marshall voted the way he did because he was extremely liberal (Segal and Spaeth 2002: 86).

> When an act of Congress is appropriately challenged in the courts as not conforming to the constitutional mandate, the judicial branch of the Government has only one duty – to lay the article of the Constitution which is invoked beside the statute which is challenged and to decide whether the latter squares with the former (*U.S. v. Butler* 297 U.S. 1, 62 [1936]).

The two passages articulate two very different understandings of judicial decision making. The former allows for the possibility that an array of extra-legal forces bear upon any individual judge's decisional behaviour, and therefore also on the outputs of any collegial court. The latter leaves room only for the law. The former emphasises predispositions and ideologies: to the greatest possible degree, judges want to make decisions that are congruent with their policy preferences. The latter emphasises the legal syllogism, axioms, and corollaries with a precision akin to mathematics (Holmes 1963). Finally, the former embraces division among judges when deciding a case, while the latter would explain any division as a consequence of errors in one or another judge's legal calculus. In this chapter we attempt to establish that in the context of the Norwegian Supreme Court, the former – that is, an extra-legal model – has the greater verisimilitude.

Now, we are by no means arguing that the decisions of Norway's Supreme Court justices are unmoored from 'the law'. Legal facts, precedent, legislative and/or constitutional intent are considered and often direct or at least mould the individual justice's votes. Yet, in a non-trivial proportion of cases before the Court, facts, dispositive precedent, and intent are not obvious. In these 'hard' cases, there is opportunity – some might even go so far as to say necessity – for the attitudinal preferences of judges to play a role. As we noted in Chapter One, the foundational elements of the legal model are not necessarily antithetical to the extra-legal model. The consideration of the facts of the case, for example, is fundamental to judicial decision making. But it matters *which* facts one chooses to emphasise, and attitudinal preferences can affect this determination. By the same token, precedent is integral to the law. It legitimises decisions and prevents the law from appearing random or capricious. However, in nations with well-developed legal systems, like Norway, it is not unusual for there to be precedents on both sides of the dispute. And here again is the opportunity for a justice's preferences to come to the fore. Faced with competing precedents, a justice's preferences can affect which precedent to invoke and which precedent to distinguish (*see* the discussion in Chapter One).

Because preferences affect the weights different justices give to certain facts or precedents, we would expect there to be disagreements in the merits voting behaviour of Norway's justices. And this is just what we find. We explore these patterns of non-unanimous decisional behaviour in greater detail in our discussion of the historical pattern of decisional disagreements among the justices, after we describe the Court's merits procedures. We turn first, however, to a brief discussion of the Court's docketing process.[1] After all, this is the step where the 'hard' cases – the cases with the greatest potential to make policy, the greatest room for the play of the justices' preferences, and the greatest likelihood of disagreement among the justices – are separated from the ordinary cases. We conclude this chapter by taking stock of the central points of the preceding discussion and setting the table for some of the systematic analyses in the chapters that follow.

The docketing stage – The 'rule of one'

As noted in Chapter Two the *Høyesterett* is both Norway's highest appellate court and a court of general jurisdiction. That is, it has the power to hear any case involving Norway's civil, criminal, administrative, or constitutional law brought to it on appeal. The Court's wide authority to hear and review cases would almost certainly overwhelm its finite institutional resources were it not for its discretionary jurisdiction, as exercised through the Appeals Selection Committee – the three-justice panel responsible for composing the Court's merits docket (*see* Chapter Two for a more complete description).[2] In other words, the Appeals Selection Committee is the Court's gatekeeper; it screens all appeals and selects a subset that it deems worthy of the Court's full attention.

To process the multitude of cases that arrive at the Court's doorstep, the Appeals Selection Committee effectively makes use of cues that indicate whether a given case is worthy of the Court's limited time and resources. Accordingly, appeals that are more likely to be docketed are ones that raise constitutional issues, that indicate conflict among the lower courts, that indicate that the law or legal doctrine is in need of clarification, or that have attracted substantial public attention – perhaps

---

1. The processes we describe and discuss in this and other chapters are based on updated documentation and recent interviews. Over the years there have been very few procedural changes. Therefore, the procedures are basically valid across the years that we analyse in this book.

2. Only three justices from the Committee actually screen any given appeal. Rotation among five justices ensures that the screening panels alternate from appeal to appeal.

in the media or in broader public discussions.[3] These are the cases that have the greatest potential social, political, or economic impact (on a court's use of its discretionary jurisdiction to 'cherry-pick' cases for their broader consequences, *see* Caldeira and Wright 1988). And these cases are relatively unique. By some estimates, the Appeals Selection Committee rejects up to 90 per cent of the cases appealed to the Supreme Court.

As we noted in Chapter Two, the clerks play an integral role in the screening process. Each appeal is assigned to a clerk, who produces a memo that summarises the appeal's claims and arguments. The memo also includes a recommendation concerning whether the case should be docketed. In general, the Appeals Selection Committee relies upon the memos in its screening decisions, and it usually adopts the clerk's docketing recommendation.

As a decision-making body, the Appeals Selection Committee is a small group that exhibits small group norms of behaviour. The justices who compose the screening panel for any given appeal circulate a written document, enclosed within a wrapper, to share their views on that case; typically, the views of the most senior justice are followed. The Committee employs what might be called a 'rule of one', inasmuch as a case is docketed when at least one justice concludes that it is worthy of a merits hearing.[4] Despite the presence of multiple decision makers, the Appeals Selection Committee is relatively efficient, usually rendering an up or down decision on whether to docket an appeal within two or three weeks. And despite the need for only one supporting justice's vote, it is ruthless in the performance of its gatekeeping function – rejecting between 80 per cent and 90 per cent of all appeals.[5]

The merits stage

All justices on the Court rotate equally between service on the Appeals Selection Committee and on the panels.[6] Normally, a panel composed of five justices hears the merits of an appeal that has survived the Court's screening process. Assignment of justices to these merits panels follows a quasi-random procedure, or a 'controlled lottery'.[7] That is, the assignment of an individual justice to a

---

3. Procedures of appeals to the Supreme Court are regulated by *The Dispute Act*, *see* Section 30.

4. In the U.S. Supreme Court, four justices (the 'rule of four') must vote to grant a petition for *certiorari*, thereby docketing a case. The U.S. Court does not employ a separate panel of justices for its gatekeeping decisions.

5. By way of comparison, between 1975 and 2009, the U.S. Supreme Court rejected approximately 95 per cent of all paid appeals (computed from Epstein *et al.* 2011: Table 2–6).

6. The exception is the Chief Justice who, due to the administrative tasks, participates less on the Appeals Selection Committee.

7. Justice Arne Christiansen coined the term 'controlled lottery' (*kontrollert loddtrekning*) in a 1981 Supreme Court decision (Rt-1981–673: 679). Theoretically, there are 15,504 combinations of five justices being selected from a pool of twenty justices to serve on a panel [$C_{20,5} = (20*19*18*17*16) / 5!$], and 1,140 combinations of three justices being selected from a pool of twenty justices to serve on the Appeals Selection Committees [$C_{20,3} = (20*19*18) / 3!$].

merits panel is, as far as practicable, removed from human choice. Of course, both mundane and more dramatic obstacles can frustrate perfectly random assignment. The Chief Justice must be conscious of managing the Court's caseload and distributing the work equally across the justices.[8] And then there are the rare personal disputes and antagonisms that can upset random assignment. Recall, for example, the 1997 Lund–Bugge feud we noted in Chapter Two where, for over a year, Justice Jens Bugge refused to sit on the same panel as Justice Ketil Lund, and where Chief Justice Smith had to intervene and replace Bugge.

Ten justices are eligible for assignment to the merits panels. These are the justices who have not been assigned to the Appeals Selection Committee; are not assigned to their 'office week'; or are not on research leave or vacation. Because ten justices are available for assignment, two parallel panels are created,[9] and it is at this stage that the principle of avoiding biased selection effects is most evident. First, the ten justices are sorted in descending order according to seniority. The Chief Justice – if among these ten justices – is automatically listed as the 'most senior'. Once sorted, the ten justices are assigned to the two panels in alternating order. This ensures that each panel is composed of justices with varying degrees of seniority and that a panel never will consist of freshmen not thoroughly socialised into the customs and practices of the court. This assignment procedure does not take into account the justices' legal specialisation and expertise. Finally, appeals are assigned to each panel without regard to the panel members' preferences or expertise.

Employing a 'controlled lottery' yields benefits to the Court, both in practice and in principle. In practice, the routinisation of the justices' panel assignments relieves the Chief Justice of this burdensome and time-consuming chore. Meanwhile, random assignment of both the justices and appeals to panels helps to ensure the public that the Court's decisions are independent of the preferences of any individual justice. This, in turn, contributes to the Court's legitimacy among the mass public.

In addition to the five-justice panels, the Court hears certain cases on their merits as a Grand Chamber or in plenary session. Only cases that involve the proper application of Court precedent, conflicts between statutes, or the determination of the constitutionality of a parliamentary act or an international treaty to which Norway is a party invoke Grand Chamber review. When a case involves an issue or question that results in a Grand Chamber being convened, eleven justices hear the appeal – ten justices drawn at random plus the Chief Justice. All of the justices – other than the Chief and those who have been exempted or with potential conflicts of interest – participate in the Grand Chamber lottery.[10]

---

8. The responsibilities for the routine administrative tasks are delegated to the Court's Director General.

9. In 1905, due to the workload at the merits stage, the Court temporarily branched into two separate panels consisting of seven justices each. In 1938 the number of justices serving on the panels was reduced to five. To accommodate immediate post-World War II workload, for a short time the Supreme Court operated three five-justice panels (see Sunde 2012: 60–63; Sandmo 2005).

10. Examples of permissible exemptions include planned vacations, research leaves, and board meetings (see, for example, Rt-2010–939).

Similar to Grand Chambers, plenary sessions of the Court are convened to hear and decide only certain types of appeal. In this instance, it is the Chief Justice who determines that an appeal raises such an extraordinary issue or legal question that the full Court should hear and decide it. Accordingly, every justice – other than those with a permissible exemption or a conflict of interest – must hear the appeal.

The effect of recusals can be striking either because of permissible exemptions or conflicts of interest. Take, for example, the landowner-to-tenant property transfer cases decided in 2007. Because of the nature of the cases and the legal questions at bar, they were heard in plenary session. Of the nineteen justices who could have participated, however, eleven were recused.[11] Another example is the 2010 *Ship Owner's Taxation* case (Rt-2010–143). In this case, five justices were deemed to have conflicts of interest, two justices were on leaves of absence, and the most junior justice had to step down in order to reduce the number of sitting justices to an uneven number. Consequently, only eleven justices participated in this case.[12] It is worth noting, however, that even the loss of nearly half of the sitting Court did not prove fatal to plenary review. Both Grand Chambers and plenary sessions must have at least five participating justices.[13]

The most public aspect of the Court's merits stage is the oral argument. Oral arguments provide a significant opportunity for the justices to glean important information about the issues and legal questions at bar. Because of the quasi-random nature of panel composition, the blinded assignment of appeals to the panels, and the Court's wide substantive jurisdictional authority, it is very likely that the justices reviewing any given appeal are not experts in the specific area

---

11. In these cases (i.e. Rt-2007–1281; Rt-2007–1306; Rt-2007–1308), six justices were recused because they or their families had been or were renters; two more justices were recused because they had recently worked on the issue as government civil servants; and three justices were recused because of close family relationships with lawyers who had been involved in the preparations of the case. Chief Justice Tore Schei and Justice Karl Arne Utgård had also declared potential conflicts of interest, but for them no such conflicts were sustained (Rt-2007–705). Finally, Clement Endresen, the junior justice of the eight remaining justices, had to abandon the case in order to establish an odd number of justices. In the end, seven justices participated in the plenary decisions that involved more than 300,000 tenant property contracts (Rt-2007–1281, paragraph 18). Professor of law, former director of the Ministry of Justice's Legislation Department (*Lovavdelingen*), and common law partner of former justice Karin Maria Bruzelius, Inge Lorange Backer, sharply criticised the Court's practices of conflict of interest issues when justices with only a 'peripheral connection' to the issue were excluded. He warned that too strict practices could result in a biased Court whose decisions could risk the Court's trust and legitimacy (Backer 2008).

12. The 2010 conflicts of interest decisions in the *Ship Owner's Taxation* case were decided in Rt-2009–1617 and the final number of justices was finalised in Rt-2010–143, paragraphs 66–68.

13. If, after all the justices with a conflict of interest or permissible exemptions are excluded, an even number of justices remains, the most junior justice is dropped. In five-justice panels, if, for whatever reason, a justice has to withdraw from a case he or she may be replaced by one of the five justices initially allocated to the Appeals Selection Committee.

of the law upon which the appeal turns.[14] Accordingly, the justices make use of the oral arguments to develop a fuller understanding of the legal issues. It is quite common for the justices to put questions to the advocates during the presentation of their cases. Also indicative of the informational purposes oral arguments serve, Norway's Supreme Court advocates are not pressed to present their cases within a rigid and tightly compressed time period, unlike their counterparts in the U.S. Supreme Court.

Following the oral argument, the justices meet to discuss the case's merits. The meetings are 'formalized discussions' that take place in the court room (Schei 2010: 15). The meetings start with the most senior justice presenting his or her views on the facts of the case, the relevant statutes in questions, and how the case should be decided. Then, in strict order of descending seniority, each justice offers his or her views on the case. In larger cases, these deliberations may take some time; second and third rounds of discussion can take place, as individual justices might describe their ratiocination at some length in an effort to convince or persuade their counterparts. In the course of deliberations, the assignment of writing the Court's majority opinion is made. The opinion assigner is the Chief Justice or – if the Chief Justice is not a member of the merits panel – the most senior justice. In general, the Court follows a norm of equal division of the opinion-writing workload and, as a result, the justices know who is next in the assignment queue. Changes in assignment can be made, however, when the justice to whom the opinion would ordinarily be assigned is in the minority. Due to the workload of being responsible for presenting the case at the start of the discussion, the Chief Justice – or the most senior justice – will never write the opinion. Before the meeting is adjourned, the justices agree on a timetable for when the decision will be announced (Schei 2010).

Voting fluidity can occur during deliberations, as a justice's position regarding the outcome of an appeal may change. After the meeting, draft opinions are circulated and commented upon, perhaps in an effort to affect the final shape of the majority opinion. Indeed, modifications are made to the Court's opinion in order to attract additional justices to the majority position as well as to maintain the original majority. Meanwhile, dissenting opinions, with an eye to separate a justice or two from the original majority, might also be circulated.

Whether there is a strong norm *against* non-unanimous behaviour operating on the Norwegian Supreme Court is moot. More certain is the presence of several forces that would militate against its appearance. First, as we have already noted, some appeals are highly technical, presenting cut and dried legal questions and controversies. In these cases, it may be easier for the justices' positions to converge on a single outcome. Second, even on the harder, more ambiguous, cases efforts

---

14. We are by no means suggesting that the Supreme Court justices are legal tyros. Many of them are legal specialists. Justice Magnus Matningsdal, for example, quite literally wrote the book on Norwegian criminal law. Justice Skoghøy and Chief Justice Schei are the experts on civil law procedure, and Justice Falkanger on property law, to name a few.

are made among the justices to arrive at a compromise position.[15] As mentioned, draft opinions are circulated and modified to accommodate dissenting views. Third, unlike their counterparts on the U.S. Supreme Court, Norway's justices do not have a stable of clerks assisting them as they write their opinions. Thus, writing a dissent imposes an additional workload on the justices. (Of course, a justice may dissent from the majority vote without writing an accompanying opinion, by supporting an opinion offered by another justice.) And finally, dissents can be costly to the Court itself, perhaps undermining its institutional legitimacy among the mass public. Yet, non-unanimous behaviour occurs. It is to a general discussion of the pattern of this behaviour on the Norwegian Supreme Court that we now turn.

Historical pattern: Non-unanimous behaviour on the Norwegian Supreme Court

We define non-unanimous decisions as those instances in which the justices voting at the merits stage fail to reach consensus. For non-unanimous decisions we include three matters over which justices may disagree. First, a justice disagrees with the substantive outcome of the case. Second, a justice offers his or her concurring opinion. Here the justice agrees with the result reached by another justice, but not necessarily with the reasoning or the logic used in reaching such a result. And third, a justice may agree on the outcome of a case and the reasoning behind it, but the justice may disagree on the amount of punishment or compensation. Three different responses are available to justices when they disagree with the majority opinion: They may (1) write a concurring opinion, (2) write a dissenting opinion, or (3) simply vote contrary to the majority while offering no explanation for their disagreement.

Since political scientists have paid little attention to the *Høyesterett* and to the judicial behaviour that underlies its non-unanimous decisions, an appropriate first step is to offer a very basic overview of the body of non-unanimous decisions in the Norwegian Supreme Court. Our goal here is not explanatory. Rather, we seek to document the empirical presence of non-unanimous behaviour on Norway's High Court. We select and concentrate on the behaviour of the five-justice panels that so dominate the Court's workload at the merits stage. The presence of non-unanimous behaviour will be the case and votes that provide the grist for the quantitative mills that follow in later chapters.

Accordingly, we begin by briefly mapping the total number of five-justice panel decisions and the total number of non-unanimous five-justice panel decisions from 1945–2012 (*see* Figure 3.1 and Figure 3.2). The Figures show the total number of cases and how these break down into civil and criminal cases. The Figures also show the total number of cases per year as data points, and the local trend of the times series as solid lines.[16]

---

15. This distinction between technical, cut and dried controversies and cases freighted with legal ambiguities echoes the distinction between 'easy' and 'hard' cases (*see* Baum 1997: 66).

16. The time series have been smoothed by the T4253H-procedure (*see* Tukey 1977; Velleman and Hoaglin 1981).

Figure 3.1: Total Five-Justice Panel Decisions (N), Norwegian Supreme Court 1945–2012

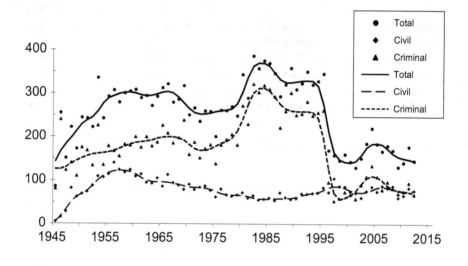

Figure 3.2: Non-Unanimous Five-Justice Panel Decisions (N), Norwegian Supreme Court 1945–2012

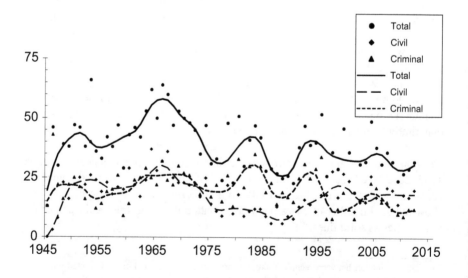

Immediately after World War II, the total number of cases grew and established a stable level of roughly 300 cases per year between 1955 and 1970 (*see* Figure 3.1). After a brief slump in the 1970s, the total number of cases peaked close to 400 per year during the 1980s. Primarily driven by the court reform of criminal case appeals in 1995, the total number of cases has normalised at around 150 cases per year. In the 1960s the total number of civil cases peaked around 120 cases per year but has stayed below 100 cases per year for the rest of the period.

The total number of non-unanimous cases climbed steadily between 1945 and 1965 (*see* Figure 3.2). Then there was a decline in such cases until the mid-1970s, followed by fluctuations until the early 1990s. For the rest of the period the number of non-unanimous five-justice panel decisions has stabilised around thirty-plus cases per year.

A complementing figure can be studied when we calculate the percentages of the Court's non-unanimous decisions (*see* Figure 3.3). Again we show the percentages of all non-unanimous decisions as well as those of criminal and civil cases both as data points and as local trend lines.

Figure 3.3 shows that there is a relatively higher number of dissents in civil cases (top line) as compared to criminal cases (bottom line). The per cent of non-unanimous criminal cases fluctuates closely with the overall per cent of non-unanimous cases. But the time series for per cent of non-unanimous civil cases shoots above the main trend in the first post-World War II decades, and also for the decade and a half that starts at the beginning of the 1960s.

Figure 3.3: Non-Unanimous Five-Justice Panel Decisions (%), Norwegian Supreme Court 1945–2012

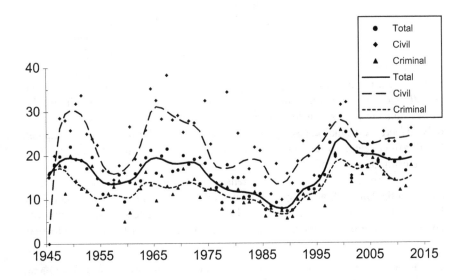

The overall time series in Figure 3.3 can be broken down into four more or less distinct segments. First, early in the time series there are two peaks of non-unanimous decisions, one in 1950 and another in 1965. The 1965 peak roughly corresponds with the time period that political historians have identified as the endpoint of the post-World War II era of reconstruction and consensus among the political parties (Bergh and Pharo 1987). Second, between 1968 and 1989 there is a general decline in the relative incidence of non-unanimous decisions. Third, this era of harmony among the justices comes to an abrupt end in 1990, and throughout the subsequent decade there is a steep increase in non-unanimous decisions. Finally, there is a levelling off of non-unanimous decisions during the first decade of the twenty-first century.

The flip side of non-unanimous behaviour on the Supreme Court is the extent to which there is consensus among the justices when deciding a case. According to Sandmo's history of the Norwegian Supreme Court, there was a clear tendency for consensus during the 1950s and 1960s, with the 1970s witnessing the dissolution of the social democratic order – a pattern that would continue apace through the 1980s (Sandmo 2005: 518–523). Sandmo argues that the loss of consensual norms accelerated with Gro Harlem Brundtland's Labour government appointment of Carsten Smith as Chief Justice in 1991. Smith was known for subscribing to the view that the Supreme Court is a political institution. Indeed, in what amounted to his judicial-political manifesto in 1975, he had stated that there should be greater recognition that the Court has a political function (Smith 1975). And, it was on Chief Justice Carsten Smith's watch that the Court in 1996 explicitly defined its main task as, 'to ensure uniformity, clarity and development of law'.[17]

The reduced number of minor criminal cases reaching the High Court following the 1995 judicial reforms (see Matningsdal 1996; and Chapter Two in this book) may also have militated for an increase in the rate of the Court's non-unanimous decisions. First, this reform permitted Chief Justice Smith – who had advocated for it in 1975 – to pursue his goal of greater discussion of legal principles rather than, in Smith's own words, wasting the energies of bright legal minds on the technical minutiae of criminal appeals on a case-by-case basis. Second, and perhaps more importantly, it ensured that run of the mill criminal appeals were not crowding the Court's docket. Worthy of mention, Figure 3.3 shows that the forces that lead to the increase in non-unanimous decisions not only affected criminal cases, but civil cases as well. Initially, then, a Carsten Smith effect seems to provide a broader explanation than an explanation based on the criminal court reform.

Interestingly, a similar loss of consensual norms was observed a half-century earlier in the United States Supreme Court, after the appointment of Harlan Fiske Stone as Chief Justice (Walker et al. 1988). Stone's leadership style, however, appears to have had a greater impact on rates of dissent in the U.S. Court than

---

17. This mission, stated in four different languages, is now clearly presented to all who visit the Court's web pages. Online. Available http://www.domstol.no/no/Enkelt-domstol/-Norges-Hoyesterett/ (last accessed 15 November 2014).

can be observed in Smith's leadership style on the Norwegian Supreme Court. In any event, based upon Sandmo's (2005) historical assessment, we would expect that the proportion of non-unanimous decisions would be very low during the 1950s and 1960s, increase appreciably during the 1970s and 1980s, and explode after 1991. Table 3.1 shows the rates of non-unanimous behaviour by the terms of the Chief Justices.[18] This permits a quick assessment of the validity of our expectations.

A cursory inspection of the data presented in the table reveals that the percentage of non-unanimous decisions was relatively high in the 1950s and 1960s – presumably a quiescent, idyllic period in Norwegian political history. Chief Justices Paal Berg, Emil Stang, Sverre Grette and Terje Wold were administering the Supreme Court during these years. This period was followed by two decades of declining rates of non-unanimous behaviour on the Court; yet, the national political consensus was crumbling. Chief Justices Rolv Ryssdal and Erling Sandene headed the Court during the 1970s and 1980s.[19] On average, during Chief Justice Carsten Smith's term, the 1990s level of non-unanimous behaviour returned to the levels exhibited in the 1950s. The new century has, during Chief Justice Tore Schei's leadership, seen the highest levels of non-unanimous behaviour in the post-World War II period. If we focus only on those years Carsten Smith was Chief Justice (1991–2002), the average level of non-unanimous behaviour climbs back to that observed for the 1960s. Thus far all we can say is that, although anything but explosive, there was a significant increase in the proportion of non-unanimous case outcomes in the 1990s and 2000s. However, Chief Justice Smith may have been an influential player in raising the level of non-unanimous votes.[20]

The plot in Figure 3.3, discussed above, reflects our summary of the incidence of non-unanimous behaviour over time. While our expectations, based upon Sandmo's evaluation of consensus in the decades following World War II, do not find a great deal of support, there is a sharp rise in the percentage of non-unanimous case outcomes once Carsten Smith becomes Chief Justice in 1991. During Smith's tenure, the overall percentage of non-unanimous behaviour reaches its apogee at 28.8 per cent in 1999; it then settles back down roughly to the level observed for the 1950s and 1960s (*see* Figure 3.3).

---

18. Chief Justice Paal Berg's tenure started in 1929, but only the two immediate post-World War II years are included in the Table. Chief Justice Tore Schei is expected to serve out his term until he reaches the age of seventy. Figures for Schei include the 2002–2012 years. The percentages are based on all years that a justice served as Chief.

19. Rolv Ryssdal, reflecting upon his period as Chief Justice from 1969 to 1984, noted that during deliberations there could be sharp differences among the justices, but that more often than not, consensus would take hold among the justices. Once an outcome was decided, he argued, it was also important that the justices did not disagree on the justifications 'to a greater extent than necessary' (Ryssdal 1984: 1041).

20. Chief Justice Carsten Smith participated in a total of ninety-two non-unanimous decisions while on the Court. He was in the majority sixty-six times (72 per cent) and the minority twenty-six times (28 per cent).

Table 3.1: Proportion of Dissents by Chief Justices' Terms

	Proportion of Dissents		
	Total	Criminal	Civil
Paal Berg 1929–1946	0.166	0.170	0.100
Emil Stang 1946–1952	0.190	0.151	0.276
Sverre Grette 1952–1958	0.151	0.121	0.195
Terje Wold 1958–1969	0.167	0.120	0.263
Rolv Ryssdal 1969–1984	0.144	0.115	0.225
Erling Sandene 1984–1991	0.088	0.073	0.154
Carsten Smith 1991–2002	0.176	0.145	0.227
Tore Schei 2002–2012	0.195	0.160	0.237

Conclusion

Several points bear emphasis from this brief discussion of the decisional processes of the Norwegian Supreme Court and its non-unanimous behaviour. First, the nature of the Court's jurisdiction militates for it boring with a large policy-making auger. The *Høyesterett* has extensive substantive appellate jurisdiction. And more importantly, it has great control over which appeals ultimately find their way onto its merits docket. In concert, these two jurisdictional features all but ensure that the Court will be able to concentrate its finite resources on those appeals that present the most consequential political, social, or economic issues.

Second, the quasi-random procedures used in the assignment of both justices and appeals to the merits panels virtually guarantees that the merits panels will comprise justices that have differing attitudinal preferences with respect to the case stimuli before them. To put this a bit more concretely, the random procedures will throw together justices who are liberal and conservative, male and female, from the center and from the periphery, and who will respond very differently to at least some of the cases that have been randomly assigned to the panel. Thus, we would expect – and in fact we found – non-trivial rates of non-unanimous merits decisions.

Third, non-unanimous behaviour is certainly not foreign to the *Høyesterett's* decisional outputs. To be sure, there is an ebb and flow to the proportion of non-unanimous decisions over the time series we inspect. But there is never a term in which the Court issued only unanimous decisions. The legal model does not adequately account for this behaviour.[21] We contend that the composition of the Court – the nature of the justices occupying the High Bench – is the more likely explanation for the Court's regular lack of unanimity. In the next chapter, therefore, we turn to a systematic exploration of the Court's changing composition.

---

21. More precisely, legal methods acknowledge the presence of dissent among justices, but legal methods are inconclusive as to legal explanations for the dissent. *See*, for instance, Nygaard's influential volume on the legal method and the brief discussion on this topic (2004: 172–174).

References

Backer, I. L. (2008) 'Habilitet i Høyesterett', *Lov og Rett* 47 (10): 577–578.

Baum, L. (1997) *The Puzzle of Judicial Behavior,* Ann Arbor: The University of Michigan Press.

Bergh, T. and Pharo, H. Ø. (eds) (1987) *Vekst og Velstand: Norsk Politisk Historie 1945–1965,* Oslo: Universitetsforlaget.

Caldeira, G. A. and Wright, J. R. (1988) 'Organized Interests and Agenda Setting in the U.S. Supreme Court', *American Political Science Review* 82 (4): 1109–1127.

Epstein, L., Segal, J. A., Spaeth, H. J. and Walker, T. G. (2011) *The Supreme Court Compendium: Data, Decisions, and Developments*, Washington DC: CQ Press.

Holmes, O. W. (1963) *The Common Law,* Cambridge Mass.: Belknap Press of Harvard University Press.

Matningsdal, M. (1996) *To-instansreformen,* Oslo: Universitetsforlaget.

Nygaard, N. (2004) *Rettsgrunnlag og Standpunkt,* Bergen: Universitetsforlaget.

Ryssdal, R. (1984) 'Høyesterettsjustitiarius Rolv Ryssdal', *Retstidende* Rt-1984–1029, 1037–1041.

Sandmo, E. (2005) *Siste Ord: Høyesterett i Norsk Historie 1905–1965,* Oslo: Cappelen.

Schei, T. (2010) 'Arbeidet med domsskriving i Høyesterett', in Bergli, W. K., Fauske, L., Garborg, M., Fliflet, J. G. and Rørvik, I. H. (eds) *Domsnøkkel. Privatrettslige emner,* Oslo: Gyldendal Akademisk, pp. 13–16.

Segal, J. A. and Spaeth, H. J. (2002) *The Supreme Court and the Attitudinal Model Revisited,* New York: Cambridge University Press.

Smith, C. (1975) 'Domstolene og rettsutviklingen', *Lov og Rett* 14: 292–319.

Sunde, J. Ø. (2012) 'Dissenting Votes in the Norwegian Supreme Court 1965–2009: A legal cultural analysis', *Rechtskultur* 1: 59–73.

Tukey, J. W. (1977) *Exploratory Data Analysis,* Reading: Addison-Wesley.

Velleman, P. F. and Hoaglin, D. C. (1981) *Applications, Basics, and Computing of Exploratory Data Analysis,* Boston: Duxbury Press.

Walker, T. G., Epstein, L. and Dixon, W. J. (1988) 'On the Mysterious Demise of Consensual Norms in the United States Supreme Court', *The Journal of Politics* 50 (2): 361–389.

Chapter Four

Policy Making by Appointment: The Composition of the Norwegian Supreme Court 1945-2009

Underlying the discussion in the previous chapter of the Norwegian Supreme Court's decisional processes and rates of non-unanimous behaviour is the notion that there are attitudinal differences among the justices that manifest themselves in different voting behaviour. In this chapter we examine the Supreme Court's composition, since the characteristics of the sitting justices capture some of the experiences that shape their political views. Three broad sets of forces bear upon the appointment of justices to sit upon Norway's highest bench – legal training, social/demographic attributes, and the political attitudes of those responsible for the recruitment of individuals to the Court. These forces combine to define the specific nature of the justices, which in turn affects their attitudes and preferences. In other words, the way the Court decides cases of political, social, and economic significance is a consequence of who sits on the Court. The forces that condition appointment obviously affect who sits on the Court.

One characteristic common to all the justices is a law school education. Indeed, judges spend some of their most formative years in law school, being socialised into the prevailing legal system and incorporating those values into their political frame of reference. In fact, Supreme Court justices are recruited from that small pool of individuals who compiled the very strongest records in law school. Consequently, judges interpret public policy in light of the considerations emphasised in their legal education – considerations such as precedent, the meaning of laws under scrutiny, parliamentary goals embodied in legislation, and equitable considerations. There is little doubt that law school equips its graduates with the ability to engage in sophisticated legal reasoning that distinguishes lawyers from the population at large and from other professional groups. Certainly, Supreme Court justices employ legal analysis when deciding cases. That is a given.

Of course, as intimated earlier, the legal is not divorced from the political. Take the matter of equitable consideration – a criterion grounded in fair play. While a strict legal interpretation might inform a Court decision, equitable consideration paves the way for extra-legal forces to influence the outcome.[1] In fact, too much reliance

---

1.   We do not intend to address the demarcation problem between legal and extra-legal forces. In general we refer to 'forces' as all independent variables that are expected to influence judges' decisions (Brace and Hall 1997), as, for instance, when Dworkin (1988) uses the term 'gravitational force' when precedents narrow judges' voting options, or when food-breaks influence judges' rulings (Danziger *et al.* 2011). For example, if legislators include the term 'reasonable' ('*rimelig*')

on matters of 'fairness' would be unsettling to scholars committed to what we call the 'legal model' of judicial decision making (Magnussen 2005). However, even what appears to be purely legalistic justifications may be cherry-picked to support the ideological preference of a justice (Skoghøy 2010). Be that as it may, many a judge will opt for a purely 'legal' rationalisation for staking out a policy position. Given that the judicial community is particularly homogeneous (Hjellbrekke *et al.* 2007), if graduating from law school was the relevant characteristic of sitting justices, they would be equally homogeneous in their decision-making behaviour. But, as we showed in the previous chapter, they are not. They manifest differences in legal opinions that reveal a diversity of interpretation springing, in part, from their law school training, but also from socio-political factors impinging upon their judicial pronouncements.

Although fundamentally constrained by the requirement to appoint the best trained lawyers in the land, for some time now there has also been a concerted effort to select people of varying backgrounds, in order to incorporate a wide range of interests and life experiences (Domstolkommisjonen 1999). The extent to which this selection criterion is employed can produce a mix of justices more representative of the social, economic, and political predispositions of the broader public. Certainly, those interests include political ideology, gender-based issue positions, and regional orientations.

Whether or not explicit recruitment – of, say, northerners or women – results in a more 'representative' Court is an intriguing question. Do they bring different perspectives to bear upon legal and constitutional reasoning? Many feminists would make a persuasive case that women bring an outlook distinct from that of their male colleagues. Likewise, the legal community outside of the Oslo national elite could plausibly maintain that the views of geographically peripheral regions of the country should find expression on the highest court in the land. What this intimates is that in Norway it is not just about legal training, which is fairly uniform across the nation's law schools. Indeed, life experiences, and the concomitant values thereof, could shape jurisprudential understanding. If selecting applicants with an eye to diversity does not have attitudinal implications, then appointing more women or aspirants from the far north might only be a politically correct charade of descriptive representation.

Finally, it is perhaps to state the obvious that those responsible for judicial recruitment are not immune from political preferences. The reader should keep in mind that since World War II, the executive through the Ministry of Justice has dominated Court appointments (*see* Chapter Two). There are two stages of the process during which the government could influence, if not control, the appointment of justices: (1) application and (2) recommendation.

---

in a statute and leave the interpretation to the judge, does 'reasonable' amount to a legal or extra-legal force? On the other hand, 'legal sources' refers to e.g. laws, precedents, and legislative intent that invariably present facts and arguments that may or may not offer an anchoring for legal reasoning.

Applications are accepted upon the announcement of a Court opening. In more than one instance, potential candidates have been asked, perhaps even lobbied, to apply.[2] No doubt a purely sincere legal motive might encourage a well-placed member of the Norwegian elite – perhaps someone sequestered in the Ministry of Justice – to urge an eminently qualified individual to apply. However, in addition to legal *bona fides* and satisfying the norm of diversity, an applicant may be recruited who shares values important to the executive.

Once all applications, usually a limited number, have been submitted, a committee endorses those to be reviewed by the Ministry of Justice. The Minister of Justice also accepts the evaluation of candidates offered by the Chief Justice of the Supreme Court. Upon evaluating the candidates through interviews and reference letters, the Minister of Justice submits a recommendation, which is approved by the King in Council.

In 2002 the appointment process was reformed to increase the autonomy of the Court by establishing an independent entity – the Judicial Appointments Board. The Appointments Board evaluates the applicants and then sends a rank ordering of the three most qualified candidates to the Ministry of Justice, which in turn makes a recommendation to the King in Council.[3] Presumably, this reorganisation insulates the process from the political objectives of the executive (Gangnes 2010; Smith 2003) . However, there are pathways through which political forces remain in play. For instance, while the Appointments Board is not permitted to seek applicants, there is nothing stopping others from doing so. (*See* Chapter Two for a more detailed discussion of the appointment process.)

Although the selection of justices may be fair and balanced at both stages of the process, one 'can also imagine that the executive responds to the court's tendencies of legislating from the bench by appointing friendly justices' (Eckhoff 1964: 132), and indeed, may do so with unabashedly political goals in mind (Willoch 2002). Effectively, then, there is more to appointment than populating the Court with the best legal minds; since justices also harbor ideology, values and attitudes, appointment is also an opportunity to affect constitutional law and public policy in an ideologically congenial direction (Torgersen 1963). Simply put, extra-legal attitudes are, in effect, appointed to the bench.

If variability in the descriptive characteristics of sitting justices predisposes them to disagree on important legal decisions heard on appeal, then an examination of the post-World War II trends in the Supreme Court's composition should provide some insight into attitudinal dispositions that inform judicial decision-making behaviour. During the sixty-five odd years since 1945 that we study here,

---

2. The most familiar example is the Labour government's strong invitation in late 1990 and early 1991 to law professor Carsten Smith to apply to the upcoming vacancy of Chief Justice. Prominent among the solicitors was Minister of Defence, Thorvald Stoltenberg, whose family were close friends with the Smith family.

3. The process also involves the applicants being interviewed by the Chief Justice and the most senior justice on the Supreme Court (Aschehoug 2010).

there have been a total of 214 appointments to the Court – i.e. acts in which the King in Council has appointed an interim or permanent justice to the Court. Fifty-two lawyers have been appointed as interim justices a total of 116 times. Ninety-one lawyers have been appointed as either associate or Chief Justices to the Court a total of 98 times.[4] Six lawyers have first been appointed as interim justices and were then subsequently appointed as permanent justices. Our analysis includes only the permanently appointed justices.

We now turn to a descriptive analysis of the proportion of justices appointed by governments led by socialist or non-socialist parties. Quite naturally, we would prefer a more immediate and direct measure of political ideology; sadly, however, such a measure does not exist for all post-World War II justices. We therefore employ the nature of the appointing government as a reasonable proxy for ideology. The statistical analysis presented in the remainder of this chapter explores the appointments to and the composition of the Supreme Court from 1945 to 2009. Occasionally, however, we make reference to developments that have occurred after 2009. These references are useful illustrations of analytical points that we are making and are continuations of 1945 to 2009 trends.

Historical pattern: Socialist and non-socialist appointment

The mapping of post-World War II descriptive patterns begins with the proportion of justices appointed by socialist-led governments (*see* Figure 4.1).[5] Even a cursory examination of Figure 4.1 suggests that the political centre of gravity moved significantly over the time period under study. For instance, what must have been the politics of the Court from 1945 through the mid-1960s, a period during which Labour dominated the government? One could argue that this was a time that consensual politics ruled the day in Norway (Elder *et al.* 1988). The public and the political parties shared what seemed to be an unshakeable commitment to the welfare state. Furthermore, for much of this period, other political parties were pessimistic about the prospects of replacing Labour as the governing party (Rokkan 1966).

---

4.   This number includes the six permanently appointed justices who later were elevated to Chief Justice (Emil Stang, Sverre Grette, Terje Wold, Rolv Ryssdal, Erling Sandene, and Tore Schei; Paal Berg was appointed Chief Justice before the start of our time series); as well as O.C. Gundersen, who served two non-contiguous terms as associate justice (in addition to several intermittent ambassadorial and ministerial positions).

5.   The values by year for the Supreme Court justices are based on all justices who served on the Court within any given year. Note that the proxy for the justices' ideology is coded binary by the political ideology of the government – i.e. socialist-led (or social democratic-led, or Labour-led) versus non-socialist-led governments. In the half-year period after World War II, Einar Gerhardsen of the Labour Party (i.e. Gerhardsen I) headed a broad-based caretaker-type government representing 147 of Parliament's 150 members, and all but two political parties, including representatives from the underground resistance movement. Judicial appointments in this period were coded as non-socialist.

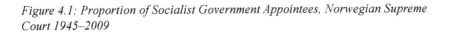

Figure 4.1: Proportion of Socialist Government Appointees, Norwegian Supreme Court 1945–2009

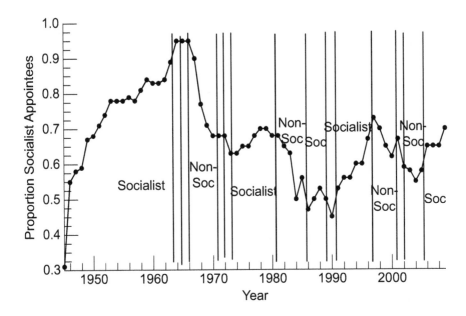

The appearance of an apparent consensus might suggest a lack of significant conflicting interests. We are reminded of Rokkan's admonition, however, that 'votes count in the choice of governing personnel but other resources decide the actual policies pursued by the authorities' (Rokkan 1966: 106). And, during this time period, there was no paucity of divergent interests – whether economic, social or religious. The potentially conflicting demands, however, were not manifested in electoral politics. Rather, the pursuit of different policies occurred through a kind of corporatism, where boards comprised of business, labour, and government negotiated policies and regulations, which in turn were approved by various governmental institutions, typically Parliament. In the end, political conflict was managed, and there was no serious electoral challenge to Labour's control of the instruments of government.

In any event, prior to the early 1960s, Labour governments merrily appointed justices so that the proportion of socialist government appointees rose from 46 per cent in 1945 to 95 per cent in 1964. In 1965, the installation of Per Borten's non-socialist coalition government comprising the Conservative, Centre, Christian People's, and Liberal Parties, coupled with the steady retirement of Labour-appointed justices, saw a sharp decline in the presence of socialist-appointed justices on the High Bench, dropping from a high of 95 per cent in 1966 to 68 per cent in 1970.

Although Labour was restored to government, the tranquillity of consensus politics did not accompany the restoration. A variety of issues – like membership in the European Community (EC), and the Alta Valley hydroelectric project (Urwin 1997: 34) – continued to churn Norwegian political waters throughout Labour's eight-year stint at the helm of government. Navigating these waters would prove difficult, as the 1981 election would demonstrate. Nevertheless, with Labour in charge, the proportion of socialist-appointed Court justices rose modestly, but steadily.

Two issues – taxation and abortion policy – dominated the election of 1981. Lowering taxes was a major campaign theme for the Conservative and Progress Parties (Kuhnle *et al.* 1986), while on the question of abortion – an important issue in the previous election (Valen 1992) – the agrarian Centre Party was split and the Christian People's Party assumed the most staunchly pro-life stance. The combined outcome was to bring all non-socialist parties into a centre-right position on the left–right continuum, giving them a solid parliamentary majority, and control of government until mid-1986 (Shaffer 1998). Returning to our story, once again the Court's composition tracked with the party in power. Retirements from the Court allowed the Conservative-led government of Kåre Willoch to reduce the proportion of socialist appointed justices below the 50 per cent mark for the first time since 1945 (*see* Figure 4.1).

By the time the 1985 election rolled around taxation was no longer a salient issue, having been replaced by health policy and care of the elderly (Shaffer 1998). While the non-socialist bloc enjoyed a numerical advantage, the parliamentary coalition was extremely fragile, and Conservative Prime Minister Kåre Willoch was unable to hold together the deeply divided parties of the right. In addition, there was evidence of a leftward shift among three putatively non-socialist parties – the Liberal, Christian People's, and Centre Parties (Shaffer 1998). The historical anti-tax and anti-welfare state Progress Party became the downfall of the Willoch government when its two members of Parliament failed to support the Willoch government's oil tax proposal, occasioned by the need to craft an austerity budget. The Willoch government collapsed and was replaced by Gro Harlem Brundtland's (Labour) second cabinet. Accordingly, during Brundtland's 1986–1989 stint as Prime Minister, there was a slight uptick in the proportion of socialist government appointees.

Economic and social issues remained salient in the 1989 election, but the addition of environmental quality to the list of voter concerns (Valen 1990) significantly benefitted the Socialist Left Party, seen as the party most likely to protect the environment. Meanwhile, however, the dramatic increase of seats held by the Progress Party, offsetting Conservative losses, gave the non-socialist bloc brief control of government. No one really expected this government to last long, given the fact that other right-of-centre parties viewed the Progress Party with great scepticism. The other right-of-centre parties expected the Progress Party to contribute to a parliamentary basis for a non-socialist government, but they were not considered *salonfähig* for participation within a cabinet. Moreover, the Centre Party was completely at odds with the Conservatives over membership in the European Union. The non-socialist government collapsed after one year. Nevertheless, it survived long enough to bring about a slight drop in the proportion of socialist government Court appointees.

With the collapse of the non-socialist government in 1990 and the restoration of a Brundtland government, the percentage of socialist appointees rose from a post-World War II low of 45 per cent to 73 per cent. Then, in anticipation of the 1994 referendum on EU membership, the Centre Party nearly tripled its parliamentary presence, becoming the largest non-socialist party in the *Storting* in the process. The resulting majority enjoyed by the centre-right parties led to the selection of Christian People's Party leader Kjell Magne Bondevik as Prime Minister, and the proportion of socialist government appointees to the Court dropped steadily through 2005.[6]

The 2005 election was unique in that for the first time in the post-World War II era, a 'red–green' coalition took the reins of government. This time Labour and its allies emphasised spending on public services and raising taxes, which marked a departure from Labour's more restrained fiscal policies of the previous election. When Progress Party leader Carl I. Hagen withdrew support for any Christian People's Party-led government, there was little standing in the way of a socialist dominated red-green government (Sitter 2006).[7] Naturally, the percentage of socialist Supreme Court appointees increased during the remainder of the period under study.

From the preceding, brief sketch of Norway's electoral history, it is obvious that socialist or non-socialist appointments are linked directly to which bloc heads the government. Since the Labour Party has been the major player throughout most of the post-Word War II era, it is no surprise that socialist regimes appointed two-thirds (67.8 per cent) of the Supreme Court justices. The proportion of socialist government appointees never dropped below 45 per cent of the Court's membership and rose as high as 95 per cent. In addition, for every year a socialist government was in place, the proportion of socialist appointed justices increased by 5.5 percentage points.[8]

---

6. Non-socialist control of the government was interrupted for more than a year in 2000–2001 when Labour leader Jens Stoltenberg served as Prime Minister as a result of a no confidence vote in which Labour, the Conservative, and the Progress Parties supported the construction of gas-burning power plants – a move inconsistent with Norway's commitment to CO_2 emissions controls (Madeley 2002: 213). Although Labour had taken a more conservative position on taxation, centre-right parties upped the ante by proposing to use oil revenues to finance government programs and lower taxes (Madeley 2002: 214). In the end the results of the 2001 election gave the centre-right parties the advantage, yielding another non-socialist government with Bondevik (Christian People's Party) restored as Prime Minister.

7. In 2005, the Centre Party joined a coalition government with the Labour Party. In so doing the clean-cut left–right government formation was blurred for the first time since 1945.

8. The correlation between the increase in socialist appointments and the government in power is .554, with no evidence of serial correlation (Durbin Watson = 1.938). The associated regression equation is $Y = -.089 + .055X$, where Y is the change in the percentage socialist appointees and X is whether or not a socialist party or coalition headed government.

The fact that the proportion of socialist government appointees varies depending on whether or not a socialist government is in place is, in and of itself, uninteresting. However, it is a crucial link in the political chain that constitutes our theoretical foundation for hypothesising that some Court decisions reflect the ideological predispositions of the justices. As the following chapters demonstrate, an extra-legal model of decisional behaviour holds for the Norwegian Supreme Court, and there are systematic differences between justices appointed by socialist and non-socialist governments (*see* especially Chapters Five, Seven and Eight). In other words, there seems to be a relationship between the party controlling the selection choice at the time of any particular justice's appointment and that justice's attitudinal preferences. Thus, the more justices that a government can appoint, the more it would tip the collective ideological propensity of the Court in one way or another.

This also suggests that the preferences of the mass public, at least indirectly, bear upon the composite attitudinal disposition of the Supreme Court. After all, there is a wealth of empirical evidence that voter partisanship and attitudes on important political issues determine which bloc controls the government in any given election period. Any direct connection between voters' opinions and judicial ideology, however, probably exists only to the extent that justices of different backgrounds may share policy predispositions with those of a similar background, such as a common regional background. Of course, politically insulated justices, such as those serving on the Norwegian Supreme Court, will not be as strongly influenced by public sentiment as those securing judicial positions through an electoral process (Baum 2008).

Historical pattern: Appointment of women to the Supreme Court

While, in order to incorporate social and political diversity, serious efforts have been made to create greater gender balance on the Court, applicants were required to be prominent members of the legal profession. One consequence of this is that although women constitute a segment of the population roughly equal to that of men, it was not until 1968 that a woman joined the High Court. Of course, while there may have been a relatively small percentage of female lawyers at the time, gender equality in politics and government was also not as pervasive as it has become.

That said, Norway is considered to be among the most egalitarian societies in the world, and the presence of women in the country's political life is quite impressive (Andrews and Hoekstra 2010; Inglehart and Norris 2003). In the national executive, Gro Harlem Brundtland was a very popular Prime Minister. Of the seven political parties holding seats in the Parliament (as of spring 2013), four have female party leaders. One is clearly on the left – Liv Signe Navarsete (Centre Party); two are decidedly on the right – Siv Jensen (Progress Party) and Erna Solberg (Conservative Party); and one is centrist – Trine Skei Grande (Liberal Party). During the 2005–2013 period, the Prime Minister was a male – Jens Stoltenberg (Labour). During the final years of his term, women headed ten of the seventeen government ministries.[9] In the September 2013 election, the non-socialist parties won the election and a woman – Erna Solberg of the Conservative Party – became Prime Minister with Siv Jensen, the leader of the Progress party, serving as the *de facto* deputy prime minister. In this government, half of the ministries are headed by women.

A good deal of research has focused upon the incidence of women in national legislative bodies, and much of that work can be invoked to account for the trend over more than three decades of Norwegian elections. We have plotted that trend in Figure 4.2, along with the corresponding trend in the inclusion of women on the Norwegian Supreme Court. Norway is one of the nations with the highest proportion of women in Parliament, and earlier studies suggest two general factors that we think have facilitated the election of women to the *Storting* – cultural values and institutional practices.

Assessing the role of culture, Inglehart *et al.* (2002) demonstrate that nations with well-developed egalitarian values elect women to national legislatures in far greater numbers than more traditional cultures, or those more concerned

Figure 4.2: Proportion of Women Appointees, Norwegian Supreme Court 1967–2009

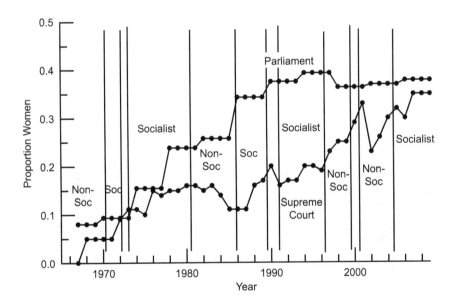

9. Those ministries include: Labour; Children, Equality and Social Inclusion; Fisheries and Coastal Affairs; Government Administration, Reform and Church Affairs; Defence; Justice and Public Security; Local Government and Regional Development; Culture; Education and Research; and Transport and Communications.

with survival issues. Such societies have developed economically to the extent that they can move beyond 'survival' to greater 'self-expression' values. With a greater commitment to egalitarian norms, more women are elected to Parliament. Undoubtedly, Norway has a longstanding commitment to political equality, and the demand for gender equality was viewed as 'legitimate' (Bystydzienski 1988: 77). The egalitarianism of Norwegian political culture created a congenial environment for the inclusion of women in national politics.

However, taking advantage of a favourable cultural climate, the activity of strong women's organisations provided the impetus for the increased election of women to Parliament. The concerted efforts of women's groups in the 1960s and through the 1970s energised the push to elect more women to the *Storting* (Bystydzienski 1988: 77). Institutional arrangements also contributed to this growth. For example, Norway's proportional representation system provided opportunities to slate and elect a significant number of women on party lists, an effect that has been observed in PR systems generally (Norris 2004), at least in more developed nations (Matland 1998).

Of course, there are various structural features in proportional representation systems that offer opportunities for high levels of inclusion. For example, multi-member districts allow for diversity on a party ticket, resulting in more opportunities for women, not so much because of high district magnitude, but more likely because of greater 'party magnitude' (i.e. the size of a party's parliamentary delegation in a multi-member district, Matland 1993). In addition, there is considerable turnover of members of Parliament in PR systems, whereas dislodging incumbents in majoritarian systems can be a long, tortuous project (Norris 2004). In Norway opportunities were plentiful, and with a strong push within civil society, the trend of substantial increases in the election of women was jump-started.

Returning to Figure 4.2. We begin in the late 1960s when in 1968 the percentage of female Supreme Court justices moved from 0 to 5 per cent with the appointment of the first female justice, Lilly Bølviken. An absence of women was true also in the Parliament. The first noticeable increase in female MPs occurred in the early 1970s, and came in response to the concerted mobilisation efforts of women's organisations (Bystydzienski 1988). A significant increase can be observed following the 1977 election when the Socialist Left and Liberal Parties adopted gender quotas, after which a levelling off occurred during Conservative Kåre Willoch's first and second cabinets. The proportion of female MPs remained in a more or less steady state until 1985, by which time the Labour Party decided to include a high percentage of women on its party lists. Thus, after the 1985 election, the presence of women in the *Storting* jumped to nearly 35 per cent. Without a doubt, the reservation of party list positions for women goes a long way towards explaining the dramatic upward trend from the late 1970s through the middle 1980s (Narud and Valen 2008).

Another institutional variable of note is what Matland (1993) labels 'party magnitude'. This is simply the size of a party's parliamentary delegation in a multi-member district. If a party has a sizeable number of MPs, it will have more opportunity to slate women on its election list. Indeed, at least through the early 1970s, party magnitude was linked to the presence of women in the *Storting* (Matland, 1993). Overall, then, the combination of an egalitarian culture, a proportional representation electoral system, a sizeable 'party magnitude', and gender quotas implemented by the political parties fostered the steady increase of women in the Parliament through most of the period under study. However, during the last twenty years, the proportion of women MPs has remained stable.

While the Supreme Court functions in the same cultural milieu, the increase in the proportion of women justices was considerably dampened, in large part due to institutional impediments. Justices may serve until the age of seventy and – unlike MPs – are not subject to elections. Consequently, the opportunities to elevate women to the nation's highest court are sharply limited. Typically, a sizeable number of men and women cannot be slated for multiple openings on the Court – a task that would have been challenging throughout most of the time period under analysis, since women were not heavily represented in the legal profession in the early years of this period. So, this much slower process of placing women on the Court has had to rely upon the general embrace of equality in Norwegian political culture.

As we noted, the first woman was appointed to the Court in 1968. From then until 1980, there was a gradual increase in the number of women on the High Court, primarily during the Labour Party's control of government. During Willoch's first and second cabinets, the proportion of women on the Supreme Court declined slightly, which in a way paralleled the levelling off of women in the *Storting*. From 1988 through the end of 2009 there was a slow but steady increase in the proportion of female Supreme Court justices, until that percentage nearly matched the percentage of women in the Parliament.

That the pace at which the inclusion of women reaches an apparent steady state – at slightly less than 40 per cent in both Parliament and the Supreme Court – can in all likelihood be explained by structural differences in the two national branches of government. Although the proportion of women on the Supreme Court is quite impressive by comparative standards (Andrews and Hoekstra 2010), Chief Justice Tore Schei still thinks the inclusion of women on the Court ought to reflect their presence in the general population (Schei 2006). Embracing this goal, Knut Storberget – a Minister of Justice in the Stoltenberg's second government – sought to ensure that at least 40 per cent of the Court's members should be women (NTB 2008). That goal has nearly been achieved, as the plot in Figure 4.2 demonstrates.[10]

While the Norwegian culture of equality combined with the influence of civil society (e.g. women's groups) can be brought to bear on the composition of both Parliament and the Court, institutional features can account for the much more

---

10. And below the institutional radar, female students at Norwegian law schools compose more than 50 per cent, sometimes up to 70 per cent, of the student body.

rapid growth in the *Storting*. Clearly, proportional representation and its attendant party magnitude, as well as the adoption of gender quotas, increased the number of opportunities for women to win parliamentary seats. By contrast, changing recruitment rules to increase the percentage of women on the Supreme Court was simply not an option. The smaller number of positions, along with the long tenure of sitting justices, guarantees a very gradual replacement process. Institutional impediments, however, only seem to have slowed down the inclusion of women on the Court; they did not wholly short-circuit it. In the long run, an egalitarian culture has produced a legal profession populated by many more women, and a corresponding commitment to the appointment of women to the Supreme Court.

Historical pattern: Centre–periphery and the Supreme Court

Rokkan (1967) has made a strong case that regional differences assist in explaining Norwegian politics. For instance, the 'counter culture' of the periphery of western and southern Norway translated into new parties. Although Rokkan's analysis may appear dated, we can still find political variation by region. In the 1994 European referendum, for example, the eastern region anchored by Oslo gave a very large majority of its support to joining the European Union. More specifically, 67 per cent of Oslo voters backed membership in a referendum in which membership was rejected by 52.2 per cent of the recorded votes. Likewise, the communities of Bærum and Asker, conventionally included in the Oslo-West legal community, cast 75 and 72 per cent of their votes in favour of EU membership.[11] There were certainly many other factors at work in that referendum (Pettersen *et al.* 1996), but the centre–periphery division noted by Rokkan was relevant to the struggle over EU membership.

In the Norwegian jurisprudential community, the centre–periphery effect should emerge in a manner similar to the one observed by McGuire (1993) for the role of a Washington-centric legal elite in the United States. Focusing upon the dominant role of Washington-based lawyers in arguing cases before the Supreme Court, McGuire asserts that we 'need to take account of the social alliances that exist among the legal, as well as political, actors who shape the direction of the choices made by the federal government' (McGuire 1993: 388).

We strongly suspect a centre–periphery effect in the Norwegian legal community, with the most elite players concentrated in the capital.[12] A significant number of Supreme Court justices come out of this jurisprudential milieu,

---

11. The Asker and Bærum municipalities in the county of Akershus are located immediately west of Oslo. They are often included in the greater Oslo area. These communities are not coded as part of the Oslo (until 1925: Kristiania) variable we use here.

12. Until the University of Bergen established its law school in 1969, the country's only law school was at the University of Oslo. The University of Tromsø started the third and final law school in 1987. These three universities also accept bachelor degrees in law from other colleges and permit these students to complete their master's degrees in law at their law schools.

and we hypothesise that 'social alliances' may shape the policy preferences of those eventually elevated to the Supreme Court. There is reason to believe that interpersonal interactions within this elite circle occur on a regular basis (Kristjánsson 2010b).

Such discussions may set the 'Oslo-West' legal community a bit apart from lawyers located outside the greater Oslo region. For example, there is at least anecdotal evidence that the Oslo legal milieu might be tied to the government.[13] Indeed, law professor Eivind Smith has pointed out that far too many justices have been employed in the Ministry of Justice or some other governmental office. He claims that it is quite understandable that a justice could be influenced by work experience and environment (Kristjánsson 2010a; Pedersen 1994). The narrow nature of the legal community becomes evident when Supreme Court justices have to recuse themselves because they are married to the government's prosecuting attorney arguing a case before the Court and other key governmental civil servants (Kristjánsson, 2010a). This portrayal certainly plays into Fleischer's characterisation of the Supreme Court as government friendly (Fleischer 2006).

Turning to the pattern of post-World War II Oslo appointees, we can readily observe that there has been a general, long-term decline over the last half century (*see* Figure 4.3).[14] Initially, from 1945 through most of the 1950s, there was a steady rise in the percentage of Oslo-born justices, making up from about 40 per cent to over 60 per cent of the Court membership. 60 per cent, however, was the high water mark. Since the 1950s, the proportion of Oslo-born justices has dropped until it settled at about the level it was at immediately after World War II. If (1) being part of the Oslo social matrix explains, at least in part, judicial decision making and (2) about 40 per cent of all justices are part of that legal milieu, then this variable is of particular interest to students of the Norwegian Supreme Court – a possibility we explore in several of the analytical chapters that follow.

Historical pattern: Centre–periphery and the 'inside track'

If ever there is a centre–periphery division relevant to the Norwegian Supreme Court, it might well be reflected in key departments of the Oslo-based Ministry of Justice – the Legislation Department (*Lovavdelingen*) and the Public Prosecutor's Office (*Riksadvokaten*).[15] Toiling away in the bowels of these

---

13. Professor Asbjørn Strandbakken – Dean of the University of Bergen Law School – argued that the Supreme Court should be relocated to the small town of Kristiansand in order to increase its independence from the government institutions in Oslo, and to limit the recruitment to the Court from Holmenkollåsen in 'Oslo West' (Garvik 2008).

14. In 1956, the Oslo-born Carl Rode, having been chief district court judge (*sorenskriver*) in the Vesterålen area in the 1945–1953 period, was selected for a justiceship on the Court in part because of his 'knowledge about Northern Norway' (The National Archives of Norway, files).

15. The Public Prosecutor's Office (*Riksadvokaten*) may also be referred to as the Director General of Public Prosecutions and more officially as '*The Higher Prosecution Authorities*'.

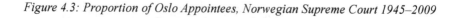

Figure 4.3: Proportion of Oslo Appointees, Norwegian Supreme Court 1945–2009

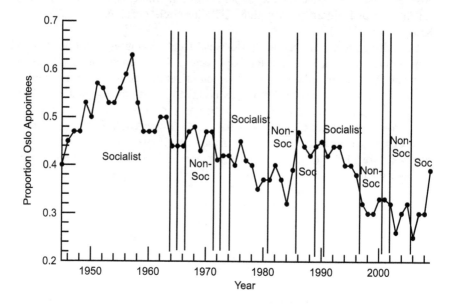

critically important central government organs might well encourage sympathy for the political centre, and of the two, previous experience in the Legislation Department might have the greater relevance for the full range of legal and constitutional issues brought to the Supreme Court. Clearly, a substantial number of justices are drawn from the Legislation Department (Kjønstad 1999), and it would be naïve to think that this on-the-job socialisation does not leave a lasting impression (Eckhoff 1964). These are the very people who write, or assist in writing, the laws, and who interpret the laws – with or without a request from other governmental officials (Andenæs 1986). If indeed the Legislation Department decides 'what the law is' (Skarpnes 1986: 195), then justices recruited from this division of the Ministry of Justice may well continue to know what the law is when elevated to the High Court. The post-World War II trend in recruiting Supreme Court justices from the Legislation Department is exhibited in Figure 4.4.

Generally speaking, the post-World War II period was marked by an approximately six decade long increase in the presence of former Legislation Department employees on the Supreme Court. From 1945 until the mid-1980s, the presence of these appointees was gradual, but steady. From the mid-1980s until the mid-1990s the proportion shot up to the point that half or more of the justices had this specific type of executive branch experience. A sharp decline beginning in 1997 bottomed out in 1999. This was followed by a resurgence of the appointment of those with Legislative Department experience, so that by the end

Figure 4.4: Proportion of all Justices with Legislation Department Experience, Norwegian Supreme Court 1945–2009

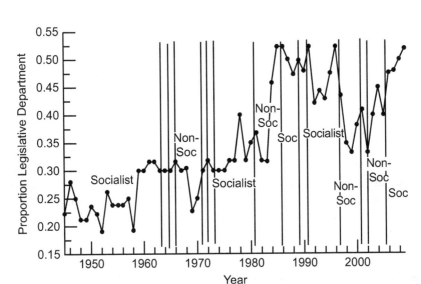

of the period, well over 50 per cent of the Supreme Court justices passed through the Department on their way to a seat on Norway's highest court.

While unquestionably highly qualified judicial candidates can be found in the Legislation Department, a caveat of systemic proportions deserves mention. What we have here is not a smooth progression within, say, the court system. Justices are not necessarily moving from experience as judges in lower courts, which could easily be regarded as a logical career path, in which ascension would proceed within a politically independent domain. Instead, we are witnessing a potential breach of the judiciary's independence from the executive branch of government. Governments simply can elevate members of the executive branch to the High Court. Under such circumstances, can we credibly assert that there is a meaningful degree of judicial independence from the executives controlling the appointment process?[16] Perhaps, but the question deserves further attention.

---

16. Until the terrorist bombing of the Government headquarters in Oslo 22 July 2011, the offices of the Prime Minister, the Ministry of Justice, and the Legislation Department were all located in the same high-rise building, with only the building of the Treasury Department separating it from the Supreme Court building. When Toril Øie, with an eighteen year career at the Legislation Department, was appointed to the Supreme Court in 2004, she was afraid that during her first days in her new job she might be entering the wrong building (Moe 2004).

Of course, experience in the central government may represent, at least in part, reinforcement of some basic values embedded in the law school curriculum. Perhaps a bias tipped in favour of the government and more powerful economic interests is a natural consequence of a legal education (Eckhoff 1964; Fleischer 2006). If so, law schools are, in effect, teaching more than legal principles and reasoning. They are equipping prospective lawyers and judges with some of the very extra-legal predispositions we seek to address in this book.

Historical pattern: The ivory tower

Academia has been another route to a seat on the High Bench, particularly over the past two decades. Torgersen (1963) counts five law professors on the Court in the 1814–1884 period, primarily stemming from the disorganised situation at the University of Oslo at the beginning of that period. Professors were absent from the Court for the next one hundred years. But during the last two decades, a number of law professors themselves – not just their students – have found their way onto the High Court.[17] As depicted in Figure 4.5, not a single law school professor was permanently appointed to the Supreme Court from 1945 through 1990. That pattern was altered in 1991 when Carsten Smith – a University of Oslo law school professor – was appointed to the Supreme Court as Chief Justice.[18] After Smith's appointment, the presence of law professors on the Court rose steadily, peaking at 20 per cent in 1998. It remained at that level for several years, only to be cut in half at the tail end of the time series (*see* Figure 4.5).

At this juncture, we would tentatively hypothesise that the increase in law professors on the Court might have helped produce more dissent and a modest step toward increased institutionalisation. As indicated in the previous chapter, Chief Justice Smith considered the Supreme Court to be a political institution, and thought that full discussion and dissent were appropriate elements of the deliberative process. It is at least intuitive, and perhaps also stereotypical, to think that professors revel in extended discussion, debate, disagreement, and embellishment. In such a decision-making environment, dissenting becomes an accepted – and perhaps even valued – standard of conduct. The slow, but steady increase in the proportion of academics on the High Bench might reinforce the practice of dissenting from the Court's rulings.

On the second point, we surmise that the Norwegian Supreme Court is reasonably well institutionalised. Employing McGuire's (2004) trichotomous typology, we note that the Court is 'differentiated' in that it is distinct from other

---

17. In 1982, Axel Hærem, an esteemed law professor at the University of Bergen, applied for a permanent position on the Court, but was turned down by the Ministry of Justice. Obviously, the professorial era on the Court had not yet arrived.

18. In 1981 Carsten Smith's wife Lucy Smith became the first woman to hold a PhD in law; in 1987 she became the first female Law Professor at the University of Oslo; and during 1993–1998 she served as the first female rector of the University of Oslo.

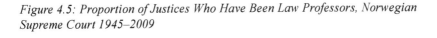

Figure 4.5: Proportion of Justices Who Have Been Law Professors, Norwegian Supreme Court 1945–2009

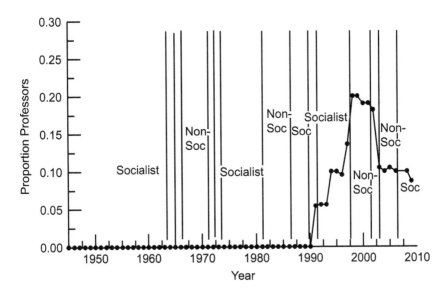

branches of government and has a clear role in the political system. However, a sizeable number of justices have not had a great deal of experience as judges prior to their appointment – a key indicator of differentiation. The Supreme Court is also 'durable' in that it is an acknowledged governmental coequal with 'internal norms and regularised procedures for decision making' (McGuire 2004: 132).[19] Finally, with respect to 'autonomy', the Court does exercise control of its docket, but – given the judicial appointment process and the regular ascent to the Bench of individuals with experience in the Legislation Department – it may be more dependent on the executive branch.

It is on this final dimension of autonomy that the presence of law professors might make an important contribution. Clearly, some law professors, being intellectually grounded in constitutional law, might be predisposed to engage in judicial activism when deliberating cases. One scholar notes that 'especially during the past few years, the Judiciary has shown a more dynamic understanding of its own power of judicial review of legislative acts and a renewed 'activism' in its interpretation of the Constitution' (Nguyên-Duy 2011: 10). The greater presence of law professors may have encouraged such behaviour, which, in turn, seems to stimulate an increased institutionalisation of the Norwegian Supreme Court.

---

19. A law clerk, however, is not assigned to each individual justice – a form of staffing that should contribute to durability.

Conclusion

In this chapter, we have assumed that national policy ruled upon by the Supreme Court is, in part, determined by appointment. We contend that it matters whether a socialist or non-socialist government runs the appointment process, whether a male or female is selected, whether the candidate is part of the Oslo legal elite network, and whether the justice served in the Legislation Department or was a faculty member of one of the country's law schools. That said, we have reported a descriptive analysis of appointments with respect to the nature of the government, the presence of female justices, the distribution of justices from the 'centre' and the 'periphery', Legislative Department service, and previous experience as a law school professor.

First, we presented a graph that tracked the proportion of those appointed by either socialist or non-socialist governments. As would be intuitively obvious, we find that for each year a socialist-led government is in place, there was a 5.5 percentage point increase in the presence of socialist appointees on the Court. Naturally, a similar pattern would hold for non-socialist appointments.

Second, tracking the proportion of women serving on the Supreme Court with the proportion elected to the Parliament, we find that while both percentages were comparable at the end of the period under study, women entered the *Storting* much more rapidly than they did the Court. Institutional differences in the recruitment processes seem to account for this difference in rate of growth. We suggest that the egalitarian nature of Norwegian culture eventually led to a greater percentage of women being appointed to the Supreme Court.

Third, some observers argue that there is a centre–periphery effect, in which those in the national centre of Oslo might – as elites gathered in the nation's capital – behave differently. Near the beginning of the post-World War II period, an extraordinarily high proportion of justices were Oslo-born, followed by a long-term decline. Nevertheless, even by 2009 nearly 40 per cent of the justices were born in Oslo.

Fourth, while the Supreme Court is a relatively autonomous institution, the fact that we find a remarkable increase in the proportion of Legislation Department employees being elevated to the High Court might quite possibly compromise its independence. These appointees bring a great deal of executive experience outside of judicial channels, providing adequate grounds to at least hypothesise that they bring government-friendly behaviour. We explore this possibility in greater detail in Chapter Seven. We suspect that this appointment pattern might not only diminish autonomy, it could also suggest a reduced level of institutional differentiation.

Finally, we noted that law professors – after well over four decades of complete absence from the Supreme Court – began to have a presence on the Court. Indeed at the time of writing, one in five justices were recruited from the professoriate of the nation's law schools. This may result in a greater measure of judicial independence. We have, for example, witnessed the Court's recent increased willingness to flex its judicial muscle on some controversial constitutional issues (*see* Chapter Eight).

Overall, the political, social, and professional backgrounds of justices must shape their perceptions of the law and its application in the adjudicative process. To the extent that justices are not machine-like drones cranked out by the nation's law schools, their fundamental ideological attitudes do inform their decision-making behaviour. Most importantly for present purposes, if and when appointment decisions are made on the basis of gender, party, centre–periphery origins, or professional background, the government is to some degree making policy by appointment.

References

Andenæs, Ø. (1986) 'Et tilbakeblikksbillede fra 1946. En fest og en lærdom for livet' in Bugge, H. O., Coward, K. and Rognlien, S. (eds) *Festskrift Lovavdelingen - 100 år 1885–1985*, Oslo: Universitetsforlaget, pp. 170–171.

Andrews, E. and Hoekstra, V. (2010) 'The Selection of Women on Constitutional Courts: The Impact of Judicial Selection Mechanisms and Party Quotas on Court Composititon', Paper prepared for the 2010 Southern Political Science Conference, Atlanta, Georgia.

Aschehoug, M. (2010) 'Rekordmange nye dommere i Scheis periode', *Advokatbladet* 90 (10): 26–27.

Baum, L. (2008) *Judges and Their Audiences: A Perspective on Judicial Behavior*, Princeton: Princeton University Press.

Brace, P. and Hall, M. G. (1997) 'The Interplay of Preferences, Case Facts, Context, and Rules in the Politics of Judicial Choice', *The Journal of Politics* 59 (4): 1206–1231.

Bystydzienski, J. M. (1988) 'Women in Politics in Norway', *Women and Politics*, 8 (3–4): 73–95.

Danziger, S., Levav, J. and Avnaim-Pesso, L. (2011) 'Extraneous Factors in Judicial Decisions', *Proceedings of the National Academy of Sciences* 108 (17): 6889–6892.

Domstolkommisjonen (1999) 'Domstolene i samfunnet: Administrativ styring av domstolene. Utnevnelser, sidegjøremål, disiplinærtiltak. Midlertidige dommere. Oslo, Justis- og politidepartementet'. Online. Available https://www.regjeringen.no/nb/dokumenter/nou-1999–19/id141812/ (last accessed 25 November 2014).

Dworkin, R. (1988) *Taking Rights Seriously*, Cambridge Mass.: Harvard University Press.

Eckhoff, T. (1964) 'Noen refleksjoner om domstolens uavhengighet' in *Festskrift tillägnad professor, juris doktor Karl Olivecrona vid hans avgång från professorämbetet den 30 juni 1964*, Stockholm: Norstedt, pp. 109–147.

Elder, N., Thomas, A. H. and Arter, D. (1988) *The Consensual Democracies? The Government and Politics of the Scandinavian States*, Oxford: Basil Blackwell.

Fleischer, C. A. (2006) *Korrupsjonskultur, Kameraderi og Tillitssvikt i Norge*, Oslo: Koloritt Forlag.

Gangnes, O.-M. (2010) 'Smith and Jussen', *Juristkontakt* 45: 6–11.

Garvik, O. (2008) 'Jussprofessor vil flytte Høyesterett til Kristiansand', *Bergens Tidende*, 7 March.

Hjellbrekke, J., Roux, B. L., Korsnes, O., Lebaron, F., Rosenlund, L. and Rouanet, H. (2007) 'The Norwegian Field of Power Anno 2000', *European Societies* 9 (2): 245–273.

Inglehart, R. and Norris, P. (2003) *Rising Tide: Gender Equality and Cultural Change Around the World*, Cambridge: Cambridge University Press.

Inglehart, R., Norris, P. and Welzel, C. (2002) 'Gender Equality and Democracy', *Comparative Sociology* 1 (3): 321–345.

Kjønstad, A. (1999) 'Er Høyesterett statsvennlig?', *Lov og Rett* 38: 97–122.

Kristjánsson, M. (2010a) 'Er gift med staten', *Klassekampen*, 20 February.

— (2010b) 'Høyesterett delt på midten', *Klassekampen*, 18 February.

Kuhnle, S., Strøm, K. and Svåsand, L. (1986) 'The Norwegian Conservative Party: Setback in an Era of Strength', *West European Politics* 9 (3): 448–471.

Madeley, J. T. S. (2002) 'Outside the Whale: Norway's Storting Election of 10 September 2001', *West European Politics* 25 (2): 212–222.

Magnussen, A. M. (2005) 'The Norwegian Supreme Court and Equitable Considerations: Problematic Aspects of Legal Reasoning', *Scandinavian Political Studies* 28 (1): 69–89.

Matland, R. E. (1993) 'Institutional Variables Affecting Female Representation in National Legislatures: The Case of Norway', *Journal of Politics* 55 (3): 737–755.

— (1998) 'Women's Representation in National Legislatures: Developed and Developing Countries', *Legislative Studies Quarterly* 23 (1): 109–125.

McGuire, K. T. (1993) 'Lawyers and the U.S. Supreme Court: The Washington Community and Legal Elites', *American Journal of Political Science* 37 (2): 365–390.

— (2004) 'The Institutionalization of the U.S. Supreme Court', *Political Analysis* 12 (2): 128–142.

Moe, E. (2004) 'Toril M. Øie gleder seg: Ung, kvinne og høyesterettsdommer', *Rett på Sak* 2 (2): 16–17.

Narud, H. M. and Valen, H. (2008) 'The Norwegian Storting: 'People's Parliament' or Coop for "Political Broilers"?', *World Political Science Review* 4 (2): 1–34.

Nguyên-Duy, I. (2011) 'From Parliamentary Sovereignty to Constitutional Democracy? [What is the scope of constitutional judicial review of legislation in Norway in the light of the Shipping Tax case and the OVF case of 2010?]', Paper presented at the 2nd International Conference on Democracy as Idea and Practice, Oslo 13–14 January 2011.

Norris, P. (2004) *Electoral Engineering: Voting Rules and Political Behavior*, Cambridge: Cambridge University Press.

NTB (2008) 'Storberget vil ha flere kvinner til Høyesterett', *Norsk Telegrambyrå*, 31 October.

Pedersen, D. (1994) 'Hvor 'blind' er fru Justitia?', *Aftenposten*, 10 May.

Pettersen, P. A., Jenssen, A. T. and Listhaug, O. (1996) 'The 1994 EU Referendum in Norway: Continuity and Change', *Scandinavian Political Studies* 19 (3): 257–281.

Rokkan, S. (1966) 'Norway: Numerical Democracy and Corporate Pluralism' in Dahl, R. A. (ed.) *Political Oppositions in Western Democracies*, New Haven: Yale University Press, pp. 70–115.

— (1967) 'Geography, Religion, and Social Class: Crosscutting Cleavages in Norwegian Politics', in Lipset, S. M. and Rokkan, S. (eds) *Party*

Systems and Voter Alignments: Cross-National Persepctive, New York: Free Press, pp. 367–444.

Schei, T. (2006) 'Høyesterett må ha de beste', *Aftenposten*, 21 February.

Shaffer, W. R. (1998) *Politics, Parties, and Parliaments: Political Change in Norway*, Columbus: Ohio State University Press.

Sitter, N. (2006) 'Norway's Storting Election of September 2005: Back to the Left?', *West European Politics* 29 (3): 573–580.

Skarpnes, O. (1986) 'Minner fra Lovavdelingen', in Bugge, H. O., Coward, K. and Rognlien, S. (eds) *Festskrift Lovavdelingen - 100 år 1885–1985*, Oslo: Universitetsforlaget, pp. 711–726.

Skoghøy, J. E. A. (2010) 'Dommeratferd og dommerbakgrunn. Særlig om yrkesbakgrunnens betydning for utfallet av tvister mellom private og det offentlige', in Lambertz, G., Lindskog, S. and Möller, M. (eds) *Festskrift till Torgny Håstad*, Uppsala: Iustus.

Smith, C. (2003) 'Domstolsadministrasjonen – Bakgrunn og Prinsipper for Reformen', *Jussens Venner* 38: 1–7.

Torgersen, U. (1963) 'The Role of the Supreme Court in the Norwegian Political System', in Schubert, G. (ed.) *Judicial Decision-Making*, New York: The Free Press of Glencoe, pp. 221–244.

Urwin, D. W. (1997) 'The Norwegian Party System from the 1880s to the 1990s', in Strøm, K. and Svåsand, L. (eds) *Challenges to Political Parties: The Case of Norway*, Ann Arbor: University of Michigan Press, pp. 33–59.

Valen, H. (1990) *Endring og Kontinuitet: Stortingsvalget 1989*, Oslo: Statistisk Sentralbyrå.

— (1992) *Valg og Politikk: Et Samfunn i Endring*, Oslo: NKS-Forlaget.

Willoch, K. (2002) *Myter og Virkelighet: Om Begivenheter frem til Våre Dager med Utgangspunkt i Perioden 1965–1981*, Oslo: Cappelen.

Chapter Five

Public Economic Interests vs.
Private Economic Rights

As we noted in the conclusion of the preceding chapter, our theoretical perspective is that the composition of the Court, in terms of the justices' attitudes and attributes, affects its outputs. In other words, Norway is a nation of laws, operating under a constitution, but ultimately the laws and the Constitution are what the justices say they are.[1] This theoretical perspective, in turn, suggests that there should be systematic differences in the individual justices' decisional behaviour. In this and the next three chapters we put this overarching theoretical expectation to the test. In this chapter, we examine the association between the nature of the government appointing a given justice and that justice's votes in cases involving public versus private economic rights.

In the social welfare states of Scandinavia, few issues are more salient or orient the political system more clearly than does the relationship between public economic interests and private economic rights (Shaffer 1998: 87). Norway is certainly no exception. Heidar notes that throughout the second half of the twentieth century, a major (perhaps *the* major) fault line in Norwegian electoral politics has been the role of the state in the economy (2000: 62). Indeed, the public–private economic cleavage has been dominant in all election studies since the late 1950s (*see*, for example, Aardal 2011). Shaffer's analysis of the changing Norwegian political landscape at the close of the twentieth century confirmed its endurance (Shaffer 1998: 78, 80; Heidar 2000: 83). Not surprisingly, the scope of state involvement in the economy also appears to define Norway's party system, dividing the parties into socialist and non-socialist blocs (Heidar 2000: 27). The 'policy and ideological predilections of the parties' core interest groups and elites' reflect a basic left/right economic dimension that positions the competing parties in Norwegian political space (Shaffer 1998: 18; and more generally Chapter Five). According to Strøm and Leipart, the left/right policy dimension 'powerfully constrained' coalition building between parties in parliament (1989; 1993).

Given the prominence of the economic cleavage in Norwegian politics, we would not expect that justices always see eye to eye on public/private economic issues. Moreover, when justices disagree on economic issues, we would expect their preferences to track very closely with their political ideology, as well as with the identity of the political party that appointed them. The association between the justices' votes in economics cases and the nature of their appointing party should

---

1. This is a modification of U.S. Supreme Court Chief Justice Charles Evans Hughes' characterisation of the power of the judiciary: 'We are under a Constitution, but the Constitution is what the judges say it is' (Hughes 1908: 139).

be a relatively easy test, then, of our primary research hypothesis that appointments matter. In other words, if we are going to see 'policy making by appointment' with respect to the Norwegian Supreme Court, we should see it here. As noted above, in this chapter we explore the role of the individual justices' policy preferences as defined by the colour of the appointing party, by analysing their decisional behaviour in the issue area of economic rights.

Now, we are by no means arguing that Norway's Supreme Court justices are partisan operatives who merely vote according to the policy directives of whichever party's leadership was responsible for their appointment. Rather, we are using the nature of each justice's appointing party as a crude proxy for that justice's attitudinal preferences. Certainly, a more direct (and valid) measure of a justice's ideology would be preferable. However, no such measure is readily available. This problem is made even more acute in that we seek to analyse over six decades of the justices' decisional behaviour. Given the absence of a direct measure of judicial ideology and the need to deploy an instrument that can be operationalised across sixty-plus years of Norwegian judicial history, then, we are left to rely upon the political colour of the justices' appointing governments. Accordingly, we hypothesise that justices who were appointed by social democratic governments are more likely to support the litigant claiming a public economic interest than are their non-socialist appointed counterparts.

We test this hypothesis in three, increasingly rigorous, steps. First, we examine the justices' behaviour in a recent landmark decision that unambiguously pitted the proponents of public economic interests against the defenders of private economic rights. As briefly discussed in the first chapter, this case concerned the government's right to impose retroactive taxes on ship owners, and the justices' votes show a clear division that is strongly related to the identity of the political party that appointed them. We then turn to a multi-dimensional scaling analysis of the six non-unanimous, plenary decisions involving economic rights handed down by the Court between 2000 and 2010. That analysis locates the justices in three-dimensional space, and the specific coordinates of any individual justice reveal a close connection between the justice's ideology and the nature of his or her appointing government. Finally, we subject the individual justice's vote in all of the Supreme Court's non-unanimous decisions concerning economic issues handed down between 1948 and 2009 to a multivariate logit analysis. The results of that analysis show that, even under multivariate controls, there is a strong and predictable relationship between the partisan identity of a justice's appointing government and his or her vote in cases involving economic rights.

The *Ship Owner's Taxation* case

In 2010 the Norwegian Supreme Court handed down its decision in the *Ship Owner's Taxation* case (Rt-2010–143). To a small polity, it was the political and financial equivalent of *Bush v. Gore*.[2] Some identified the decision as arguably

---

2.   531 U.S. 98 (2000).

involving, 'in monetary, legal and political terms the largest, most important and most fundamental legal dispute between the state and business that Norway has seen for many decades.' To the legal experts close to the case, the Court's decision portended significant ramifications for the state's capacity to control the economic system, curbing the government's power to enact legislation that would have 'material consequences for individuals, companies, or industries' (Schjødt, nd). Others demurred, pointing out that although the case was a showdown between the branches of government, the legal and political impact of the decision itself was undermined by the facts that the decision was rendered by less than a full Court, only eleven of the nineteen justices participated in the decision, and that the participating justices were so sharply divided in its 6–5 decision. (Høgberg 2010).[3]

The gravamen of the case concerned whether the social democratic led government's requirement that the nation's shipping industry pay approximately twenty-one billion kroner (about \$3.547 billion[4]) in back taxes as part of a transition to a new taxation regime was permissible, despite being in violation of Section 97 of the Norwegian Constitution – the provision against *ex post facto* laws. Indeed, there was unanimity among the Court's members that the transition tax ran afoul of Section 97.[5] Differences among the justices arose, however, over whether this constitutional violation could pass muster under the doctrine of 'equitable considerations' – that is, as an instance where changing social and political conditions empower the justices to actively interpret the Constitution in order to reach a decision that they identify as fair and appropriate. (For a more detailed discussion of the 'equitable considerations' doctrine, *see* Chapter One.)

The government's position in the *Ship Owner's Taxation* case was that the 'transition tax' was utterly fair and appropriate in light of the changed tax regime that was in effect. In 2007 Norway had adjusted its tax on shipping tonnage so as to bring it into line with the prevailing European taxation system on shipping (Ward and Wright 2010). This resulted in a substantial loss in tax revenues, and the state argued that its concomitant effort to collect billions of kroner in back taxes was 'merely a "justified" demand for taxes previously deferred' (Schjødt, nd). Essentially, the government defended its back-tax requirement on the grounds of the 'equitable considerations' doctrine. A minority of the justices supported the government's position on the explicit basis of the Court's 1996 *Borthen* decision and its unanimous view that the government needed revenues to fund the welfare state (Rt-2010–143, paragraph 208).

---

3. Of the total number of nineteen justices on the Court at that time, five justices were recused due to conflict of interest (Rt-2009–1617), two justices had leaves of absence, and the youngest remaining justice, Justice Arnfinn Bårdsen, had to leave the case in order to meet the legally required odd-number of justices in any case (Rt-2010–143, paragraphs 67 and 68).

4. Based on the average exchange rate of 5.92 NOK/USD in February 2010. Online. Available http://www.norges-bank.no/Statistikk/Valutakurser/valuta/USD/ (last accessed 15 November 2014).

5. The minority's position was that the new tax regime was retroactive, but permissible in the present case.

To state the matter somewhat more directly, the justices agreed that the transition tax violated the constitutional protection from *ex post facto* legislation; they disagreed, however, as to whether this violation was a *legitimate* and/or *reasonable* exercise of government power given the context in which that power was being applied. Although in terms of legislative intent and the facts at bar, the case was relatively transparent, it was by no means an 'easy' one to decide. To be sure, the *Ship Owner's* case presented the justices with an act of government on the one hand, a constitutional provision on the other, and the charge to determine if the former squared with the latter;[6] yet, complex questions abounded concerning what was 'fair' and 'equitable' with respect to state power over the economy and the appropriate relationship between the state and the individual in economic matters. Consequently, the justices had to navigate these complexities, and as human decision makers it is highly probable that their own attitudinal preferences would play a role in charting their course.[7]

As just noted, the minority bloc of justices in the ship-owner case interpreted the 'equitable considerations' doctrine in line with the 1996 *Borthen* decision, in which the Court developed the standard that Section 97 of the Constitution prohibits only retroactive laws that are 'clearly unreasonable or unfair' (Rt-1996–1415 at 1426). The majority of the justices in the *Ship Owner's* case, on the other hand, interpreted the 'equitable considerations' doctrine in line with a more recent plenary decision (*Arve's trafikkskole*, Rt-2006–293), in which the Court developed the standard that Section 97 could only be put aside if 'compelling societal interests' were found. The majority did not find this to be the case in the present instance.[8]

The outcome of the *Ship Owner's Taxation* case was that five of the justices agreed with the position of the state, and six justices agreed with the position of the ship owners. Thus, the state lost by a razor-thin 6–5 margin. In that vote, two phenomena are evident. First, it is clear that invoking equitable considerations provides ample opportunity for the justices' individual policy preferences to play a role in their decisional behaviour. Second, these policy preferences are closely associated with the identity of the political party that appointed each justice. All of the voting justices who were appointed by non-socialist governments found for the ship owners. Meanwhile, five of the seven justices appointed by social democratic governments voted for the state. In short, the division among the justices was almost perfectly collinear with the partisan identity of their appointing government. In other words, the *Ship Owner's Taxation* case is a manifest example of policy making by appointment.

---

6. This classic formulation of legal formalism is, perhaps, best articulated in *U.S. v. Butler* (297 US 1 at 62 [1936]).

7. *See* Baum (1997) on the opportunity complex cases provide for justices to pursue their policy preferences.

8. Finer legal discussions on the interpretation of Section 97 also include the terms 'true retroactivity' ('*egentlig tilbakevirkning*') and 'quasi-retroactivity' ('*uegentlig tilbakevirkning*') neither of which we shall pursue here. *See also* Chapter Eight on judicial doctrines of Section 97.

Indeed, the justices' ideological predilections appear to have been their 'lodestar', as a clear and systematic pattern emerges in the justices' vote on the merits. In her close analysis of the *Ship Owner's Taxation* case, legal scholar Benedikte Moltumyr Høgberg notes that the majority and the minority factions of the Court seemed to have made up their minds on the outcome of the case *before* they began to discuss its legal elements. These decisions had consequences for which standard of the 'equitable considerations' doctrine they decided to apply to the case and how they construed the case in light of the broader circumstances. Pertinently, Høgberg questions the degree to which the justices' discussion in the decision was a 'play for the gallery' (Høgberg 2010: 713, 715).

The social democratic coalition government had invested a lot in the ship owners' decision. It also believed that it had secured its position since the Ministry of Justice's own legal citadel, the Legislation Department, sanctioned the legislation. The social democratic dominated majority in Parliament also expected that the Supreme Court would defer to the Parliament, since in the 1976 *Kløfta decision* the Court had established the standard that deference to the first branch of government in economics cases was the appropriate *modus vivendi*.[9] The minority bloc of justices in the *Ship Owner's decision* did defer to the Parliament, but the majority chose to distinguish between *types* of economic interests in order to diminish the quality of the Parliament's preparatory works regarding the tax legislation. This decisional manoeuvre allowed the majority to disregard Parliament's views since the legislators had used a different decisional standard than the one chosen by the Court (Høgberg 2010: 729–731). When Justice Karl Arne Utgård, writing on behalf of the majority, brushed away all discussions and claimed that there can be 'no doubt' (Rt-2010–143: paragraph 173) that the Parliament's new tax regime violated Section 97 of the Constitution, legal scholar Erik Gjems-Onstad respectfully requested that the Supreme Court be less arrogant (qtd. in Høgberg 2010: 742).

Of more immediate consequence for our analytical purposes, however, is the consistency between the ideological direction of the justices' votes and the manifest policy preferences of the different parties' core elites and interests with respect to economic issues. To put it concretely, social democratic appointed justices voted for public economic interests – the economic issue position most identified with the socialist bloc of parties. Non-socialist appointed justices voted for private economic rights – a policy preference most identified with the non-socialist bloc.

Appointing party and a justice's ideology: A spatial analysis

The voting divisions and the justices' substantive vote choices in the *Ship Owner's Taxation* case are very suggestive of the relationship between the justices' attitudinal preferences on economic issues and the identity of the political party that appointed them. A single case, in and of itself, however, does not provide

---

9.   The economic standard in the *Kløfta decision* (Rt-1976–1) was subsequently upheld in both the plenary *Borthen decision* (Rt-1996–1415) and the *Øvre Ullern Terrasse decision* (Rt-2007–1281). *See* Chapter Eight.

a great deal of analytical leverage (*see* King *et al.* 1994, on the importance of designing research in order to maximise leverage). It is said that '[g]reat cases, like hard cases, make bad law',[10] and in this instance, great cases might also make bad social science. That is, the *Ship Owner's* case may be so unique, may invoke such sharpened attitudes among the justices, that it is in reality an outlier. The behaviour of the justices in the *Ship Owner's* case, and the relationships underlying that behaviour, might stand at some appreciable distance from the justices' typical behaviour and underlying relationships. In other words, it may be that in the great bulk of cases (even the non-unanimous ones) there is no genuine systematic pattern or relationship between the partisan identity of the governing coalition in power at the time of a justice's appointment and that justice's policy preferences.

To test this possibility, we conducted a spatial analysis of the justices' votes on economic issues decided in plenary session between 2000 and 2010. Specifically, we applied multi-dimensional scaling (MDS) to eight cases that raised economic issues and were decided non-unanimously in plenary sessions of the Court.[11] The fifteen justices who participated in at least half of these decisions provide the input for the analysis. For each case, a justice's vote was assigned a value of 1 if the vote was in support of the litigant claiming a public economic interest; a value of -1 if the vote was in support of the litigant arguing a private economic right; and a value of 0 if the justice did not participate. These scores were then used to compute Euclidean distances among the justices, and an MDS procedure was applied to the inter-justice distances to derive a one, two, or three-dimensional solution.

Using the Stress one goodness-of-fit measure, we determined that a three-dimensional solution is the best representation of the economic policy space we are mapping (stress index = .10). The substantive interpretation of each dimension in the MDS solution is based upon the degree to which it is related to the different types of economic cases and thus represents a different aspect of economic rights. Accordingly, we identify the first dimension as a *Government Overreach* dimension because it comprises two cases in which the Court found for a private individual or company and where the government was seen as exceeding its proper authority. We identify the second dimension as *No New Taxes* since three cases concerning the government's power to impose new taxes are associated with it. And we identify the third and marginal dimension as *Added Tax* since it doubles up on taxes already imposed.

---

10. *Northern Securities Co. v. U.S.* (197 US 197 [1903]).

11. Rt-2002–509; Rt-2002–557; Rt-2005–1365; Rt-2006–293; Rt-2006–1409; Rt-2007–1308; Rt-2010–143; Rt2010–535. Focusing on non-unanimous decisions gives us greater traction in our effort to identify the relationship between the justices' attitudinal preferences and the nature of the governing coalition that was in power at the time of their appointment. This is not to say that the justices' attitudes are necessarily absent in unanimous cases. Rather, it might be that the justices find themselves at the same point on the ideological continuum in unanimous cases or the unanimous cases present such clear legal facts that the justices are effectively driven to a particular outcome or the unanimous cases concern a set of questions that do not trigger a justice's policy preferences (Baum 1997).

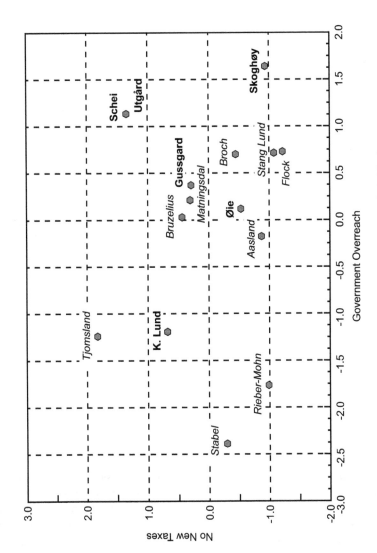

Figure 5.1: Two-Dimensional Plot of MDS Coordinates. 'No New Taxes' Plotted on 'Government Economic Overreach', Eight Plenary Sessions 2000–2010

Note: Socialist appointees in italics and Non-Socialist appointees in bold print.

With a satisfactory MDS solution in hand, we can plot the individual justice's coordinates on each of the two most important dimensions (omitting *Added Tax*) to represent their position in ideological space (*see* Figure 5.1). Since our goal is to determine whether ideology – as measured by the nature of the appointing governing coalition – is related to a justice's position in economic policy space, correlating those coordinates with a variable measuring the identity of the appointing government produces soundings of the strength of that relationship. Those correlations reveal a moderate, but substantively meaningful, association between a justice's positions on each dimension and the identity of the appointing government.

The strongest relationship between the partisan identity of the appointing government and a justice's ideological position on economic issues exists for the *Government Overreach* dimension. This makes good sense inasmuch as this dimension substantively seems to be most on point with respect to the central lines of cleavage in this issue domain, i.e. the place and role of the state in the economy; the relationship between the state and the individual in economic matters; and the allocation or redistribution of society's finite resources. Five of the six leftmost justices were social democratic appointees, while the majority of the justices on the right were non-socialist appointees. The relationship is by no means perfect, but with a correlation coefficient of .389, there is statistical support that knowledge of a justice's appointing government improves the prediction of that justice's ideological position.[12]

Nevertheless, the reader should note that even a casual glance at Figure 5.1 is enough to see that Ketil Lund is a dramatic outlier on the *Government Overreach* axis. In fact, the correlation between *Government Overreach* and appointing government jumps from .389 to .533 when Lund is removed from the calculation. Although our crude measure of ideology (appointing government) identifies Lund as a conservative, we are not convinced that we have properly included him among the Court's conservative justices, at least with respect to *Government Overreach*.

Appointed during the brief term of Jan Syse's conservative-led government, Lund would be expected to be located to the right of center on the *Government Overreach* continuum. In a sense, the attenuated link between appointing government and a justice's position on this particular economic dimension when Lund is included does not negate the political connection we posit in this chapter. To the contrary, the outcome when Lund is included seems to reflect, in part, the fact that appointing government is a crude indicator of the ideological proclivities of the justices. Indeed, if we had a more refined and valid measure of ideology, we contend that the ideological grounding of judicial decisions would be even more apparent.

For that matter, some of Lund's earlier political contributions suggest that his ideological predilections would place him considerably to the left of a Conservative government's agenda. In two studies of Supreme Court justices' sentencing inclination in criminal cases, Jostein Bakke, a lawyer at the Oslo Police Department, twice rated Justice Ketil Lund among the most lenient justices on the High Court. Bakke demonstrated that Lund voted very consistently in favour

---

12. The correlations here are based on a small non-random sample where we emphasise the substantive significance.

of the criminal defendant (2002; 2007). Also Hans Petter Graver, the Dean of the University of Oslo law school, identified Justice Lund as one of the most famous of the left wing lawyers coming out of the radicalised political era of the 1960s and 1970s (Lunde 2013). Against this backdrop, we might suggest that being a non-socialist government appointee produces some measurement error, and our hypothesised relationship between political ideology and decisional behaviour on economic policy is in fact more robust than can be observed when we employ appointing government as a proxy for ideological proclivities.

The relationship between ideology and a justice's voting is moderate on the *No New Taxes* dimension. The correlation coefficient is .319, a bit below the correlation for the *Government Overreach* dimension. Along with the weaker measure of association, the justices are, on this dimension, placed less clearly according to ideology. As a group, the social democratic appointees were more likely to have low scores, but justices with higher scores were more evenly distributed between social democratic and non-socialist appointees.

Finally (but not shown in Figure 5.1), the justices' positions on the *Added Tax* dimension evince the weakest ideology/appointing government relationship in the economic policy domain. The simple correlation is a very weak -.141. Thus, this dimension does not appear to be a function of a justice's ideological orientation.

In the end, this spatial analysis suggests a compelling link between a justice's policy preferences and the ideological nature of their appointing government. Thus, it adds some empirical weight to our argument that the ideological proclivities of the Court's composition – as defined by the identity of the appointing government of the justices – affect the nature of its outputs. To state the matter concretely, there is some evidence of policy making by appointment, at least in the issue domain concerning the economy. Justices appointed by social democratic governments have been more likely to fall at the public economic interest end of an economic interests versus rights continuum, while their non-socialist appointed counterparts have been more likely to fall at the private economic rights end of that same dimension, just as we saw exemplified in the *Ship Owner's Taxation* case.

The plot of the justices' positions on the *No New Taxes* and *Government Overreach* dimensions – the two dimensions with a moderate association with ideology, in Figure 5.1 – provides a visual representation of the potential link between ideology and voting in economic cases. As noted above, with a couple of exceptions socialist government appointees are generally located on the left side of a continuum, while those appointed by non-socialist governments are a little more likely to be on the right.

Deliberation in five-member panels

While ideology informs the decisional behaviour of Supreme Court justices when considering economic cases in plenary session, most appeals are subject to deliberation in the five-member panels. While many five-member panel hearings may not involve fundamental constitutional questions, we nevertheless expect the ideology to have a direct bearing on the rulings handed down on public *vs.*

private economic disputes. A stark example involves the 2002 *Nesset decision* (Rt-2002–94), a brief description of which follows.

In 1995, the small municipality of Nesset, located on the northwestern coast of southern Norway, decided that the national telecommunication company Telenor should pay property taxes. The municipality's justification for the new taxation was the reorganisation of Telenor the previous year from a government owned and controlled service to a government owned corporation serving the public. The legal question was whether, after its reorganisation, Telenor could still be exempted from paying property tax.

In 1999, Telenor lost the case in Romsdal District Court, and appealed the decision to the Frostating Appeal Court. In 2000, the Frostating Court reversed the lower court's decision, ruling unanimously that Telenor's activity was more of a service than a business, and that the law did not permit a municipality to tax this type of company.

In its appeal to the Supreme Court, the municipality of Nesset argued that the part of *The Property Tax Act* in question could not be limited in the way ruled by the court of appeal. The tax law offers incomplete guidance, since the list of types of businesses and cases to which the law explicitly applied could not be considered exhaustive. Nevertheless, modern telecommunication companies are by their very nature industrial in size, complexity and function, and thus subject to taxation.

Telenor argued that the municipality could not tax its business and disputed Nesset's interpretation of the tax law. The old tax laws in question failed to be relevant to the objects that the municipalities wanted to tax. Since no statute could be firmly applied to impose property tax, the legal principle was not met in the present case. Telenor also argued for the relevance of the 1995 *Kvitsøy decision* (Rt-1995–980). The communication lines and services that were ruled untaxable in that decision were applicable to the facts of the present case.

Justice Kirsti Coward wrote the 3–2 majority opinion, arguing that the 1975 tax statute in question could be interpreted to support the taxation of the type of corporation that Telenor represented. She also argued for the preparatory works of tax laws – a fully acknowledged legal source – back in 1882 and 1911, even though the specific examples of industries used in the old laws did not exactly match modern telecommunication corporations. The 1995 *Kvitsøy decision* was problematic for the present case, since the justices in that decision failed to agree on the interpretation of the same tax statute. Coward pointed out that the municipality emphasised the difference between its case and the non-unanimous *Kvitsøy decision*, while Telenor emphasised the similarities. Coward, joined by Justices Lars Oftedal Broch and Georg Fredrik Rieber-Mohn, concluded that Nesset was correct in imposing taxes on Telenor.

Interim justice and law professor Henry John Mæland wrote the minority opinion, in which he argued that previous tax laws did not provide a coherent legal basis for taxing a reorganised Telenor. Given the long legal history of taxation, Mæland found it to be unfortunate that the Supreme Court ruled to the disadvantage of Telenor. Mæland emphasised that it had to be up to the lawmaker, and not the Court, to decide when the technical development of service industries came within the reach of property taxation. Justice Ketil Lund joined Mæland's opinion.

What might explain the justices' votes in this decision? As we demonstrate here and elsewhere, left–right ideology informs the voting on many cases involving a dispute between a public and private economic interest. We employ the colour of the government during which a justice is appointed as our proxy measure of ideology. Thus the non-socialist government appointees Lund and Mæland both sided with Telenor, while Coward, Oftedal Broch and Rieber-Mohn – who had all been appointed by socialist governments – supported Nesset's right to tax Telenor. Probably reinforcing this outcome was the legal background of the justices: (1) the non-socialist appointed justices ruling in favour of the company had a great deal of private practice experience, while (2) the socialist appointees in this case had years of service as government employees in the Legislation Department and/or the Prosecutor General's Office.

But a key question remains: Does this plausible pattern for individual justices hold under multivariate controls that more accurately reflect the complex matrix of forces that can affect a justices' decisional behaviour? It is to this question that we now turn.

A multivariate analysis of the justices' votes

The literature points to several forces that might affect a justice's vote in cases concerning economic rights. Occupation is certainly one of them (Tate 1981; Tate and Sittiwong 1989; Tate and Handberg 1991). As we pointed out in Chapter Four, occupational pursuits have political socialising effects. They engender experiences, relationships, and memberships in social networks that produce or at least reinforce worldviews and therefore political attitudes (*see also* Grendstad *et al.* 2012; Lazarsfeld *et al.* 1944). Tate (1981), for example, finds that lawyers who held elective office prior to ascending to the U.S. Supreme Court are more economically liberal than their counterparts who were recruited directly from private practice. He suggests that the explanation for this is that justices who managed to win electoral support from what is typically a more liberal mass electorate will be more apt to relate to those liberal views. Justices taken directly from private practice, on the other hand, are more likely to relate to the elite, and the more conservative socio-economic interests that they had previously represented.

Likewise, Tate explains the greater economic conservatism of justices who had been prosecutors in terms of their occupational experience: 'Prosecutors spend most of their time defending the position of the 'haves' against the criminal attacks of the 'have nots'. Such experience would logically engender sympathetic attitudes toward economic 'top dogs' (Tate 1981: 363). Although in cases where the government is a party we have found that alumni of the Director General of Public Prosecutions (*Riksadvokaten*) tended to support the government (Grendstad *et al.* 2011b), this may not be true in cases involving economic issues because of their obligation to employ the powers of the state to protect private economic rights against criminal attacks. We hypothesise, therefore, that justices who were in private practice or served in the office of the *Riksadvokaten* before ascending to

Norway's High Bench are more likely to identify with private economic interests, perhaps the interests of members of the socio-economic elite, and as a result, justices with these occupational backgrounds and socialisation experiences will be more apt to identify with and vote for litigants claiming a private economic right.

Justices whose prior occupational experience was with the Legislation Department of the Government's Ministry of Justice (*Lovavdelingen*), on the other hand, may be socialised into support for the public interest (on the relationship between public service careers and support for the government, *see* Kjønstad 1999, but modified by Tellesbø 2006; *see also* Grendstad *et al.* 2011b). The typical public service career path among Supreme Court justices has been employment in the Legislation Department (Kjønstad 1999). As shown in Chapter Four, throughout most of the post-war period, former employees of the Legislation Department accounted for at least one-quarter of the sitting justices, and by the mid-1980s, consistently more than one-third of the justices were Legislation Department alumni.

Of particular importance to our purposes here, experience in the Legislation Department likely brings with it more than a mere tendency or inclination to side with the government or public interest. Employment in the Legislation Department engenders actual identification with the government and its policies. The Legislation Department drafts the nation's laws. This gives rise to the perception that it is the 'legal authority and brain of the administration' (Andenæs 1986: 170). Moreover, since the Department was there at a law's creation, it is in a unique position to act as the 'internal supreme court of the executive branch' (Grendstad *et al.* 2011b: 10). In effect, then, the Legislation Department 'decides what the law is' (Skarpnes 1986: 195). A likely result is that former employees of the Legislation Department have a strong predisposition to accept the public interest or government position in Supreme Court cases questioning the constitutionality of economic legislation. Thus, we hypothesise that justices recruited from the Legislation Department will be more apt to support the public economic interest claim.[13]

Chapter Four also established that since the early 1990s academia – specifically Norway's law schools – became another source of appointees to the High Bench. A handful of professors were appointed as interim justices to the Supreme Court a total of ten times, all within the 1946–1969 period. Within the 1987–2012 period, another handful of professors were appointed and reappointed as interim justices to the Court a total of 29 times. At best, each of these appointments was scheduled to last only a couple of months. Law professors have, however, begun to take permanent seats on the Court with more regular frequency since the 1991 appointment of Carsten Smith as Chief Justice (1991–2002). Indeed, as of 2010, six law professors have migrated from positions in the ivory tower to permanent stations on the Court.

It is difficult to predict what effect membership in the ivory tower might have on an individual justice's attitudes toward private economic rights versus

13. In Chapter Seven we return to many of these specific hypotheses. There, we put to a more direct test the notion that the appointment process tends to result in an especially 'government-friendly' Supreme Court.

public economic interests. On the one hand, one might surmise that the general liberalising effect of higher education might induce the former law professor to be prone to support the public economic interest. Yet, on the other hand, it is possible that legal education introduces areas of the law (e.g. contracts, realty) that might make one more attentive to private economic rights. In the end, then, we expect a background in academia to affect a justice's decisional behaviour, but we cannot hazard a directional hypothesis.

Other than the socialising effect of the experiences of a career, a dimension associated with a particular type of career on the Bench might affect the behaviour of some Supreme Court justices – namely, interim appointees. For these justices, concerns over career advancement might enter into their decisional calculus. (*See* Segal and Spaeth 1993: 69–72 on the absence of ambition for higher office's effect on the U.S. Supreme Court justices' pursuit of policy goals.) Although the Supreme Court sits at the apex of the Norwegian judicial system, and there are effectively very few opportunities to pursue higher judicial office, interim justices are not permanent members of the Court. Consequently, they might perceive their temporary appointment to the High Bench as an 'opportunity to audition' for a permanent justiceship. Indeed, former Chief Justice Terje Wold (1958–1969) observed 'that appointments of interim justices opens a shortcut for later appointments of justices' (Wold 1964: 397), and some interim justices have eventually found their way into permanent seats on the Court. Other interim justices applied, but were not selected.

Several observers of the Norwegian legal system have expressed reservations over the interim justices' possible lack of independence from the government (*see*, for example, Wold 1964; Eckhoff 1964; Hylland 2009). They question whether interim justices could be expected to decide against the government's legal position when it is in fact the *government* that has the power to 'reward' them for a 'correct decision' with a permanent justiceship upon the next Court vacancy.

Empirical tests of the decisional behaviour of interim justices have produced mixed results regarding the interim justices' 'government friendliness'. Østlid (1988) found that in civil cases interim justices did not vote for the litigant claiming a public interest any more frequently than did permanent justices. In criminal cases involving sentencing adjustment, however, interim justices voted in favour of the prosecution at a rate of ten percentage points higher than did their permanently appointed counterparts. Using more rigorous analytical techniques, Grendstad and his coauthors have shown that even under multivariate controls, interim justices are significantly more likely to find for the government in *all* non-unanimous civil cases involving the state as a litigant decided between 1945 and 2009 (Grendstad *et al.* 2011a; *see also* Chapter Seven in this book). However, their preliminary test of the interim justices' support for the government as an instance of 'strategic behaviour' yields no evidence of interim justices adjusting their votes in order to improve their chances of gaining a permanent seat (on judges acting strategically, *see* Epstein and Knight 1998). Given our earlier findings, we hypothesise that interim justices are more apt to find for the public interest in cases involving economic issues,[14] but we cannot offer a hypothesis grounded in empirical findings that this behaviour is an instance of a justice making a strategic calculation.

Another attribute for which the extant literature documents an association with attitudes towards economic redistribution, welfare, and public services is sex (e.g. Inglehart and Norris 2000; Listhaug *et al.* 1985). With respect to judicial decision making, Østlid (1988) found that in Norway women judges tended to be more lenient regarding sentencing adjustments than their male counterparts (*see also* Hansen 2011; Østbye 2011). Women judges also appear to support more liberal positions in the American judicial context (*see*, for example, Gruhl *et al.* 1981). Although more recent empirical evidence casts some doubt on a general causal connection between a judge's sex and his or her decisional behaviour (*see* Boyd *et al.* 2010), the possibility of a relationship between sex and attitudes to economic issues has not been fully put to rest. To guard against omitted variable bias, then, we are persuaded to include the justice's sex in our model specification and hypothesise that women justices will be more likely to find for the party claiming the public economic interest.[15]

Geography is related to the decisional behaviour of the justices on the U.S. and Canadian Supreme Courts (*see* Tate 1981; Tate and Sittiwong 1989), and we would expect it to affect the voting decisions of Norway's justices as well. As we discussed in Chapter Four, there is a distinct and historical tension between the 'centre' and the 'periphery' in Norway (Rokkan 1967; Heidar 2000). This tension might be reflected in the justices' decisional outputs concerning economics cases in at least two ways. First, Oslo is the political, cultural, and social 'centre' of the nation. Government employment and the service sectors dominate its economy, and it stands in contrast to a 'periphery' whose economy is more industrial and oriented toward the development and extraction of natural resources like oil and fish. We hypothesise, therefore, that justices socialised in Oslo – that is, in the 'centre' – may be more supportive of an active and large state presence in the economy and might therefore be more sympathetic to the litigant pressing a public economic interest.

Second, in Chapter Four we pointed out that justices born and raised in Oslo are more likely to be members of a homogenous social network comprising the nation's legal elites (Hjellbrekke *et al.* 2007) – one that dominates the Norwegian judicial process, much in the same way that McGuire (1993) has suggested for the specialised Supreme Court bar operating in the United States. In both Norway and the United States, these small, elite groups of lawyers form social networks

---

14. Indeed, the salience of economic questions to the powers and behaviour of the Norwegian welfare state might make the interim justices' calculations concerning the role of the government in this specific issue domain more consonant with their calculations about the role of the state in criminal prosecutions. That is, in the issue domain of criminal law, the government is the sole legitimate regulator of criminal penalties. In the social welfare state, the government is perceived as legitimately having an expansive role in the regulation of the economy.

15. In Chapter Six we put the effect of sex on decisional behaviour to a more rigorous test.

that can affect the nature of judicial outputs (McGuire 1993: 388). There seems to be a level of interconnection among these elite bars such that their members perceive almost an 'ownership' of, or intimate identification with, key positions in the government. Thus, we hypothesise that justices socialised in Oslo will be more likely to identify with the interests of the state in economics cases and therefore will be more likely to support the litigant claiming a public economic interest.

In addition, we control for period effects and the possibility that the Supreme Court engages in an 'error-correcting strategy' when it reviews cases. Throughout the first half of the 1980s, the conservative Willoch governments, championing lower taxes and a reduced regulatory presence for the state, lead the Norwegian political system (Grendstad and Holgersen 2009; Hagtvet and Bjørklund 1981). To the extent that the formation of governments in parliamentary systems such as Norway's can be linked to the electorate's policy preferences (Shaffer 1998), it seems that the general mood of the nation during this time period was for a smaller role of the state in the economy. To tap this mood, we include a variable that measures the conservative period effect of the Willoch-era, that is the time period between 1981 and 1986. We hypothesise that the Court's outputs during this time period will be more likely to support the party claiming a private economic right.

Finally, since the Supreme Court has discretionary jurisdiction, there is the possibility that it accepts cases in order to reverse them. That is, the Appeals Selection Committee pursues an 'error-correcting strategy', docketing those cases that it believes were decided wrongly (Brenner 1997; Brenner and Krol 1989; Krol and Brenner 1990; Palmer 1992). Accordingly, we hypothesise that when the appellant is the litigant arguing in favour of a public economic interest, the justices are more likely to favour that position.

Model specification, the data and analysis

To test these hypotheses, we specify the following probability model:

$$\left(\frac{prob\ y = 1}{prob\ y = 0}\right) = \beta_0 + \beta_1\text{GOVERNMENT} - \beta_2\text{PRIVPRACTICE} + \beta_3\text{LEGDEPARTMENT} -$$
$$\beta_4\text{PUBPROSECUTOR} + \beta_5\text{ACADEMIA} + \beta_6\text{INTERIM} + \beta_7\text{SEX} + \beta_8\text{OSLO} -$$
$$\beta_9\text{WILLOCH-ERA} + \beta_{10}\text{ERROR-CORRECTING} + \varepsilon$$

The operationalisations and descriptive statistics of the variables included in the model are presented in Table 5.1. We estimated the model on the individual justice's vote for the litigant claiming a public interest (1 = yes) in all non-unanimous cases concerning a dispute between public economic interests and private economic rights decided by five-justice panels between 1948 and 2009 (n = 1,003).[16] To correct for the possibility that our standard errors are correlated

---

16. Between 1945 and 2009, a total of 290 economic non-unanimous decisions were initially identified as tapping the public–private distinction. On closer inspection, eighty decisions had indistinct outcomes as to the economic issue and/or the economic content of the cases was less salient. For some justices background information is incomplete. On the remaining 210 economic non-unanimous decisions, some justices' votes are lost due to listwise deletion.

Table 5.1: Variables, Operationalisations, Hypotheses and Descriptive Statistics

Variable	Operatio-nalisation	Hypothesised Relationship	Mean	Standard Deviation	Min	Max
Dependent Variable	0 = Private Right 1 = Public Interest		.518	.500	0	1
Appointing Government	0 = Non = Socialist 1 = Social Democrat	+	.694	.461	0	1
Private Practice	0 = No 1 = Private Practice	−	.396	.487	0	1
Legislation Department	0 = No 1 = Legislation Department	+	.374	.484	0	1
Prosecutor's Office	0 = No 1 = Prosecutor's Office	−	.070	.255	0	1
Law Professor	0 = No 1 = Law Professor	+/−	.057	.232	0	1
Interim Justice	0 = No 1 = Interim Justice	+	.021	.143	0	1
Sex	0 = Male 1 = Female	+	.110	.313	0	1
Oslo	0 = Born Elsewhere 1 = Born in Oslo	+	.460	.499	0	1
Willoch-Era	0 = Other 1 = 1981–1986	−	.070	.255	0	1
Error-Correcting	0 = No 1 = Appellant for Public Interest	+	.395	.489	0	1

Figure 5.2: Marginal Effects of Forces Explaining Justice's Vote for Public Economic Interest

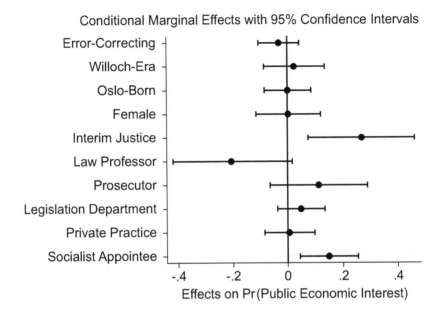

both cross-sectionally and over time, we clustered them on the individual justice and the year of each decision.[17] The results of the model estimation are reported in Table 5.2, and the marginal effects of the forces included in the model are displayed in Figure 5.2.[18]

As the Wald Chi^2 statistic indicates, the full model offers a significant improvement in explanatory power over the naïve model, which includes only the constant term. Yet, its boost to predictive accuracy is not particularly impressive – yielding an increase of only about 11 per cent. More striking, and of far greater importance to our analytical goals, is the blindingly significant coefficient estimate of our proxy measure of a justice's ideology – that is, the partisan colour of the appointing government. Justices appointed during periods

---

17. As robustness checks of the model estimates, we also clustered our observations on the justice and the case. The results are reported in Appendix 5A.

18. The logit procedure, permitting standard errors to be clustered on two dimensions, cannot be used to generate the point estimates and confidence intervals displayed in Figure 5.2. Accordingly, we estimated a conventional logit model with standard errors clustered only on the justice. The results of the model estimation are displayed in Appendix 5B. The reader will notice that the results of the two models are almost identical.

Table 5.2: Clustered Logit Estimates: Public Economic Interests

	Coef.	T-stat	P > |t|
Socialist Appointee	0.595	2.80*	0.01
Private Practice	0.011	0.06	0.95
Legislation Department	0.172	0.98	0.33
Prosecutor's Office	0.470	1.20	0.23
Law Professor	-0.869	-1.89	0.06
Interim Justice	1.317	2.45*	0.01
Female	0.032	0.14	0.89
Oslo-Born	0.018	0.11	0.92
Willoch-Era	0.106	0.74	0.46
Error-Correcting	-0.100	-0.72	0.47
Constant	-0.397	-1.42	0.16

Notes: * $p < 0.01$. DV = Support for Public Economic Interests. N = 1,003 (Listwise); Standard Errors clustered on Individual Justice and Year. Chi^2 = 37.98; Prob > Chi^2 = 0.00; Pseudo R^2 = .03. MLE Improvement = 11 per cent.

of social democratic government are significantly more likely to support the litigant pursuing a public economic interest, just as the case study of the *Ship Owner's Taxation* ruling and the multi-dimensional scaling analysis led us to expect. Moreover, substantive consequence accompanies this. Simply put, justices appointed by social democratic governments are about 36 per cent more likely to find for the public interest litigant than are their non-socialist counterparts.[19]

Interim justices are also more likely to decide in favour of the public interest litigant – a result that is consistent with a finding from some of our earlier research (Grendstad *et al.* 2011b) that interim justices are more apt to rule for the state in civil cases where the government is a party. Holding the other variables at their mean values, the probability of an interim justice finding for the litigant claiming a public economic interest is about 55 per cent greater than is the probability of a permanent justice. And if an interim justice happens to be appointed during a period of social democratic government, then that justice's support for the public economic interest is almost guaranteed. The probability of a social democratic government's interim appointee voting for the litigant pursuing a public economic interest is .82.

While ideology matters, we find no systematic evidence for interim justices acting strategically and 'changing' their voting behaviour once they have secured a permanent appointment to the Court. During the period and with respect to the

---

19. To derive the 36 per cent increase, we subtracted the probability of the non-socialist justice voting for the public interest party from the probability of the socialist justice voting for that party and then divided by the non-socialist probability – (.564–.416) / .416 = .355.

issue domain under analysis here, there were four interim justices whose elevation to permanent justiceships permits us to explore the possibility of strategic behaviour. To do so, we compared the decisional behaviour of these four justices during the year they sat on the Court as interim appointees to their behaviour during their first year on the Court as permanent justices. We found no systematic change. It seems interim justices are just more supportive of public economic rights. (We must hasten to add, however, that our data are too thin to yield any definitive conclusions.)

Although just missing conventional levels of statistical significance, the effect of a background in academia is worthy of mention. Justices recruited from the ranks of the nation's law faculty appear to be more supportive of parties claiming private economic rights. Holding the other variables constant at their means, former law professors are 39 per cent *less* likely to rule in favour of public economic interests than are their colleagues on the Bench who never inhabited the ivory tower.[20] Although our data do not permit us to offer a substantive interpretation for this statistical result, a possible and attractive explanation is in line with the speculation we offered above. Namely, justices who were recruited from law school faculties are especially sensitive to constitutional law, the separation of powers, and the special role the Supreme Court has in protecting the rights of a minority from an overreaching, yet democratic, majority.

With respect to the rest of our hypotheses, the estimated results fail to confirm any of them. Based on our logit estimation, then, it seems that the principal extra-legal force affecting a Norwegian Supreme Court justice's vote in cases involving economic issues is the justice's attitudinal preferences. Justices appointed by social democratic governments are far more likely to support a regulatory role for government in the economy, the redistribution of economic resources, and the continuation of an expansive welfare state over calls for the defence of private economic rights. In sum, a general position with respect to the economy that is consistent with the 'policy and ideological predilections of the [social democratic] parties' core interest groups and elites' (Shaffer 1998: 183).

Conclusion

In this chapter we have offered systematic evidence that policy making by appointment occurs on the Norwegian Supreme Court. Social democratic government appointees are significantly more likely to support the side claiming a public economic interest in the non-unanimous cases we have examined here. Thus, it matters who sits on the Court and – taking one step back in the appointment process – it also matters who makes the appointments. We are by no means arguing that crass partisan politics drive the selection of justices to Norway's highest court. The justices are not selected through democratic elections. They are

---

20. To derive the 39 per cent decrease, we subtracted the probability of the academic appointee justice voting for the public interest party from the probability of the non-academic justice voting for that party and then divided by the academic probability – (.322 - .531) / .531 = -.394.

not listed on a partisan slate. And, as we pointed out above, they certainly are not partisan hacks. But individuals with attitudinal preferences that are reflected in *their* partisan identification do choose the justices. And it stands to reason that these appointers will be more likely to choose justices whose attitudes and preferences are congruent with their own – either because of a selection effect (i.e. potential appointees are more apt to present themselves at times when they anticipate a greater chance of selection), or because the appointers perceive the potential nominee with whom they share preferences as having a superior 'judicial temperament' – that is, as being better qualified. In a sense, then, policy making by appointment is a collateral effect of the selection process being in the hands of the party controlling the government.

In Chapter Four, we pointed out that there has been a concerted effort to increase the presence of women on the Supreme Court. Has this appointment desideratum had a similar collateral effect? This is a question subject to empirical testing, and in the next chapter we turn our attention to doing just that.

Appendix Table 5A: Clustered Logit Estimates (Robustness Check)

	Coef.	T-stat	P > |t|
Socialist Appointee	0.595	2.68**	0.01
Private Practice	0.011	0.06	0.95
Legislation Department	0.172	0.98	0.33
Prosecutor's Office	0.470	1.19	0.24
Law Professor	-0.869	-1.82	0.07
Interim Justice	1.317	2.28*	0.02
Female	0.032	0.14	0.89
Oslo-Born	0.018	0.10	0.92
Willoch-Era	0.106	0.68	0.50
Error-Correcting	-0.100	-0.66	0.51
Constant	-0.397	-1.40	0.16

Notes: * $p < 0.05$;** $p < 0.01$. DV = Support for Public Economic Interests. N = 1,003 (Listwise); Standard Errors clustered on Individual Justice and Case. $Chi^2 = 39.14$; Prob > $Chi^2 = 0.00$; Pseudo $R^2 = .03$. MLE Improvement = 11 per cent.

Appendix Table 5B: Logit Estimates (Clustered on Justice)

	Coef.	T-stat	P > |t|
Socialist Appointee	0.595	2.64**	0.01
Private Practice	0.011	0.06	0.95
Legislation Department	0.172	0.96	0.34
Prosecutor's Office	0.470	1.22	0.22
Law Professor	-0.869	-1.86	0.06
Interim Justice	1.317	2.24*	0.03
Female	0.032	0.13	0.90
Oslo-Born	0.018	0.10	0.92
Willoch-Era	0.106	0.47	0.64
Error-Correcting	-0.100	-0.65	0.51
Constant	-0.397	-1.37	0.17

Notes: * $p < 0.05$;** $p < 0.01$. DV = Support for Public Economic Interests. N = 1,003 (Listwise); Standard Errors clustered on Individual Justice. $Chi^2 = 20.99$; Prob > $Chi^2 = 0.03$; Pseudo $R^2 = .03$. MLE Improvement = 11 per cent.

References

Aardal, B. (ed.) (2011) *Det politiske landskap. En studie av stortingsvalget 2009*, Oslo: Cappelen Damm.

Andenæs, Ø. (1986) 'Et tilbakeblikksbillede fra 1946. En fest og en lærdom for livet', in Bugge, H. O., Coward, K. and Rognlien, S. (eds) *Festskrift Lovavdelingen - 100 år 1885–1985*, Oslo: Universitetsforlaget, pp. 170–171.

Bakke, J. (2002) 'Høyesterett som politisk organ', *Politiembetsmennenes Blad* 4: 7–9.

— (2007) 'Hvor strengt skal vi straffe? Hvilken politikk vinner frem i Høyesterett?', *Politiembetsmennenes Blad* 1: 10–13.

Baum, L. (1997) *The Puzzle of Judicial Behavior*, Ann Arbor: The University of Michigan Press.

Boyd, C., Epstein, L. and Martin, A. D. (2010) 'Untangling the Causal Effects of Sex on Judging', *American Journal of Political Science* 54 (2): 389–411.

Brenner, S. (1997) 'Error-Correction on the U.S. Supreme Court: A View from the Clerk's Memos', *Social Science Journal* 34 (1): 1–9.

Brenner, S. and Krol, J. F. (1989) 'Strategies in Certiorari Voting on the United States Supreme Court', *Journal of Politics* 51 (4): 428–440.

Eckhoff, T. (1964) 'Noen refleksjoner om domstolens uavhengighet', in *Festskrift tillägnad professor, juris doktor Karl Olivecrona vid hans avgång från professorämbetet den 30 juni 1964*, Stockholm: Norstedt, pp. 109–147.

Epstein, L. and Knight, J. (1998) *The Choices Justices Make*, Washington DC: CQ Press.

Grendstad, G. and Holgersen, J. D. (2009) 'Varighet og Velstand. En prediksjonsmodell for ettermælet og omdømmet til de norske statsministrene i det 20. århundre', *Norsk Statsvitenskapelig Tidsskrift* 25 (2): 99–124.

Grendstad, G., Shaffer, W. R. and Waltenburg, E. N. (2011a) 'Judicial behavior on the Norwegian Supreme Court 1945–2009. Determining the effects of extra-legal forces on the justices' votes: The case of "government friendly" voting', Prepared for delivery at the 2nd International Conference on Democracy as Idea and Practice, Oslo, 13–14 January 2011.

— (2011b) 'Revisiting "the State Friendliness of the Norwegian Supreme Court" hypothesis', Paper presented at Nasjonal fagkonferanse i statsvitenskap, Bergen, 5–7 January 2011.

— (2012) 'Socio-Political Experiences of Norwegian Supreme Court Justices', Prepared for delivery at the Annual Meeting of the Western Political Science Association, Marriott Waterfront, Portland, Oregon, 22–24 March 2012.

Gruhl, J., Spohn, C. and Welch, S. (1981) 'Women as Policymakers: The Case of Trial Judges', *American Journal of Political Science* 25 (2): 308–322.

Hagtvet, B. and Bjørklund, T. (eds) (1981) *Høyrebølgen - epokeskifte i norsk politikk? Høyres velgerframgang og Arbeiderpartiets 80-årsdilemmaeri sosial, økonomisk og politisk belysning,* Oslo: Aschehoug.

Hansen, L. (2011) 'Varsom med ros, sparsom med ris. En analyse av høyesterettsdommernes voteringer i straffeutmålingssaker med dissens i Høyesterett i perioden 1994 til 2006', Paper, Department of Comparative Politics, University of Bergen.

Heidar, K. (2000) *Norway: Elites on Trial,* Boulder: Westview Press.

Hjellbrekke, J., Roux, B. L., Korsnes, O., Lebaron, F., Rosenlund, L. and Rouanet, H. (2007) 'The Norwegian Field of Power Anno 2000', *European Societies* 9 (2): 245–273.

Hughes, C. E. (1908) *Addresses and Papers of Charles Evans Hughes,* New York: G. P. Putnam's Sons

Hylland, A. (2009) 'Hva bør gjøres når svært mange høyesterettsdommere er inhabile?' *Lov og Rett* 48 (2): 112–118.

Høgberg, B. M. (2010) 'Grunnloven § 97 etter plenumsdommen i Rt. 2010 s. 143 (Rederiskattesaken)', *Tidsskrift for Rettsvitenskap* 123 (4–5): 694–744.

Inglehart, R. and Norris, P. (2000) 'The Developmental Theory of the Gender Gap: Women's and Men's Voting Behavior in Global Perspective', *International Political Science Review* 21 (4): 441–463.

King, G., Keohane, R. O. and Verba, S. (1994) *Designing Social Inquiry: Scientific Inference in Qualitative Research,* Princeton: Princeton University Press.

Kjønstad, A. (1999) 'Er Høyesterett statsvennlig?', *Lov og Rett* 38 (2): 97–122.

Krol, J. F. and Brenner, S. (1990) 'Strategies of Certiorari Voting on the United States Supreme Court: A Reevaluation', *Western Political Quarterly* 43 (2): 335–342.

Lazarsfeld, P. F., Berelson, B. R. and Gaudet, H. (1944) *The People's Choice,* New York: Duell, Sloan and Pierce.

Listhaug, O., Miller, A. H. and Valen, H. (1985) 'The Gender Gap in Norwegian Voting Behaviour', *Scandinavian Political Studies* 8 (3): 187–206.

Lunde, A. F. (2013) 'Radikalt Vakuum', *Morgenbladet,* 27 September.

McGuire, K. T. (1993) 'Lawyers and the U.S. Supreme Court: The Washington Community and Legal Elites', *American Journal of Political Science* 37 (2): 365–390.

Palmer, J. (1982) 'An Econometric Analysis of the U.S. Supreme Court's Certiorari Decisions', *Public Choice* 39 (3): 387–398.

Rokkan, S. (1967) 'Geography, Religion, and Social Class: Crosscutting Cleavages in Norwegian Politics' in Lipset, S. M. and Rokkan, S. (eds) *Party Systems and Voter Alignments: Cross-National Persepctives,* New York: Free Press, pp. 367–444.

Schjødt (nd) 'Battle for Billions of Norwegian Kroner'. Online. Available http://www.schjodt.com/news-insights/work/battle-for-billions-of-norwegian-kroner.aspx (last accessed 5 March 2012).

Segal, J. A. and Spaeth, H. J. (1993) *The Supreme Court and the Attitudinal Model*, New York: Oxford University Press.

Shaffer, W. R. (1998) *Politics, Parties, and Parliaments: Political Change in Norway*, Columbus: Ohio State University Press.

Skarpnes, O. (1986) 'Minner fra Lovavdelingen' in Bugge, H. O., Coward, K. and Rognlien, S. (eds) *Festskrift Lovavdelingen - 100 år 1885–1985*, Oslo: Universitetsforlaget, 194–196.

Strøm, K. and Leipart, J. Y. (1989) 'Ideology, Strategy, and Party Competition in Postwar Norway', *European Journal of Political Research* 17 (3): 263–288.

— (1993) 'Policy, Institutions and Coalition Avoidance: Norwegian Governments, 1945–1990', *American Political Science Review* 87 (4): 870–887.

Tate, C. N. (1981) 'Personal Attribute Models of the Voting Behavior of U.S. Supreme Court Justices: Liberalism in Civil Liberties and Economics Cases, 1946–1978', *American Political Science Review* 75 (2): 355–367.

Tate, C. N. and Handberg, R. (1991) 'Time Binding and Theory Building in Personal Attribute Models of Supreme Court Voting Behavior, 1916–1988', *American Journal of Political Science* 35 (2): 460–480.

Tate, C. N. and Sittiwong, P. (1989) 'Decision Making in the Canadian Supreme Court: Extending the Personal Attributes Model Across Nations', *Journal of Politics* 51 (4): 900–916.

Tellesbø, O. (2006) 'Hvorfor Høyesterett er statsvennlig', *Retfærd* 29 (4): 65–78.

Ward, A. and Wright, R. (2010) 'Norwegian Shipping Lines Win Back-Tax Case', *Financial Times*, 13 February.

Wold, T. (1964) 'Domstolenes deltakelse i justisforvaltningen', *Lov og Rett* 3: 385–400.

Østbye, I. M. (2011) 'Fra "Høyst ærverdige herrer" til "Høyst ærverdige rett" – betydningen av kvinnelige dommere i Norges Høyesteret', Paper, Department of Comparative Politics, University of Bergen.

Østlid, H. (1988) *Dommeratferd i Dissenssaker,* Oslo: Universitetsforlaget.

Chapter Six

The Presence and Effect of Women on the Court: Family and Criminal Law

As discussed in Chapter Four, the egalitarian nature of Norwegian culture and society has facilitated the notable presence of women in Norway's political life. Norway granted a qualified franchise to women in 1901, and it extended the vote to all of its citizens who were at least twenty-five years of age in 1913 – earlier than almost any other European nation.[1] In the 1970s, with the emergence of the women's movement and the concomitant mobilisation of female political activists, political parties began to recruit women to elected office. Soon thereafter women began to have a substantial presence in the *Storting*. By the mid-1970s, two of the nation's major parties (the Liberal Party and the Socialist Left Party) adopted quota rules for their party organisations and party lists at elections.[2] Not too long after, three other parties followed suit: the Labour Party (traditionally Norway's largest party) in 1983; the Agrarian Centre Party in 1989; and the Christian People's Party in 1993. No such formal rules exist for the conservative parties Høyre and Progress (Teigen 2011: 88–89), but the other parties have, through their practices, 'put some pressure on' the conservative parties (Matland 2004: 6). One result of this is that women are well integrated into Norway's electoral and partisan elites, in many cases occupying significant leadership roles (Heidar 2000: 86–88; Chapter Three).

In some sense the parties' quota rules were efforts to institutionalise gender equality. Requiring that women constitute some minimum proportion of a party's organisation guaranteed women a hand in shaping the party's policy agenda, thereby ensuring women's concerns would not be ignored. What is of particular importance to our purposes is that this egalitarian effort to guarantee women a seat at the policy-making table eventually extended beyond the party organisations and parliamentary representation to another significant national political institution: the Supreme Court. This is not surprising given the Court's substantial policy-making role. As already discussed, it acts as a guardian of fundamental political rights. It determines winners and losers in the allocation of finite resources. And – perhaps most importantly – it decides the constitutionality of legislation. As a result, hard-fought policy victories in Parliament can be both consolidated or undone at the bar of the Court.

---

1.   Finland permitted near universal suffrage in 1906. In fact, if we only consider *free and independent* countries (Finland, Australia and New Zealand did not qualify as such at the time of their suffrage extension), Norway was the first country in the world to introduce universal suffrage.

2.   Each party adopted a rule requiring that women account for at least 40 per cent of the party organisation.

Women first occupied a seat on the Supreme Court in 1968, with the justiceship of Lilly Bølviken. Since then there has been a determined effort to appoint women to the Court, and this effort has yielded dividends in terms of women's representation in that institution. As shown in Chapter Four, within four decades, the proportion of women justices was nearly equal to the proportion of women MPs, while in a comparative context Norway stands especially tall.[3] Examining nine European constitutional courts over the past three decades, Andrews and Hoekstra (2010) report that Norway consistently ranks at or near the top in terms of the proportion of women making up its highest court.

That women have constituted an appreciable presence on the Norwegian Supreme Court since 1968 raises an important research question: What, if any, has been the effect on the Court? Now, we would not necessarily expect the effect on the Court's decisional outputs to be uniform across issues (Boyd *et al.* 2010; Songer *et al.* 1994) or time. By their nature, some issues (e.g. *ex post facto* laws or expropriation without just compensation) are unlikely to be perceived as any more salient to women than they are to men. Other issues (e.g. welfare policies or family law), however, are likely to be closely associated with women's interests, and thus, we might expect the presence of women on the Court to be evident in its decisional behaviour in these issue domains. With respect to time dimension, it seems unlikely – if not impossible – for women to exert much sway on the Court's decisional outputs before the number of women justices achieves some 'critical mass' (Songer *et al.* 2010; Peresie 2005). As the only woman on the Court in 1968, it was unusual for Lilly Bølviken even to be present on any given panel. And when she did find herself on a panel, her male brethren would always outnumber her four to one.

In this chapter we focus on the presence and decisional behaviour of women on the Norwegian Supreme Court. We begin by exploring in some detail their appointment to the High Bench. First, we describe the relative presence of women on the Court through 2009. We show that despite appreciable gains made by women, there remains a strong tendency to select men to the High Court, especially for interim appointments. We then compare female appointees to their male counterparts across a variety of background attributes that have been shown to be associated with a justice's decisional behaviour. We find several significant differences. Finally, we turn to a systematic examination of the individual justice's votes in two issue areas where 'gendered judging' seems likely.

Given the differences we find between male and female appointees, we might expect to unearth evidence of gendered judging. Our findings, however, do not offer much support for that expectation. First, when it comes to behavioural differences between male and female justices, the evidence is mixed at best. In one of the issue domains we examine, there is no statistical evidence for the notion

---

3. A recent government proclamation that at least 40 per cent of the Court's justices should be women would effectively ensure that the presence of women on the Court would not dip below its current level (NTB 2008).

that male and female justices vote differently. The other issue domain, however, does manage to yield a cloudy pearl among all the oysters. Second, when we turn to a causal test of the effect of women on the Court's decisional outputs, we find no support for the hypothesis that the presence of women has 'changed' the Norwegian Supreme Court by leavening the decisional behaviour of male justices in an issue domain about which women might be expected to have especially valid and valuable information. Thus, consistent with the 'organisational hypothesis' (Boyd *et al.* 2010), it appears that male and female justices appointed to the Norwegian Supreme Court share sufficient educational and professional backgrounds and face similar institutional expectations and constraints 'to overcome biological, psychological, or experience-based differences between the sexes' (Steffensmeier and Herbert 1999: 1165, quoted in Boyd *et al.* 2010: 392).

Women on the Court

Between 1968 (the year Lilly Bølviken was named to the High Bench) and 2009, a total of 120 temporary and permanent appointments were made to the Norwegian Supreme Court; eighteen of them (15 per cent) were women.[4] At first blush, this suggests that men were strongly favoured in the selection process. Indeed, during this time period there were only four years in which at least one Court vacancy occurred and no man was appointed, while a woman failed to be appointed in twenty-four such occurrences. Further, in the ten years when there was only one vacancy to be filled, a man was chosen six times.[5] Overall, across the past four decades, the male to female ratio of appointments to the Court has been nearly seven to one.

This general pattern changes a bit, however, when one focuses on permanent appointments. Of the 120 appointments under review, 59 were to permanent justiceships, and with respect to these, there is some indication that women were more apt to be chosen. 67 per cent (n = 12) of the women appointed to the Court have been named as permanent justices, while only 45 per cent (n = 44) of the male appointees have taken permanent seats on the bench (Chi^2 = 2.76; p = .10; V = .15). And this difference stands to reason. As discussed earlier, interim justices are not named to the Court through the same formal process of appointment as are permanent justices. No announcement is made with respect to a vacancy, and the Judicial Appointments Board does not interview or rank a set of candidates. Rather, the Court identifies a 'need' for an interim appointment, and then the Court and/or the civil servants communicate the name of a single appointee to the Minister of Justice, who almost invariably confirms that selection.

---

4.   Lilly Bølviken insisted that it was her excellent grades from the University of Oslo Law School that brought her from the Oslo Urban Municipal Court to the Supreme Court (Verdens Gang 1968). At a meeting at Chief Justice Terje Wold's office, before Justice Bølviken's first case on the High Court, the participants decided to have the Supreme Court lawyers switch to a gender-neutral term when addressing the justices on the Court before arguing their cases.

5.   It is important to note, however, that we do not have data on whether or not a female nominee was in the offing in any of these instances.

Clearly, the principals in the selection process do not perceive interim appointments as especially consequential, and thus neither a great deal of time nor effort is spent on seeking out or vetting individuals for these positions. Presence in the 'pipeline' and informal associations with the Court and/or the civil service are likely the primary explanatory forces for the identification of individuals to fill the positions. Indeed, on average, an individual is appointed twice to an interim justiceship, and two individuals – Johs. Andenæs and Kristen Syvertsen – were appointed as interim justices six times.[6] What is more, interim justices are neither expected to hold their seats for long nor to affect the Court's decisional behaviour. Thus, concerns with gender distribution on the Bench and its effect on the Court's legitimacy or the degree to which the Court is representative of Norwegian society are unlikely to come to the fore in the case of these appointments.[7]

Finally, we must note that although the selection of men continues to be the modal choice in the appointment process, the presence of women on the Court has increased to the point that makes it possible to leave deep footprints. As of 2009, women constitute just below 40 per cent of the Bench. Consequently, the likelihood that at least one woman sits on a five-justice panel is virtually guaranteed, and the probability of a panel being drawn with a female majority is nearly 25 per cent – a far cry from 1968 when Lilly Bølviken was a solitary figure.

A statistical comparison of male and female justices

Clearly, the relative presence of women on Norway's highest court has increased substantially since 1968, but aside from sex, does the Bench look different with the addition of women? That is, do the female appointees to the Court have a set of attributes that might bear on decisional behaviour that systematically differs from their male counterparts? Table 6.1 reports the results of a series of tests that speak to this question.

Overall, it appears that women tend to be younger and drawn more from a narrow Oslo-centric, government-insider network. At the time of appointment, female justices are about four years younger than their male counterparts (p = .01). 72 per cent of female justices were born in Oslo, compared to only 41 per cent of their male colleagues (p = .02), and 72 per cent of the women justices had some prior governmental experience – especially in the Legislation Department – compared to 44 per cent of male justices (p = .03).[8] Finally, it bears mentioning that

---

6.   Five of Johs. Andenæs' interim appointments took place prior to 1968.

7.   Interestingly, since 1968 there have been eleven instances where an interim appointee has later been elevated to a permanent justiceship. No female justice has followed this career path.

8.   The dominant high-rise building in the government square in Oslo housed both the office of the Prime Minister and the Ministry of Justice, including the Legislation Department. The high-rise building sat within very moderate shouting distance of the Supreme Court. The government square was badly damaged by the 22 July 2011 terrorist bombing.

Table 6.1: Statistical Comparison of Background Attributes: Female and Male Justices 1968–2009

	Female	Male	Significance
Type of Party (Socialist = 1)	.72	.51	.09
Born in Oslo	.72	.41	.02
Age at Appointment	52	56	.01
Prior Gov. Experience	.72	.44	.03
Prosecutor	0	.06	ns
Government Advocate	.11	.16	ns
Legislation Department	.67	.28	.001
Private Practice	.17	.28	ns
Law Professor	.22	.26	ns
Interim Justice	.33	.55	.1
Permanent Justice	.67	.45	.1
Oslo Law School	.94	.95	ns
Prior Judicial Experience	.5	.59	ns

there is a near-significant difference in the nature of the appointing government with respect to a justice's sex. Nearly three-quarters of the female justices were appointed during periods of socialist government control, while only about half of the male justices were appointed under similar conditions ($p = .09$). In terms of other background characteristics, however, male and female justices do not exhibit significant differences. The proportion of male and female justices who graduated from the University of Oslo Law School is nearly identical, and although male justices are a bit more likely to have had some prior judicial experience and to have been employed in private practice and/or as law professors than are female justices, these differences are statistically insignificant.

A possible explanation for at least one of the potentially more consequential differences reported in Table 6.1 is the restricted career path of Norway's female lawyers. Menkel-Meadow (1996) notes that although over 50 per cent of Norway's current law students are women, few women actually practice law as a vocation, in part because Norwegian culture traditionally perceives litigation – with its emphasis on aggressive argument – as an improper role for women (p. 234). One result is that women tend to be 'overrepresented in lower ranks of the central government' (p. 237). Therefore, the pool of potential female Court appointees is predisposed to have had prior governmental experience. And this suggests that appointment considerations can have implications on the Court's decisional outputs. To state the matter concretely, an effort to appoint more women to the High Bench has resulted in seating a greater number of justices with prior governmental service; justices with this type of background are, in turn, more likely to decide in favour of the government position (*see* Chapter Seven).

However, we must note that this is but a collateral effect of the appointment process. It is the product of the nature of the pool of eligible female candidates for appointment. Any measurable impact of female justices on the Court's decisional outputs regarding government power is not the result of the addition of women per se, and simple bivariate evidence of a justice's sex affecting his or her finding for the government is most likely spurious. In other words, male justices with prior governmental experience may be just as likely to find for the government party as are female justices. The question, then, remains open: Does a justice's sex have a direct effect on his or her decisional outputs? It is to this question that we now turn.

The presence of 'gendered judging'?

Recent literature identifies three hypothetical explanations for gendered judging. As laid out by Boyd and her coauthors (Boyd *et al.* 2010, quotations on pp. 390–92), the *different voice* hypothesis holds that women 'develop [a] distinct worldview' – that is, 'a feminist perspective'. As a result they perceive themselves as being differently connected to society than men. They may be more sensitive to the interests of the disenfranchised and the less fortunate elements of society. This, in turn, might manifest itself in women voting differently than men. Women judges, for example, might be more liberal or 'radical' than their male counterparts in general. Consequently, they may be more apt to support interventionist government programs aimed at equalising social opportunities, or preventing exclusion in the distribution of society's resources (Songer *et al.* 1994: 428). The *representational* hypothesis presents women as advocating an agenda of women's issues that is pursued to protect their class or group in order to 'liberate other women'. Women justices, therefore, might emphasise different types of cases or fact patterns that would promote women's legal concerns or topics. Finally, the *informational* hypothesis claims that 'women possess unique and valuable information emanating from shared professional experiences'. This unique and distinctive reservoir of information results in women deciding cases somehow differently than their male counterparts, or that men are won over by the persuasiveness of women's information. Here, we put different aspects of these explanations to the test, first with a pair of conventional logit models where we estimate the effect of a justice's sex on his or her vote in the hurly-burly of multivariate controls, and then with a 'matching estimator' to test a causal hypothesis rooted in the 'informational explanation'.

Exploratory logit models

As we noted earlier in this chapter, we would not expect the presence of sex-based voting to be invariant across either issue domain or time. We therefore restrict our systematic analysis to a pair of issue areas – (a) cases involving *Family and Estate Law* and (b) *Sentencing Adjustments*. We also allow for the possibility that sex-based voting varies with the relative presence of women on the Court.

To begin, both Family and Estate Law and Sentencing Adjustments are issue areas that seem especially ripe for the observation of any sex-based voting effects. The former domain concerns issues that are particularly salient to women (*viz.*, marriage, divorce, child custody, inheritance, and succession), and some extant literature has found that it is in these types of issue areas that differences between male and female justices are most likely to emerge (King and Greening 2007; Peresie 2005; Martin and Pyle 2002; Allen and Wall 1987; but *see* Segal 2000; Walker and Barrow 1985; Bergset 2013). Accordingly, we expect that female justices will be more apt to vote for the litigant most associated with the 'female' or 'underdog' position in these cases. This position would be consistent with a 'feminine jurisprudence', one that emphasises the responsibility of the state to 'ensure that each of its members has the ability to participate fully in the community' (Songer *et al.* 1994: 428). Thus, in marriage, divorce, and family disputes this litigant would be the woman squaring off against the man. And along with the female party, in inheritance and probate cases, the 'underdog' litigant would be an individual opposed by an organisation or institution. After all, this is the litigant who is disadvantaged in terms of resources and who is in jeopardy of being excluded from fully sharing in society's opportunities.[9]

An excellent example of this possibility of a 'feminist jurisprudence' can be found in the so-called '*Housewife Case*', decided in 1975 (Rt-1975–220). The case dealt with the division of a married couple's assets upon divorce and the determination of the magnitude of the contribution each spouse made to the marital estate. Specifically, the Court was asked to construe a provision of *The Administration of Estates Act* that declared it was direct effort to bring value to an estate that secured the extent of ownership in an asset. Here, the Court was asked to determine how much value to place on the individual contributions of a husband and a wife to the house in which they lived during their marriage. According to the letter of the law, the husband's contribution was tangible and easily fixed: it was his salary and the physical effort he put into building or renovating the house. The majority of the justices, however, did not stop there. Writing for the majority, Justice Knut Blom concluded that the *intent* of the legislation went beyond such a simple calculus. Viewing the case through the lens of 'equitable considerations' (*see* Chapter One), he ruled that the Act sought to strengthen the position of the housewife with respect to the distribution of marital property. Consequently, homemaking, parenting, and childcare were also of significant economic value, and thus also the wife also made a material contribution to the house as property. Simply put, Blom's opinion established that a housewife's

---

9.   Obviously, female justices enter the Court with female experiences. Given their education and employment history, however, they do not have *underdog* experiences, per se. Nevertheless, the women's movement – with its emphasis on an equal role for women in politics and society – is a potent force in Norway. It pushed hard, for example, for the inclusion of women in Parliament (*see* Chapter Four). Thus, we might expect that these highly educated women have a unique insight about the importance of society making its resources and opportunities as broadly available as possible.

non-economic contributions to the family and to the household must be given weight, and therefore, she must also qualify for co-ownership of the estate, sharing equally in any division of the property. Significantly, with this decision, the Court articulated a policy bringing Norwegian family law into line with broader social attitudes and developments (Lødrup 1975: 438).

With respect to Sentencing Adjustments, the Court has the authority to increase or decrease the criminal sentence imposed. In rendering these decisions, Østlid (1988) found that female justices are more lenient than their male counterparts. Further, to the extent that compassion, caring, and connection with society play roles in a woman justice's decisions (Songer *et al.* 1994: 428), women may place greater weight on rehabilitation in sentencing adjustment votes than do their male counterparts. Consequently, we expect that female justices will be more likely to vote for reduced sentences than will male justices.

Next, we include a dynamic measure of the presence of women on the Court in the specifications of our models to account for the possibility that women justices must achieve some threshold level or 'critical mass' before they begin to distinguish themselves from their male counterparts. Peresie (2005) suggests that the initial set of female appointees to a court might perceive themselves as mere 'tokens' and will thus be apt to 'conform their views to those of their male colleagues' in order to establish their legitimacy on the bench (p. 1764, *see also* Songer *et al.* 2010). Only after their numbers have risen to a point where they can achieve effective representation will female justices vote sincerely and sex-based differences in the vote become visible. Thus, we hypothesise that as the number of women present on a Court panel increases, voting differences between male and female justices become more likely.

Of course, there are other forces that might affect a justice's decisional behaviour and that must be controlled for in order to fairly test for any sex-based effects on voting. As we have discussed throughout this monograph, a justice's attitudinal preferences is perhaps the most important of these. In Chapter Five we showed that Norwegian Supreme Court justices decide cases concerning economic rights in line with their attitudinal preferences as measured by the nature of the government that appointed them. To put it concretely, we found that socialist appointees are more likely to find for the party claiming a public interest than are justices appointed during periods of non-socialist governments. It is possible that a similar pattern exists with respect to decisions rendered in Family and Estate Law cases and/or in Sentencing Adjustments.

In the general issue domain of Family and Estate Law, there is broad consensus regarding support for parents and children in Norway. To a large degree, the major parties do not divide over the *goals* of government programs aimed at promoting the welfare of parents and children – universal coverage, the scope of services, the redistributive nature of the premiums. When party cleavages do occur, they often arise over the specific *policies* designed to implement those overarching goals (Heidar 2000: 120). Historically, socialist and non-socialist parties have offered differing approaches to support families, women, and children. The left-of-centre Labour Party, for example, has promoted a significant and direct role for government through the creation of a variety of state-supported programs to aid working parents and their children. By contrast, the right-of-centre Christian People's Party pursues a less interventionist approach (Heidar 2000: 119). It seeks to limit government's role to making cash payments to parents, for example, thereby enabling them to provide for their children as they see fit. Thus, the state's design of policies concerning Family and Estate Law can take on a political or partisan tone. And this stands to reason. At bottom, these policies concern the assignment and distribution of the state's finite resources, and as such they are clearly in line with Lasswell's (1936) classic definition of politics as a struggle over 'who gets what, when, and how'.

Although there are programmatic differences between the parties with respect to Family and Estate Law, party differences are not as sharply defined when it comes to supporting women per se, as an end of any specific policy. The female or underdog position can benefit from both an interventionist and non-interventionist governmental approach in the specific legal areas under examination here. As a result, there is no chasm-like 'gender gap' in Norway when it comes to identification with the parties as pertaining to party positions on the issues of marriage, divorce, custody, inheritance, or succession. Indeed, Heidar writes, 'it would be an exaggeration to claim the existence of a political cleavage line based on gender. Women have become effectively integrated into the traditional parties based on the old cleavages' (2000: 88). Consequently, we cannot offer a directional hypothesis for the relationship between the nature of the appointing government and the individual justice's vote in Family and Estate Law cases. Nevertheless, given our prior findings showing the strong effect of attitudinal preferences on a justice's decisional calculus, we include a measure of those preferences in the model to be estimated here.

Unlike Family and Estate Law, there are sharp differences between the attitudes of party adherents over the issue of Sentencing Adjustments. Those who identify with non-socialist parties, such as the Conservative and Progress parties, tend to place greater emphasis on law and order. Consequently, they will call for more severe criminal sentences. Given our use of party of appointment as a proxy for a justice's attitudinal preferences, we would expect that justices appointed by non-socialist governments will be less likely to support reduced sentences. Socialist governments, on the other hand, tend to place greater weight on rehabilitation. Thus, we expect that justices appointed by socialist governments will be more likely to support lenient sentencing adjustments.

Place of birth, and the social networks into which a justice is absorbed, might also have some bearing upon a justice's decisional calculus in these issue domains. With respect to Family and Estate Law, being born into the Oslo-centric social milieu may have implications for a justice's support of a more interventionist government role in family policies. These justices are more likely members of the national legal and governing elite, and they may well have served in government before joining the Court. Consequently, their sense of the role of government is almost certainly a positive one. Here again, however, since it is impossible to definitively state whether an interventionist or non-interventionist policy benefits the female or underdog position in the specific legal questions of marriage, divorce, custody, inheritance, and succession, we cannot hazard a directional hypothesis. But the possibility that a justice's place of birth affects his or her decisional behaviour leads us to include it in our model specification.

With respect to Sentencing Adjustments, the nature of the expected relationship between place of birth and a justice's decision seems more clearly determined. It is nearly axiomatic that violations of the criminal law are attacks on the social order, the fabric of which is woven by government. Again, justices born in Oslo are more likely to perceive themselves as essential members of that social order and to identify with the government or the centralised administrative state. Consequently, they should be less tolerant of attacks on that social order. Thus, we hypothesise that, all other things being equal, justices born in Oslo will be less lenient in Sentencing Adjustment cases than will justices born elsewhere.

Prior governmental experience can have an effect on a justice's decisional behaviour, inasmuch as the justices who have served in government might identify either with the government, broadly defined, or with the specific governmental institutions that produced the policies they are being asked to judge. In either case, these justices may be predisposed to support the government (*see* Chapter Seven). The Office of the Government Advocate (*Regjeringsadvokaten*), for example, is the government's lawyer in civil cases. Justices who have amassed some years of experience there may be more sympathetic to the government's legal position in cases under review, and they will therefore be more apt to come down on the side of the government. Service in the Legislation Department (*Lovavdelingen*) entails offering assistance both in writing the nation's laws and the interpretation or clarification of legal issues. The Legislation Department has been characterised as an internal supreme court for the executive branch (Andenæs 1986), and its opinions are often used to determine 'what the law is' (Skarpnes 1986: 195). Thus, justices with a background in the Legislation Department may have a special fealty to government action. After all, the Legislation Department quite likely offered an opinion as to the legality of any particular government policy under which the government action is occurring.

Once more, we cannot offer a clear directional hypothesis for the effect of prior governmental experience on a justice's decisions in the issue domain of Family and Estate Law. For example, a per-child subsidy given to support public nurseries (an interventionist policy of centre-left parties such as Labour) is intended to improve the lot of women, but so too would be the distribution of cash payments to parents of all children under a certain age (a non-interventionist policy advocated by the Christian People's Party and adopted in 1997). In the issue area of Sentencing Adjustments, on the other hand, we would expect prior governmental service to predispose a justice to find for the government position and against the appeal of the criminally convicted.[10]

Finally, we also control for forces that are specific to each issue domain. In the area of Family and Estate Law, we include a measure of a justice's age. Heidar points out that the strongest differences in terms of policy attitudes between the genders occur among the young (2000: 88). Thus, we hypothesise that, all other things being equal, sex-based voting will be more visible among younger women. Specifically, younger female justices should be more likely to find for the female litigant in the case.

For the Sentencing Adjustment issue domain, we include two variables intended to tap the legal and political context in which the Court hears the appeal of the sentence. First – as discussed in Chapter Two – the Court's jurisdiction was altered in 1995, substantially reducing the number of criminal appeals that the Court was required to hear. With their greater discretionary authority, the justices could 'cherry-pick' those cases that they wanted to review and embark on an 'error-correcting' strategy (*see,* for example, Krol and Brenner 1990), setting right the cases that they believed were wrongly decided in the lower courts. Thus, we hypothesise that the justices will be more likely to vote to reduce criminal sentences following the change in the Court's criminal procedure jurisdiction in 1995.

Second, just as the winds of Thatcherism and Reaganism blew across the political landscapes of England and the United States, Norway experienced its own conservative season in the 1980s. Two conservative Willoch-governments dominated Norwegian politics between 1981 and 1986 (Grendstad and Holgersen 2009; Hagtvet and Bjørklund 1981). It seems more likely than not that these governments were reflections of the general mood of the nation. Furthermore, it is possible that this conservative mood resonated with the justices, and they – perhaps born out of their concern with the Court's legitimacy or the result of an enduring shift in the public's temper (Flemming and Wood 1997; Mishler and Sheehan 1993) – adjusted their decisional behaviour accordingly. Thus, we hypothesise that during the conservative Willoch-era, justices will be less likely to support appeals for reduced sentences.

The data and model specification

We test these hypotheses by conducting a pair of logistic regressions. In the first model, we estimate the effects of sex, the number of women justices present on the panel, political preferences, place of birth, prior political experience, and

---

10. A third office in which an eventual justice might have chalked up some governmental service is in the office of the Director General of Public Prosecutions (*Riksadvokaten*). This office deals explicitly with criminal cases, and thus service in it would seem to bear especially on a justice's decisions concerning sentencing adjustments. Unfortunately, there is virtually no variation with respect to backgrounds in this office during the time period under examination here (*see* Table 6.1).

age on the likelihood of the individual justice voting in favour of the female or underdog position in all non-unanimous Family and Estate Law decisions handed down between 1968 and 2009 (1 = vote for the woman / underdog position; n = 634). To account for the possibility that both age and the number of female justices on a panel could have moderating effects on the voting behaviour of a woman justice, we also computed interaction terms between these variables and sex.

The dependent variable in our second model is the individual justice's vote for a reduced criminal sentence (1 = yes). Here again we examine only the non-unanimous decisions and its accompanying votes that the Court rendered between 1968 and 2009 (n = 2,008). With the exception of the justice's age (and its interaction with sex), we employ the same array of independent variables (including the interaction term between sex and the number of women justices on a panel). We replaced the omitted variables with two categorical variables intended to tap the change in the Court's criminal jurisdiction – the legal context – and the effect of the conservative Willoch-era – the political context. Tables 6.2 and 6.3 display the operationalisations, summary statistics, and expected relationships for the variables included in both models.

Finally, we clustered our standard errors on two dimensions (the individual justice and year) to correct for correlated residuals both cross-sectionally and over time. The results of the model estimations are presented in Table 6.4.

Table 6.2: Operationalisations, Summary Statistics, Expected Relationships (Family and Estate Law)

Variable	Operationalisation	Mean	Range	Standard Deviation	Expected Relationships
Sex	1 = Female	.09	0/1	.29	+
Number of Women per Panel	Actual number of women on the panel	.46	0/4	.80	+
Sex * Number of Women	Sex * number of women	.17	0/4	.62	+
Age	Actual age of justice	59.70	42/76	6.40	–
Sex * Age	Sex * age	5.30	0/70	16.70	–
Nature of Party	1 = Socialist	.69	0/1	.46	–/+
Born in Oslo	1 = Born in Oslo	.50	0/1	.50	–/+
Prior Experience in Government	1 = served in national government before Court appointment	.36	0/1	.48	–/+

Table 6.3: Operationalisations, Summary Statistics, Expected Relationships (Sentencing Adjustments)

Variable	Operationalisation	Mean	Range	Standard Deviation	Expected Relationships
Sex	1 = Female	.18	0/1	.38	+
Number of Women per Panel	Actual number of women on panel	.88	0/4	.83	+
Sex * Number of Women	Sex * number of women on panel	.29	0/4	.70	+
Nature of Party	1 = Socialist	.60	0/1	.49	+
Born in Oslo	1 = Born in Oslo	.40	0/1	.49	−
Prior Experience in Government	1 = served in national government before Court appointment	.51	0/1	.50	−
Change in Court's Criminal Jurisdiction	1 = case decided after 1996	.19	0/1	.39	+
Willoch-Era	1 = case decided between 1981 and 1986	.16	0/1	.37	−

Results and discussion

We turn first to the results of the model on Family and Estate Law decisions. These results can be summarised rather briefly. Neither the full model nor the coefficient estimating the effect of a justice's sex approaches even the most forgiving levels of statistical significance. Indeed, no variable attains statistical significance, although the measures of the nature of the appointing party and being a member of the Oslo social milieu do approach significance. At bottom, our findings demonstrate that despite the (presumed) close association between the subject matter of this issue domain and the gender-specific interests of women, there is *no* evidence that women justices are more likely to vote in support of the female/underdog litigant than are their male counterparts. To the extent that a concerted effort has been made to appoint women to the Norwegian Supreme Court so that they may 'seize decision-making opportunities to liberate other women' (Cook 1981: 216, qtd in Boyd *et al.* 2010: 391), that effort appears to have come a cropper. In short, women justices in Norway do not appear to perceive themselves as special representatives of women, and they do not seek to protect and promote the interests of women as a class through litigation, or at least not with respect to the interests embedded in this issue area.

The parameter estimates for the model examining a justice's decisions on Sentencing Adjustments, on the other hand, offer some evidence for gendered judging. At best, however, even these results only squint towards statistical significance. The full model's Wald Chi^2 statistic just misses conventional levels

Table 6.4: Clustered Logit Estimates: Family and Estate Law, Sentencing Adjustments

	Family and Estate Law		Sentence Adjustment	
	Coef.	SE	Coef.	SE
Female	-3.13	2.76	.55*	.31
# Women per Panel	0.01	0.14	.03	.06
Sex * Number of Women per Panel	-0.18	0.40	.21	.20
Age	-0.02	0.01	–	–
Sex * Age	0.06	0.05	–	–
Social Dem Appointee	0.43	0.28	.13	.11
Born in Oslo	0.33	0.20	.07	.11
Prior Governmental Experience	-0.27	0.21	.02	.10
Change in Jurisdiction	–	–	.24	.16
Willoch-Era	–	–	-.04	.14
Constant	0.98	0.84	-.16	.12
Dependent Variable	1 = Vote for Female		1 = Reduce Sentence	
N	634		2008	
Log Pseudolikelihood	-432.9		-1.384e+03	
Wald Chi2; p =	10.6; .23		13.8; .09	
MLE Improvement	.04		0.03	

Notes: *$p < 0.10$. Standard errors clustered on both year and individual justice.

of statistical significance ($\chi^2 = 13.8$, $p \leq .09$), suggesting that the full model does manage to offer a bit more explanatory power than a model including only the constant term. Yet, a measure of the model's improvement in predictive accuracy is only .03, indicating just how meagre a boost the full model yields.

Moving our attention to the coefficient estimates of the model's independent variables, we see that only sex approaches a relaxed threshold of significance. Consistent with Østlid's (1988) findings and our own expectation, women justices are more likely to vote to reduce criminal sentences (.55; $p \leq .08$). Indeed, being a woman justice increases the likelihood of voting to reduce the sentence by 13.5 per cent, holding the remaining variables constant at their mean values. There is no evidence, however, for a 'critical mass' effect regarding the number of women on the reviewing panel. The interaction term is both insignificant and incorrectly signed. There is some support for our hypothesis that the justices' greater discretionary authority in the area of criminal appeals gave them more freedom to review the sentences that they thought should be corrected. Following the change in the Court's criminal jurisdiction, an individual justice was nearly 6 per cent more likely to vote for a reduced sentence (.24; $p \leq .14$). There is, however, no statistical traction for the effect of the categorical variable measuring the effect of the nation's general mood. The measure of a justice's attitudes also fails to meet significance thresholds, although it is signed correctly.

Exploring a causal relationship

Although the exploratory logit models yielded only meagre evidence of distinctive voting patterns associated with sex-based effects, it remains possible that the addition of women to Norway's High Bench has affected the Court's decisional outputs by influencing the votes of male justices on issues about which women are presumed to have unique and specialised knowledge. Based on the 'informational explanation', the notion here is that in particular issue domains (such as Family and Estate Law), the unique life experiences of being a woman produces a contextual overlay such that 'female judges possess information that their male colleagues perceive "as more credible and persuasive" than their own knowledge'. As a result, 'females can directly or even indirectly alter the decisions made by males' (Boyd *et al.* 2010: 392). Accordingly, we adopt Boyd and her colleagues' (2010) research strategy and hypothesise that male justices are more likely to vote for the female or underdog litigant in Family and Estate Law cases when they sit on a 'mixed panel' (i.e. a panel composed of both male and female justices) than when they sit on an all-male panel.

This is essentially a *causal* hypothesis subject to empirical testing. Now, a powerful device for testing such a hypothesis is the classic, randomised experiment. Here, the nature or direction of the male justices' votes is the phenomenon of interest, and the presence or absence of a mixed panel is the experimental stimulus. Random assignment into the two conditions the test stimulus effects results in a control group (male justices voting in the absence of a mixed panel) and a test group (male justices voting on a mixed panel). The effect of the experimental stimulus (the presence of a mixed panel) could then be assessed with a difference in means test. Significant differences between the two groups in the phenomenon of interest would be identified as the results of the experimental stimulus because random assignment ensures that the two groups are statistically identical in every salient respect. So long as the number of subjects included in the experiment is sufficiently large, any causal inferences that are drawn would be valid (*see* Nie and Waltenburg 2014: 9).

Unfortunately, however, we do not have data that permit this analytical approach. We cannot control the application of the experimental stimulus (the presence of a mixed panel); nor can we randomly assign Norway's male justices into cases where a mixed panel is either present or absent. Instead, we must make do with the observational data at hand, and this results in consequential differences between the stimulus and control groups. Analysts typically turn to parametric models – as we did in the exploratory logit models above – to control for a variety of confounding forces in an effort to account for these differences. But, perhaps inevitably, differences between the groups remain. As a result, causal claims must be viewed with scepticism. (This point is pithily summarised in the familiar aphorism: correlation does not prove causation.)

Recently, social scientists have turned to non-parametric matching procedures to overcome the constraints imposed by observational data on testing causal hypotheses. The basic logic behind matching procedures is rather simple. The analyst seeks to pre-process the data so that there is at least one observation in the control group that matches an observation in the treatment group on every property, *except for the treatment effect itself.* These matched observations are then retained. The result is a 'balanced' dataset, and so an unbiased estimate of the causal effect of the test stimulus can be determined (Iacus *et al.* 2012: 1; Nie and Waltenburg 2014: 9–10).

Several matching procedures have been developed (*see,* generally, Guo and Fraser 2013). Many of these, however, suffer from excessive loss of data. Too many observations are discarded in the search for matches, especially when pre-processing of the data is done on a large number of covariates (Nie and Waltenburg 2014: 10). The procedure we employ here – Coarsened Exact Matching (CEM) – attempts to overcome the 'loss of data' problem by using an approximate matching algorithm that exactly matches observations in the treatment and control groups after the observations have been 'coarsened' or binned into 'substantively meaningful groups' on selected variables (Blackwell *et al.* 2009: 527; Nie and Waltenburg 2014: 10).

'CEM matches data with respect to the full joint distribution of pre-treatment covariates in statistically equal strata' (Nie and Waltenburg 2014: 10; *see also* Blackwell *et al.* 2009: 6; Groves and Rogers 2011: 580). CEM also produces an $L1$ statistic, which is used to assess the degree of multivariate imbalance in the full joint distribution of the data. $L1$ is bounded at 0.0 and 1.0. If the joint distribution is perfectly balanced, then $L1 = 0.0$; if the data are perfectly imbalanced, then $L1 = 1.0$. Importantly, however, $L1$ should not be interpreted as an absolute measure of imbalance. Rather, it should be used to determine the effectiveness of the matching solution, such that the $L1$ statistic of the processed data should be less than the $L1$ statistic of the unprocessed data (Blackwell *et al.* 2009).

Matching

We employ the Coarsened Exact Matching procedure to pretreat our data in order to test our research hypothesis regarding the causal effect of mixed panels on the voting behaviour of male justices in issue areas where women would be presumed to have especially unique and credible information. Specifically, we hypothesise that male justices on mixed panels are more likely to find for the female or underdog litigant in Family and Estate Law cases. On the other hand, we expect no effect of mixed panels on the voting behaviour of male justices in the Sentencing Adjustment issue domain, inasmuch as it is unlikely that women judges would be presumed to have any special insight or more credible knowledge when it comes to criminal behaviour, penal rehabilitation or retribution.

Since we are interested in the possible effect of the presence of women justices on the decisional behaviour of male justices, our treatment variable is the nature of the panel. A mixed panel (i.e. a panel with at least one female justice present) is the 'treatment condition', while an all-male panel is the 'control condition'.

Applying Coarsened Exact Matching to the treatment and control groups, we chose age, our proxy for judicial attitudes (*viz.*, the nature of the appointing government), being born in Oslo, and prior governmental experience as possible predictors of voting for the female or underdog position in Family and Estate Law cases. For the Sentencing Adjustment domain, we matched on judicial attitudes, prior governmental experience, being born in Oslo, and a pair of time dummies – one marking the change in the Court's criminal appeals jurisdiction, the other the Willoch-era.[11] The pre- and post-treatment $L1$ statistics are reported in Table 6.5. After the data are matched, approximately 26.5 per cent of the 509 Family and Estate Law 'male-justice votes' are in the treatment condition, while about 54.9 per cent of the 1659 Sentencing Adjustment 'male-justice votes' are in the treatment condition.

Clearly, the coarsened matching yielded better-balanced data. For both issue domains, the $L1$ statistics are appreciably less than their pre-processed counterparts. Indeed, in the case of the Sentencing Adjustments issue domain, the $L1$ statistic is almost indistinguishable from 0, and here a simple difference in means test could be used to estimate the sample average treatment effect of a mixed panel. In an abundance of caution, however, we follow the suggestion of Blackwell and his coauthors and

Table 6.5: CEM Test of Causal Effect of Mixed Panels on the Votes of Male Justices

	Family and Estate Law		Sentencing Adjustment	
	Coef.	SE	Coef.	SE
Mixed Panel	0.12	0.25	.06	.10
Age	0.00	0.03	–	–
Social Dem Appointee	0.42	0.33	.06	.11
Born in Oslo	0.62*	0.28	.16	.11
Prior Governmental Experience	-0.07	0.27	.14	.10
Change in Jurisdiction	–	–	.18	.12
Willoch-Era	–	–	-.15	.15
Constant	-0.85	1.48	.22	.13
Dependent Variable	1 = Vote for Female		1 = Reduce Sentence	
N	509		1653	
Log Pseudolikelihood	-347.42		-1141.35	
Wald Chi2; p =	5.02; .41		9.54; .15	
L1 Pre; L1 Post	.32; .16		.22; 0	

Notes: *$p < .05$. Standard errors clustered on the individual justice.

---

11. We used the procedure's automated coarsening routine for each of the pretreatment variables.

estimate a parametric model on the matched data to account for any remaining imbalance (2009: 537). Likewise, we estimate a parametric model on the matched data for the Family and Estate Law issue domain, inasmuch as the $L1$ statistic is .16.

Empirical findings

The results of the matching procedure are reported in Table 6.5. They indicate no support for our causal hypothesis. To state the matter concretely, there is no evidence that the presence of women affects a male justice's vote. In both Family and Estate Law cases and in Sentencing Adjustment cases, the treatment effects fail to even hint at significance. Thus, it appears that the addition of women to the Norwegian Supreme Court has not affected the final vote on the merits, even in issue domains where women justices might be expected to possess credible and especially persuasive information.

We should note, however, that in the Family and Estate Law issue domain, being part of the Oslo social milieu has a measurable effect when the data are better balanced (*see* Table 6.5). To state its effect concretely, male justices who were born in Oslo are 15 per cent more apt to support the disadvantaged litigant in these cases.

Conclusion

In this chapter we have explored the presence of women on the Norwegian Supreme Court. A woman's voice was first added to the chorus of male justices in 1968. Since then, the number of women on the High Bench has slowly grown to a relative level nearly equal to that of their presence in the Parliament. Importantly, both concerted efforts among political elites and formal governmental action[12] have propelled women onto the Bench. And this, in turn, has affected the Bench's character. The policy of emphasising the appointment of women, by definition circumscribes the pool of potential appointees. Selecting a woman increases the likelihood of appointing a justice with prior governmental experience, a justice born in Oslo, and (quite likely) a justice with more liberal or 'radical' inclinations.

These, clearly, are collateral effects – even unintended consequences.[13] They might affect the Court's decisional outputs by changing the relative mix of attributes present on the Bench. Male justices can and do share these attributes (and the predilections to which they give rise), but the appointment of male justices would not remake the mix as quickly because male justices are not as

---

12. Former Chief Justice of the Supreme Court, Carsten Smith believed it was essential to appoint women to the Court to ensure the Court's representativeness. The government, for example, has issued a formal proclamation that the proportion of women on the Supreme Court will not drop below 40 per cent (NTB 2008).

13. They are similar in effect to Republican presidents' emphasis of appointing 'pro-life' justices to the U.S. Supreme Court. The collateral effect here has been the elimination (for the first time in the Court's history) of justices with a Protestant religious background.

homogenous with respect to these attributes. By the same token, there was at least one motivation underlying the policy of appointing women, acted on by Norway, that was intended to affect the Court – namely, the belief that the addition of women would add an important and previously missing perspective to the Court's deliberations. The 'different voice' women would bring to the Court, and the unique and credible information of women, would shape and influence the Court's consideration of the legal issues before it.

Whether collateral or intended, then, the addition of women could affect the Court's articulation of policy. However, our analysis found little support for this proposition. All the same, it is important to note that we have not addressed all of the ways in which the addition of women to the Supreme Court could affect its creation of policy. First, we have looked only at the justices' decisions on the merits of the cases before the Court. To be sure, on this score there is little evidence of men and women behaving differently. But perhaps the presence of women affects the *nature* of the cases being brought to the Court in the first place. It might be that certain cases and controversies, previously left unchallenged, are being appealed because litigants perceive a better chance of success. In other words, while the presence of women justices may not have a profound effect on the Court's outputs, they may be influencing its inputs. Second, our focus on the votes misses another important aspect of the Court's outputs – the nature of its decisions. Perhaps the addition of women has changed the rationale for the majority decision. Women might be emphasising different issues and legal arguments for a vote that is in the same direction of their male colleagues. In other words, men and women justices might vote the same way but for different reasons. Finally, we must recognise that one of the motivations for appointing women to the Court was a belief that their presence would promote the Court's 'social legitimacy' (Boyd *et al.* 2010: 390). This, in turn, would increase the likelihood that the Norwegian mass public would accept or at least tolerate unpopular Court decisions. Thus, the addition of women might have worked to augment the Court's overall policy-making power.

References

Allen, D. W. and Wall, D. E. (1987) 'The Behavior of Women State Supreme Court Justices: Are They Tokens or Outsiders?', *Justice System Journal* 12 (2): 232–244.

Andenæs, Ø. (1986) 'Et tilbakeblikksbillede fra 1946. En fest og en lærdom for livet' in Bugge, H. O., Coward, K. and Rognlien, S. (eds) *Festskrift Lovavdelingen - 100 år 1885–1985*, Oslo: Universitetsforlaget, pp. 170–171.

Andrews, E. and Hoekstra, V. (2010) 'The Selection of Women on Constitutional Courts: The Impact of Judicial Selection Mechanisms and Party Quotas on Court Composititon', Paper prepared for the 2010 Southern Political Science Conference, Atlanta, Georgia.

Bergset, K.-R. (2013) 'Gender in the Supreme Court of Norway: Judicial Behaviour in Child Custody Cases 1968–2011', Master's Thesis. Department of Comparative Politics, University of Bergen.

Blackwell, M., Iacus, S., King, G. and Porro, G. (2009) 'CEM: Coarsened Exact Matching in Stata', *The Stata Journal* 9 (4): 524–546.

Boyd, C., Epstein, L. and Martin, A. D. (2010) 'Untangling the Causal Effects of Sex on Judging', *American Journal of Political Science* 54 (2): 389–411.

Cook, B. B. (1981) 'Will Women Judges Make a Difference in Women's Legal Rights?' in Rendel, M. (ed.) *Women, Power, and Political Systems*, London: Croom Helm.

Flemming, R. B. and Wood, B. D. (1997) 'The Public and the Supreme Court: Individual Justice Responsiveness to American Policy Moods', *American Journal of Political Science* 41 (2): 468–488.

Grendstad, G. and Holgersen, J. D. (2009) 'Varighet og Velstand. En prediksjonsmodell for ettermælet og omdømmet til de norske statsministrene i det 20. århundre', *Norsk Statsvitenskapelig Tidsskrift* 25 (2): 99–124.

Groves, J. R. and Rogers, W. H. (2011) 'Effectiveness of RCA Institutions to Limit Local Externalities: Using Foreclosure Data to Test Covenant Effectiveness', *Land Economics* 87 (4): 559–581.

Guo, S. and Fraser, M. W. (2013) *Propensity Score Analysis: Statistical Methods and Applications*, Los Angeles: Sage.

Hagtvet, B. and Bjørklund, T. (eds) (1981) *Høyrebølgen – epokeskifte i norsk politikk? Høyres velgerframgang og Arbeiderpartiets 80-årsdilemmaeri sosial, økonomisk og politisk belysning*, Oslo: Aschehoug.

Heidar, K. (2000) *Norway: Elites on Trial*, Boulder: Westview Press.

Iacus, S. M., King, G. and Porro, G. (2012) 'Causal Inference Without Balance Checking: Coarsened Exact Matching', *Political Analysis* 20 (1): 1–24.

King, M. L. and Greening, M. (2007) 'Gender Justice of Just Gender? The Role of Gender in Sexual Assault Decisions at the International Criminal Tribunal for the Former Yugoslavia', *Social Science Quarterly* 88 (5): 1049–1071.

Krol, J. F. and Brenner, S. (1990) 'Strategies of Certiorari Voting on the United States Supreme Court: A Reevaluation', *Western Political Quarterly* 43 (2): 335–342.

Lasswell, H. D. (1936) *Politics: Who Gets What, When and How*, New York: Whittlesey House.

Lødrup, P. (1975) 'Familierett i utvikling', *Lov og Rett* 14: 437–438.

Martin, E. and Pyle, B. (2002) 'Gender and Racial Diversification of State Supreme Courts', *Women and Politics* 24 (2): 35–52.

Matland, R. E. (2004) 'The Norwegian Experience of Gender Quotas', Paper presented at the International Institute for Democracy and Electoral Assistance (IDEA)/CEE Network for Gender Issues Conference The Implementation of Quotas: European Experiences. Budapest, Hungary, 22–23 October 2004.

Menkel-Meadow, C. (1996) 'The Feminization of the Legal Profession: The Comparative Sociology of Women Lawyers' in Label, R. and Lewis, P. S. C. (eds) *Lawyers in Society: An Overview*, Berkeley: University of California Press, pp. 221–281.

Mishler, W. and Sheehan, R. S. (1993) 'The Supreme Court as a Countermajoritarian Institution? The Impact of Public Opinion on Supreme Court Decisions', *American Political Science Review* 87 (1): 87–101.

Nie, M. and Waltenburg, E. N. (2014) 'Media Impact on Diffuse Support for the Supreme Court: The Black Media', Paper prepared for presentation at the annual meetings of the Midwest Political Science Association, Chicago, IL.

NTB (2008) 'Storberget vil ha flere kvinner til Høyesterett', 31 October.

Peresie, J. L. (2005) 'Female Judges Matter: Gender and Collegial Decisionmaking in the Federal Appellate Courts', *Yale Law Journal* 114 (7): 1759–1790.

Segal, J. A. (2000) 'Representative Decision Making on the Federal Bench: Clinton's District Court Appointees', *Political Research Quarterly* 53 (1): 137–150.

Skarpnes, O. (1986) 'Minner fra Lovavdelingen' in Bugge, H. O., Coward, K. and Rognlien, S. (eds) *Festskrift Lovavdelingen - 100 år 1885–1985*, Oslo: Universitetsforlaget, pp. 194–196.

Songer, D. R., Davis, S. and Haire, S. (1994) 'A Reappraisal of Diversification in the Federal Courts: Gender Effects in the Courts of Appeals', *Journal of Politics* 56 (2): 425–439.

Songer, D. R., Szmer, J., Christensen, R. K. and Johnson, S. W. (2010) 'Conflict, Voice and Critical Mass: Examining Gender Diversity and Dissensus in the Supreme Court of Canada', manuscript prepared for the 81st Annual Southern Political Science Conference, Atlanta, Georgia, 7–9 January 2010.

Steffensmeier, D. and Herbert, C. (1999) 'Women and Men Policymakers: Does the Judge's Gender Affect the Sentencing of Criminal Defendants', *Social Forces* 77 (3): 1163–1196.

Teigen, M. (2011) 'Kvoteringstradisjon og styringsekspansjon', *Tidskrift for kjønnsforskning* 35 (2): 84–101.

Verdens Gang (1968) 'Første kvinne i Høyesterett – Lilly Bølviken tar plass', *VG*.

Walker, T. G. and Barrow, D. J. (1985) 'The Diversification of the Federal Bench: Policy and Process Ramifications', *Journal of Politics* 47 (2): 596–617.

Østlid, H. (1988) *Dommeratferd i dissenssaker*, Oslo: Universitetsforlaget.

Chapter Seven

Government Friendliness of Supreme Court Justices

In the previous chapter, we showed that the presence of women per se has little or no effect on the Norwegian Supreme Court's decisional outputs in two issue areas where gendered judging would seem most likely to occur. In that particular instance, then, an intentional effect of targeted appointment to the Court has not panned out, but what of an *unintended* effect? In this chapter we turn our attention to whether the appointment process tends to staff the *Høyesterett* with justices predisposed to find for the government in cases where it is a litigant.

In the U.S. context, it is well established that the national government (as represented by the Office of the Solicitor General, the SG) fares exceptionally well as a litigant before the Supreme Court (*see* Black and Owens 2012). A primary causal explanation for this high rate of success rests on shared attitudinal preferences between the Court and the government.[1] As Black and Owens summarise it, this ideologically based

> theory holds that policy goals largely explain the relationship between the SG and the Court. When a majority of justices and the SG (and, by definition, the president) share a worldview, the Court will be more likely to side with the SG. Conversely, when the SG and the Court majority disagree, the Court will be less likely to side with the government (2012: 42).

A similar dynamic may well be at work in the case of Norway where the government wins roughly 60 per cent of the cases in which it is a party (Fagernæs 2007; Ryssdal 2006). That is, either because of concerted government efforts to identify and appoint justices who share its policy preferences, or because of some type of selection effect – where qualified candidates for a seat on the High Bench opt in or out depending on the degree to which they agree with the appointing government – there is the likelihood that there are sitting justices who are especially sympathetic to the government's position.

Now, this potential relationship is subject to empirical testing, and we do so here. Accordingly, we have collected data on all non-unanimous civil cases from 1945 to 2009 in which the Norwegian government was a litigant. Our primary hypothesis is that justices appointed by socialist or social democratic governments

---

1. There are alternative explanations for the success of the government, including its credibility as a litigant, its resource advantages, and its capacity to undermine a recalcitrant Court's institutional legitimacy as well as frustrate the individual justices' policy preferences (*see* Black and Owens 2012: 32–45).

will be more likely to support the government and its claims of greater authority in civil cases than will their non-socialist appointed counterparts. Of course – as we have demonstrated in previous chapters – other forces affect the justices' decisional behaviour, and in the section of this chapter where we begin to cobble together an explanation for a justice's support for the government, we identify and discuss these forces. Building upon this discussion, we then specify and estimate a model of judicial behaviour in order to test our appointment hypothesis. Finally, we conclude by taking stock of some of the implications of this chapter's findings. We turn first, however, to a brief discussion or review of the institutional context in which Norway's Supreme Court operates.

The Norwegian Supreme Court and its legal environment

In the 1850s, Norway was a small homogenous country that viewed the state as a benevolent actor. Its uncomplicated legal system was both a pragmatic system similar to the common law systems and to a codified legal system similar to civil law countries (Nylund 2010). Norway displays a moderate-to-low degree of procedural formalism in its legal system (Rosenthal and Voeten 2007). The advent of social democracy blurred the public–private distinction and offered fertile ground for what would become the culture of 'Scandinavian legal realism', since it offered a legal theory that dovetailed with an ideology of pragmatism and egalitarianism. Legal realism permitted, and still permits, lawyers to dodge legal theories and principles of law and to develop freer considerations of what is fair, appropriate, and reasonable (Magnussen 2005; Nylund 2010). The great formal shift in Norwegian legal method came in the 1960s when Eckhoff (1971) jettisoned the existing state of legal reasoning that formally accepted law and practice as legal sources only. In its place he identified a total of seven legal sources from each of which lawyers could draw when presenting and construing a legal case.[2] Significantly, Eckhoff claimed that no single source – not even the law itself – was *sine qua non* in the justices' decision making. Thus, the decisional behaviour of Norway's justices can be quite malleable, so much so that one Supreme Court justice, some years before he was appointed to the Court, averred that '[p]redictability in the application of law may be just as much tied to knowledge about the justices as to knowledge about legal rules and methods' (Lund 1987: 217).

So how do the justices join the Court and what kind of attitudes do they bring with them?[3] The post-World War II appointment process in Norway has taken place in a political multi-party system that still displays recognisable characteristics of a small consensual unitary state. Members of Parliament are seated according to electoral districts in the sequence by which they are elected in multi-member districts. Generally, parliamentary majorities have served as the basis for minimum winning, even minority, one-party or coalition governments. Except for the first

---

2. More recent legal sources include international law such as human rights and EU statutes. *See* e.g. Wiklund (2008), Bernt and Mæhle (2007), and Boe (2010).

3. For a more detailed and technical discussion of the appointment process, *see* Chapter Two.

six months after the Second World War and the years since the 2005 election, sixty years of government formation can be cleanly divided between a socialist and non-socialist government bloc.

The appointment of Supreme Court justices is assumed to be a purely non-political exercise and has also been tacitly accepted by the political opposition as the domain of the parties in government and, specifically, of the Ministry of Justice. From 1945 until 2002 the Ministry of Justice and the government exercised complete discretion over the entire recruitment process. The process was – and still is – largely invisible to the general public (Torgersen 1963). It begins with a public announcement that there is an opening on the Court, applicants are sought, and candidates are then subjected to an evaluation with the Ministry of Justice. Throughout the whole post-World War II period, the applicants were also subjected to an informal assessment by all justices on the Court. Afterwards, the Chief Justice meets with the Minister of Justice in order to convey the Court's views on the applicants.[4] Then the Minister of Justice offered the name of the successful candidate to the King in Council for formal appointment. When the position of Chief Justice is vacant, the process is formally more open and involves discussions with leaders of parliamentary political parties before the government sends the nomination to the King in Council. When interim justices are needed for a limited period – due to the Court's workload or leaves of absence among the permanent justices – the Chief Justice makes a direct request to the Ministry of Justice, which in turn handles the temporary appointment and brings it to the King in Council for perfunctory confirmation.

A change took place in 2002 in order both to increase the independence of the courts as well as to reduce, if not eliminate, the increasingly 'politicised' Ministry of Justice from the recruitment process.[5] The National Courts Administration was established in the city of Trondheim under which the Judicial Appointments Board was to take care of the recruitment process of permanent justices. The council cannot solicit applications, but screens and interviews applicants. The Council returns a ranked list of three applicants to the Ministry of Justice. Effective as of 2004, the Council's rankings of candidates have not been altered either by the Ministry of Justice or the King in Council.

Towards a model of judicial support for the government

Our thesis is that the appointment process results in the elevation of justices who share policy preferences with the appointing government – either because the government has sought to place individuals on the High Bench for the purposes of establishing a judiciary that is more sympathetic to its policy goals (Vaubel 2009) or as a result of 'self selection', wherein qualified candidates choose to apply for a

---

4. In 2010, Chief Justice Tore Schei decided to publicise the Court's opinion on the applicants (Gjerde 2010).

5. The 'politicisation' argument was advanced by law professor Carsten Smith who in 1991 was appointed Chief Justice of the Supreme Court (Gangnes 2010; Smith 2003).

Court position on the basis of the degree to which they agree with the appointing government.

Regardless of the causal mechanism, studies of the American judiciary confirm that the appointing party is closely related to a justice's ideology (*see* Pinello 1999) and that ideology is the force that best predicts a justice's decisional behaviour (Segal and Spaeth 2002), although that effect varies a bit by legal subfield (e.g. Zeisberg 2009). Importantly, the relationship between party and ideology or ideology's predictive quality does not appear to be a uniquely American phenomenon (*see* Dyevre, 2010). Hönnige (2009), in his study of the German and French supreme courts, and Magalhaes (2003), in his study of the constitutional courts in Spain and Portugal, conclude that the ideology of justices can be measured by the party affiliation of the appointing authority, and that ideology predicts justices' votes. Hanretty (2011) shows that judicial dissent on Spanish and Portuguese Constitutional Tribunals can be explained by their ideal points along a left–right dimension.[6] Voeten (2007; 2008) finds that a degree of judicial behaviour on the European Court of Human Rights (ECHR) is primarily attributable not to any legal culture but to the preferences of their appointing governments.

With respect to Norway's judiciary, there is less systematic evidence for these relationships, but something of an anecdotal case can be made. Torstein Eckhoff – law professor and advocate of legal realism – argued that the government, in its appointments of justices, should take into consideration the candidates' 'political attitude' in order to ensure a more politically balanced Court (1964: 143n41). He pointed to the judicial appointments of the liberal Knudsen governments in the 1908–1909 and 1913–1920 periods as notable examples of this logic.

Kåre Willoch (2002) – former member of the *Storting* for the Conservative Party, two-time Minister of Commerce (1963, 1965–1970), and Prime Minister 1981–1986 – claimed that several appointments to the Supreme Court were politically motivated. Specifically, he pointed to his conservative colleague Elisabeth Schweigaard Selmer, who very shortly after stepping down as Minister of Justice in 1970 was appointed to the Supreme Court by her own government.[7] Her leadership on the Court, Willoch argues, secured the 9-8 majority for the 1976 landmark ruling (*Kløftadommen*, Rt-1976–1), requiring full compensation for the expropriation of private property.[8]

Given the empirical findings regarding the relationship between party, ideology, and judicial behaviour, and the circumstantial evidence that can be compiled for Norway, we hypothesise that justices appointed by socialist or social democratic governments – whose traditional policy agenda has been regulation and redistribution – more often than not vote for the upper-dog government party in civil cases. But in addition to the effect of attitudinal preferences on the votes

---

6.   *See also* a similar study by Pellegrina and Garoupa (2012) for Italy.

7.   Six former Ministers of Justice have served as justices on the Supreme Court in the 1945–2009 period; none since 1990.

8.   *See* Chapter Eight where the important *Kløfta decision* is analysed in a broader context.

of individual justices, there are other forces (background attributes, socialisation experiences, and the like) that have been shown to bear upon the behaviour of Norway's justices (*see* the analyses in Chapters Five and Six) and should therefore be included in the specification of the model of judicial behaviour.

One such force is the nature of a justice's position on the High Bench itself. Section 88 of the Constitution states that the Supreme Court shall consist of a Chief Justice (*Formand*) and at least four other members. While the position of Chief is fixed, the number of associate justices may vary. In the formal government hierarchy, the Chief Justice – along with the President of the *Storting* and the Prime Minister – are ranked immediately below the King. The Chief Justice is present in matters of state and at official ceremonies. Regardless of seniority on the Court, the Chief Justice always serves as the presiding justice in the oral hearings of any panel. The Chief is the first to take the floor when justices meet to deliberate in conference (*rådslagning*). Following the Chief's summary of the case at hand, the other justices cast their votes in descending order of seniority; the Chief votes last. The prominent institutional and constitutional positions of the Chief Justice may affect how the individual sitting in that position perceives their relation with the government. As a constitutionally designated official with government rank, the Chief Justice may identify more closely with the government per se than do the other justices, all other things being equal. Therefore, in the civil cases we examine here, the Chief Justice may be especially likely to find for the government litigant. On the other hand, it is quite possible that Chief Justices perceive themselves as titular head of an independent branch of government, and will thus be particularly mindful of protecting the judiciary's separation and autonomy from the government. One clear way to achieve this is to avoid playing the role of the expected rubber stamp for contested government actions. Ultimately, we expect that the Chief Justice will exhibit a voting pattern that differs from his or her counterparts, but we cannot anticipate if that pattern is in favour of or opposition to the government.

Norwegian judicial practice and statutes permit interim justices to serve on the Court for a limited period of time. Throughout the 1945–2009 period, a total of fifty-two lawyers have been appointed as interim justices to the Supreme Court a total of 116 times. Some of these lawyers have been reappointed up to five times. Many were appointed to assist in the war trials in the immediate post-World War II period. The exact procedure as to how these appointments have taken place is neither clear nor consistent over time. Basically, interim justices have either been chosen directly by the Ministry of Justice, or specifically requested by the Chief Justice to serve in an upcoming short-term vacancy or to assist the Court during times of heavy workloads.

That interim justices may become permanent members of the Court raises the question of the Court's independence.[9] Former Chief Justice Terje

---

9. Although public records of applicants for permanent positions on the Court are limited, we can state with some certainty that at least eight interim justices have applied for a permanent position on the Court. Only six have done so successfully.

Wold (1964: 397), for example, observed that the appointment of interim justices is 'delicate and difficult [since it] concerns the principle of the court's independence [and may open] a shortcut for later appointments'. Eckhoff (1964: 137f) discussed whether interim justices would be more supportive of government interests since they may feel beholden to the government for their temporary appointment, and due to the possibility that they may be reappointed at a later occasion. Even in the Norwegian legal system where judges do not find themselves in a career system, being temporarily appointed to the Supreme Court can still be considered a promotion. Hylland (2009) is therefore concerned about the fact that the government can appoint interim justices who must cast their votes in cases where the government is a party. An analysis of non-unanimous decisions in Norway for the 1930–1979 period did not reveal any effects of interim justices in civil cases, but interim justices in criminal cases concerning sentencing adjustment were more likely to side with the prosecutor (Østlid 1988). On balance, we hypothesise that interim justices are more likely than are associate justices to vote for the government party in civil cases.

As noted in previous chapters, occupation affects the socialisation of lawyers and judges (Tate 1981; Tate and Handberg 1991; Tate and Sittiwong 1989). Our research question in this chapter directs us towards justices' pre-Court careers in the government itself. The most prominent of these careers has been in the Legislation Department (*Lovadelingen*; *see* Chapter Four), but nontrivial numbers of justices have also worked in the offices of the Director General of Public Prosecution (*Riksadvokaten*) and the Government Advocate (*Regjeringsadvokaten*).[10] Our general hypothesis is that a justice with a background in any of these government offices will be more likely to vote for the government party (*see also* Kjønstad 1999).

Education certainly imprints the individual, affecting attitudes and reference groups. Braun and Muller, for example, note that 'education is … linked with one's integration into distinctive communication networks' (Braun and Müller 1997: 168), while Eckhoff (1964: 144) has suggested that Norway's justices identify closely with the university from which they received their law degree. Presently, Norway has three law schools – the University of Oslo, the University of Bergen (the law school was established in 1969), and the University of Tromso (the law school was established in 1987). Of the three, an association with the University of Oslo may predispose a justice to support the national government as a litigant. It is located in the nation's capital and is the most likely to have alumni who are part of the national government's social network.

Since there is significant variation in the ages of sitting justices, we explore the plausible impact of age on government-friendly decisional behaviour. Employing

10. Forty-one interim and permanent justices have had experience in the Legislation Department; sixteen interim and permanent justices have had experience in the Office of the Government Advocate; six interim and permanent justices have a background in the Office of the Director General of Public Prosecution. Obviously, many of these justices have served in more than one of these offices. Another name for the Office of the Government Advocate is '*Attorney General of Civil Affairs*'.

the language of cohort analysis, we identify two types of effects we might attach to the age of a justice: age and cohort effects (Glenn 2005). Age effects simply mean that in general as people get older – irrespective of their generation – they change, perhaps in a more conservative direction (Lewis-Beck *et al.* 2008), and at some point attitudinal changes can remain relatively fixed (Jennings and Markus 1984).[11] Given that the status quo would have been the social welfare system, a conservative defence of that status quo might produce a government-friendly predisposition.

Cohort effects basically reflect shared experiences of a given generation of individuals. For example, those groups whose formative years occurred before the erosion of consensus politics in the 1970s may have internalised a more government-friendly posture that has influenced their behaviour on the Supreme Court. By way of contrast, the post-1970 cohorts may have formed a less government-friendly demeanour, given the growing predilection for increased individualism. Østlid (1988) identified an age difference in justices' voting in an important plenary case on expropriation (*Kløftadommen* Rt-1976–1). The majority consisted of younger justices who voted for full compensation, while the minority consisted of older justices who were less strict on full compensation. Eivind Smith (1993) argued that important decisions where voting patterns are related to age may herald significant shifts on the Court itself. Whether the result of age or cohort effects, we hypothesise that the older the justice, the more government-friendly he or she is likely to be.

Similar to the logic for the location of the justice's law school alma mater, we expect that a justice's place of birth might affect his or her support for the government. Birthplace is an indicator of the social network in which justices were socialised, particularly with respect to the centre–periphery divide thought to influence Norwegian political history (Heidar 2000; Rokkan 1967; Hjellbrekke and Korsnes 2010). Significantly, the Ministry of Justice has occasionally argued for justices having a background in the periphery when deciding in favour of their appointment to the Court.

We assume that Oslo-born justices are likely to be more effortlessly absorbed by the national legal elite. They have engaged in long-term personal interaction, and they continue to interact (*see* Kristjánsson 2010; Pedersen 1994). They have been trained at the same law school, have served in government together; perhaps they are related, and are therefore likely members of what has been informally referred to as the 'knee-breeches nobility' of Oslo. Thus, Oslo-born justices, assuming they resided there for a considerable period of time, may be more government-friendly.

Finally, we add controls for seniority, whether the government is a plaintiff and therefore advantaged given the likelihood that the Court accepts cases to reverse them, the changed procedure for judicial appointments, and whether the justice and the litigating government are of 'the same party'.[12] Smith (1993) suggested

---

11. For an overall review of the process of political socialisation, *see* Clawson and Oxley (2008).

12. Sex is another attribute that is typically included in models of decisional behaviour. The results of our analysis in Chapter Six, however, strongly suggest that sex has little systematic effect on the voting behaviour of Norway's justices. Therefore – following the rule of parsimony – we omit it.

that voting patterns may be linked to seniority. Experience on the Supreme Court, in and of itself, probably does not produce attitudes out of nothing, not even a more government-friendly justice. However, as one stakes out positions on issues in session after session, a justice should become more committed to his or her constitutional predispositions. Thus, radical justices will harden in their position with time in rank; similarly, conservative justices will increase their ideological consistency. Given the Court's discretionary jurisdiction, it seems likely that the Court dockets cases that it believes were wrongly decided. Thus, when the government is the plaintiff it should be advantaged. In 2002, the appointment process was changed. The intent was to remove the application process from the 'politicised' Ministry of Justice. Thus, we expect that justices appointed after 2002 would be less government friendly. Hönnige (2007) and Magalhaes (2003) suggest that the justice's votes can be affected when the government in a case is identical to the type of government that appointed the justice. For instance, a justice appointed by a socialist government would be put on the spot if a litigant party represented a socialist government. We include such a control, but expect very weak effects.

Model specification, data and analysis

As in Chapters Five and Six, we use a probability model to test these hypotheses. Specifically, we contrive the following model:

$$\left(\frac{prob\ y = 1}{prob\ y = 0}\right) = \beta_0 + \beta_1 \text{GOVERNMENT} + \beta_2 \text{CHIEF} + \beta_3 \text{ INTERIM} + \beta_4 \text{ LEGDEPARTMENT} + \beta_5 \text{PUBPROSECUTOR} + \beta_6 \text{ GOVTADVOCATE} + \beta_7 \text{ OSLOLAW} + \beta_8 \text{AGE} + \beta_9 \text{OSLOBORN} + \beta_{10} \text{SENIORITY} + \beta_{11} \text{ERROR-CORRECTING} + \beta_{12} \text{APPOINTPROC} + \beta_{13} \text{SAMEPARTY} + \varepsilon$$

Descriptive statistics and operationalisations for the variables included in the model are displayed in Table 7.1. The data on which we estimate the model consist of non-unanimous Supreme Court decisions between 1947 and 2009, on civil cases in five-justice panels where the government was a party. The *dependent variable* is the individual justice's vote (1 = for the government party). And once again, we clustered the standard errors on the individual justice and the year of the decision.[13] Estimation results are reported in Table 7.2 and Figure 7.1 displays the marginal effects.[14]

Summary statistics report that the model possesses some statistical bite. The chi^2 statistic indicates that the overall model is highly significant, although it only yields

---

13. As in Chapter Five, we conducted robustness checks of our model's estimates, clustering the observations on the justice and the case. The results are reported in Appendix Table 7A.

14. The logit procedure permitting standard errors to be clustered on two dimensions cannot be used to generate the point estimates and confidence intervals displayed in Figure 7.2. Accordingly, we estimated a conventional logit model with standard errors clustered only on the justice. The results of the model estimation are displayed in Appendix Table 7B. The reader will notice that the results of the two models are almost identical.

Table 7.1: Variables, Operationalisations, Hypotheses and Descriptive Statistics

Variable	Operation-alisation	Hypothesised Relationship	Mean	Standard Deviation	Min	Max
Dependent Variable	0 = Against Government 1 = For Government		.509	.500	0	1
Appointing Government	0 = Non-Socialist 1 = Social Democrat	+	.684	.465	0	1
Chief Justice	0 = No 1 = Chief Justice	−/+	.052	.223	0	1
Interim Justice	0 = No 1 = Interim Justice	+	.033	.179	0	1
Legislation Department	0 = No 1 = Legislation Department	+	.334	.474	0	1
Government Advocate	0 = No 1 = Government Advocate	+	.172	.378	0	1
Prosecutor's Office	0 = No 1 = Prosecutor's Office	+	.069	.254	0	1
Oslo Law Degree	0 = No 1 = Oslo Law Degree	+	.964	.187	0	1
Age	Age at Time of Decision	+	59.245	6.488	41	71
Oslo-Born	0 = Born Elsewhere 1 = Born in Oslo	+	.461	.499	0	1
Seniority	Years on Bench at Decision	−/+	8.625	6.322	0	28
Post-2002 Appointee	0 = No 1 = Yes	−	.025	.155	0	1
Government Plaintiff	0 = No 1 = Government Plaintiff	+	.421	.494	0	1
Same Government	0 = No 1 = Justice and Litigating Government, Same Party	+	.575	.496	0	1

Table 7.2: Government Friendliness, Clustered Logit Estimates

	Coef.	T-stat	P > |t|
Socialist Appointee	0.330	2.16**	.03
Chief Justice	-0.660	-2.36**	.02
Interim Justice	0.774	2.82***	.00
Legislation Department	0.344	2.48***	.01
Government Advocate	-0.077	-0.51	.61
Public Prosecutor	0.419	1.82*	.07
Oslo Law Degree	0.374	5.16***	.00
Age	0.012	0.83	.41
Oslo-Born	-0.047	-0.30	.76
Seniority	-0.016	-0.84	.40
Post-2002 Appointee	-0.242	-0.89	.38
Government Plaintiff	-0.136	-0.98	.33
Same Government	0.054	0.72	.47
Constant	-1.218	-1.55	.12

Notes: $*p < 0.10$; $**p < 0.05$; $***p < 0.01$. DV = Support for Government Litigant. N = 1,300 (Listwise); Standard Errors clustered on Individual Justice and Year. $\text{Chi}^2 = 34.85$; Prob > Chi^2 = 0.00; Pseudo R^2 = .02. MLE Improvement = 12.9 per cent.

Figure 7.1: Marginal Effects of Forces Explaining Justices' Votes for the Government as a Litigant with 95% Confidence Intervals

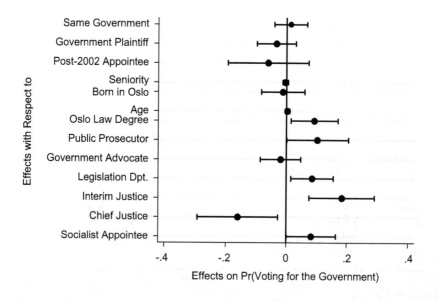

a meagre improvement in predictive accuracy. Turning to the estimated effect of the model's individual forces, there is strong confirmation that shared preferences and/or experiences with the government affect a justice's likelihood of supporting the government as a litigant. Accordingly, justices appointed by a socialist-led government – i.e. regimes given to more expansive and centralised policies and actions – are significantly more likely to support the upper-dog litigant in civil cases. This suggests, in turn, that the nature of the appointing government is a valid proxy for the ideological preferences of Norway's justices – a point that confirms the findings reported in Chapter Five. With respect to common experiences, justices who had served in the government prior to taking a seat on the High Bench are, as expected, more apt to find for the government as a litigant. Justices who had toiled in the Legislation Department are 8 per cent more likely to vote for the government, while justices drawn from the Office of the Public Prosecutor are 10 per cent more likely to favour the government in civil cases. Yet, the effect of prior government service is not perfectly uniform. Our statistical results indicate that justices with experience in the Office of the Government Advocate – the office that frequently represents the government in civil cases – are neither more nor less prone to support the government. Finally, an Oslo law degree and the concomitant likelihood of being part of the government's social network, results in a justice being 10 per cent more likely to side with the government in civil cases.

Our results also indicate that the nature of the justice's position on the Bench matters. Being Chief Justice reduces the probability of voting for the government party by nearly 16 per cent. Interim justices, on the other hand, are significantly *more* supportive of the government. An interim justice is 18 per cent more likely to side with the government litigant, all other things being equal. This tendency of greater levels of support among interim justices raises questions concerning the Court's independence. As we have noted elsewhere (and as clearly indicated in their title), *interim* justices' service on the Court is limited; and the decision to retain any one of them on the Court is, to a significant degree, at the pleasure of the Ministry of Justice. Indeed, Hylland's (2009) concern that the government can appoint interim justices who must cast their votes in cases where the government is a party, seems well grounded.

Evidence of strategic behaviour?

The significant effects exhibited in the voting patterns of both the Chief and interim justices suggest that some strategic behaviour may be afoot (on justices as strategic actors, *see* Epstein and Knight 1998). But is there? That both types of justices are dependent upon the government for their ultimate position on the Bench may precipitate strategic behaviour. That is, they are effectively *aspirant* justices on the Court prior to assuming their final positions, and as such, they might seek to adjust their behaviour with an eye to its effect on their final goal. In the case of an aspirant to the Chief's seat, it would be wise to find for the government as frequently as possible (even if a majority of the other justices vote to secure

Figure 7.2: Evidence of Strategic Behaviour of Chief Justices

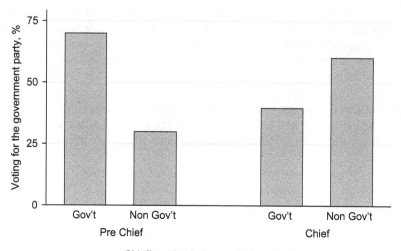

Chief's voting before and after elevation:
Non-unanimous civil cases where the government is a party
1945–2009

the opposite outcome). After all, since the government possesses the power of appointment, it would behove the strategic actor to side with government. Once the irreversible selection to Chief is made, however, the new occupant of the seat can begin to vote sincerely, or other strategic concerns – such as protection of the judiciary's independence or legitimacy – might come into play.

To test this conjecture of strategic behaviour, we compared the justices' votes as aspirant Chiefs before their elevation with their votes as Chiefs after elevation. Excluded from the analysis are three Chiefs who did not cast votes both as associate justices and Chief Justices. For the remaining five justices who later ascended to Chief, the data contain 88 votes. The votes for or against the government party were cross-tabulated with the justices' votes before and after elevation. The statistically significant result is depicted in Figure 7.2.[15]

Figure 7.2 clearly indicates that the justices changed their voting behaviour. Before elevation, the aspirant Chiefs cast 70 per cent of their votes for the

---

15. The three excluded Chiefs are Berg, who did not take part in any decisions in our data; Stang, who cast no votes as associate justice but ten votes as Chief; and Sandene, for whom we only have votes when he was associate justice. Between 1945 and 2009, five Chiefs cast 30 votes before elevation and 58 votes after elevation: Grette two and five; Wold 13 and 23; Ryssdal nine and 12; Smith one (as interim justice) and eight; and Schei – current Chief and counting – five and 10. The 88 votes were cast equally between the two parties. $Chi^2 = 7.28$; df = 1; p < .01.

government party. After elevation the Chiefs cast 40 per cent of their votes for the government party. The effect of strategic voting is 30 percentage points.[16]

As we have noted earlier, several Norwegian legal scholars have questioned whether the presence of interim justices militates against the independence of the Supreme Court (Eckhoff 1964; Wold 1964; Hylland 2009). Being handpicked and honoured to temporarily serve on the country's highest court must be considered a promotion and a career boost, which would presumably carve 'a short cut to appointment as associate justice' (Wold 1964: 397). Voting 'correctly' – that is, in favour of the government party – would likely be rewarded with additional temporary appointments or, better still, a permanent seat on the High Bench. Similarly, 'bad' behaviour would likely decrease chances of reappointment. Or so the notion goes.

To test this conjecture, we analysed the votes of the pair of individuals who have sat on the Supreme Court both as both an interim and associate justice (n = 30 votes). Carl Rode cast two votes as interim justice and 15 votes as associate justice. Per Lykke Anker cast two votes as interim justice and 11 votes as associate justice. We compared the votes that Rode and Anker cast across their two types of tenure as interim justice and associate justice. The results (not shown) indicate that there was no significant change at all in voting across their two types of tenure. The result does not support a claim that interim justices behave strategically toward the government. The conclusion remains that interim justices vote more government friendly than any other group of justices on the Court. We are mindful, however, that the very small number of justices and votes renders this conclusion highly speculative at best.

Conclusion

As we have described in detail, there are fairly generous options for the attitudinal preferences of Norway's Supreme Court justices to influence their decisional behaviour. The justices sit on the Court for terms of good behaviour and they themselves determine which cases to decide. Cases that arrive in the Court are often complex, addressing principles that raise significant policy questions. The legal method is sufficiently flexible to permit justices to elicit several legal solutions from a case – all of which are credible. In this chapter we have analysed judicial behaviour with a view to how justices on the High Court decide to cast their votes when the government is a party in their courtroom. Specifically, we have addressed justices' government 'friendliness' for the post-World War II period. We analysed which independent variables bear on the justices' votes in civil cases where consensus has not been reached and where the government is a party. This question is important because it addresses what type of justices the executive branch selects to serve on the Supreme Court and what forces influence the justices' decision making.

---

16. When we entered the justice's age and seniority as controls, the impact of which would support the ageing hypothesis, the significant relationship between the Chiefs' voting before and after elevation remained unaffected (not shown).

Our empirical results point to four important findings. First, *government appointments* matter. Justices appointed by a socialist-led government are significantly more likely to vote for the government party; the opposite is true for justices who have been appointed by a non-socialist government. These conclusions substantiate and support earlier studies that appointing party is a significant measure, or proxy, for a justice's ideology also in a European context.

Second, *careers matter*. Legal careers in the executive branch of government offices prior to appointment to the Court increase the chances of the justices voting for the government party. Although this conclusion is tempered by the fact that not all careers matter, the conclusion is valid for stints at the revered Legislation Department in the Ministry of Justice.

Third, *the hierarchy of justices matters*. Interim justices are very likely to vote for the government party. We attribute this finding to the hypothesis that interim justices may feel beholden to the government for their temporary appointment, or may side with the government with the hope of being reappointed at a later occasion. Thus, temporary appointments can be considered an audition in which justices may 'act strategically when dealing with the other branches' (Johnson 2003). On the hand, there was no evidence in the data that interim justices changed their voting when promoted to permanent positions, as only two justices in our data had taken this step.

We also conclude that Chief Justices are very likely not to vote for the government party. We attribute this conclusion to a hypothesis that Chiefs take a different view than associate justices when the Supreme Court decides cases that deal with other branches of government. Significantly, however, we did ascertain that Chief Justices are likely to vote for the government party *before* elevation to Chief, but they change their voting behaviour and decide against the government party *after* elevation. This outcome – which we interpret as strategic behaviour – was not expected and has to the best of our knowledge not been addressed in European literature on judicial behaviour.

Fourth, *alma mater* matters. We conclude that having a law degree from the capital's law school at the University of Oslo seems, more often than not, to predispose justices to support the government party. However, we limit a wider generalisation of this finding due to Norway's monocephalic structure and traditionally centralised university system.

Although we report a number of statistically and substantively significant results, we must be mindful of several limitations hobbling our conclusions. First, backgrounds and attitudes are not the only forces to influence judicial behaviour. The facts of a case also impose constraints on the justices to the degree that attitudes may often play a lesser role than the attitudinal model may lead us to believe (*see* Zeisberg 2009). Indeed, a better understanding of the facts of a case may improve statistical models of judicial behaviour (*see*, e.g. Segal and Spaeth 2002: 312–326).

By the same token, broad *legal categories* like criminal cases and civil cases may be broken down to even smaller subsets of legal categories each with their own set of dispositive legal effects. In contrast to models of political behaviour, which may perform well across different issue domains, similar general models may not necessarily be appropriate when analysing judicial behaviour.

Third, it may be argued that decisional forces of judicial behaviour may operate differently across several decades. Arguments of causal contingencies and context should be taken seriously and we welcome input from historians. But we also note that for the present analysis, the procedure of running standard errors concluded that the results were robust across the close to seven decades covered by our data.

Finally, justices and legal scholars alike agree that *attitudes* – worldviews and values – influence the justices' decision making. In this chapter – and throughout the book – we have not been able to employ direct measures of justices' attitudes and values. When those measures can be obtained, one ought to be better able to account for the justices' votes.

Appendix Table 7A: Government Friendliness, Clustered Logit Estimates (Robustness Check)

	Coef.	T-stat	P > |t|
Socialist Appointee	0.330	2.02*	.04
Chief Justice	-0.660	-2.27*	.02
Interim Justice	0.774	3.08**	.00
Legislation Department	0.344	2.38*	.02
Government Advocate	-0.077	-0.47	.64
Public Prosecutor	0.419	1.93*	.05
Oslo Law Degree	0.374	2.17*	.03
Age	0.012	0.84	.40
Oslo-Born	-0.047	-0.32	.75
Seniority	-0.016	-0.87	.39
Post-2002 Appointee	-0.242	-0.90	.37
Government Plaintiff	-0.136	-1.03	.30
Same Government	0.054	0.50	.62
Constant	-1.218	-1.49	.14

*Notes: *$p < 0.05$; **$p < 0.01$. DV = Support for Government Litigant. N = 1,300 (Listwise); Standard Errors clustered on Individual Justice and Decision. Chi^2 = 34.17; Prob > Chi^2 = 0.00; Pseudo R^2 = .02. MLE Improvement = 12.9 per cent.

Appendix Table 7B: Government Friendliness. Logit Estimate (Clustered on Justice)

	Coef.	T-stat	P > |t|
Socialist Appointee	0.330	1.97*	0.05
Chief Justice	-0.660	-2.25*	0.02
Interim Justice	0.774	3.05**	0.00
Legislation Department	0.344	2.38*	0.02
Government Advocate	-0.077	-0.56	0.57
Public Prosecutor	0.419	1.94*	0.05
Oslo Law Degree	0.374	2.31*	0.02
Age	0.012	0.85	0.40
Oslo-Born	-0.047	-0.32	0.75
Seniority	-0.016	-0.85	0.40
Post-2002 Appointee	-0.242	-0.88	0.38
Government Plaintiff	-0.136	-1.03	0.30
Same Government	0.054	0.49	0.63
Constant	-1.218	-1.54	0.12

Notes: *$p < 0.05$; **$p < 0.01$. DV = Support for Government Litigant. N = 1,300 (Listwise); Standard Errors clustered on Individual Justice. Chi^2 = 44.04; Prob > Chi^2 = 0.00; Pseudo R^2 = .02. MLE Improvement = 12.9 per cent.

References

Bernt, J. F. and Mæhle, S. S. (2007) *Rett, Samfunn og Demokrati*, Oslo: Gyldendal Akademisk.

Black, R. C. and Owens, R. J. (2012) *The Solicitor General and the United States Supreme Court: Executive Branch Influence and Judicial Decisions*, Cambridge: Cambridge University Press.

Boe, E. M. (2010) *Innføring i Juss. Juridisk tenkning og rettskildelære*, Oslo: Universitetsforlaget.

Braun, M. and Müller, W. (1997) 'Measurement of Education in Comparative Research' in Mjøset, L., Engelstad, F., Brochmann, G., Kalleberg, R. and Leira, A. (eds) *Methodological Issues in Comparative Social Science*, Greenwich: JAI Press, pp. 163–201.

Clawson, R. A. and Oxley, Z. M. (2008) *Public Opinion: Democratic Ideals, Democratic Practice*, Washington D.C.: CQ Press.

Dyevre, A. (2010) 'Unifying the field of comparative judicial politics: Towards a general theory of judicial behaviour', *European Political Science Review* 2 (2): 297–227.

Eckhoff, T. (1964) 'Noen refleksjoner om domstolens uavhengighet', *Festskrift tillägnad professor, juris doktor Karl Olivecrona vid hans avgång från professorämbetet den 30 juni 1964*, Stockholm: Norstedt.

——— (1971) *Rettskildelære*, Oslo: Tanum.

Epstein, L. and Knight, J. (1998) *The Choices Justices Make*, Washington D.C.: CQ Press.

Fagernæs, S. O. (2007) 'Vinner stat og kommune for mange saker i Høyesterett?', *Advokatbladet* 87 (3): 54–55.

Gangnes, O.-M. (2010) 'Smith and Jussen', *Juristkontakt* 45: 6–11.

Gjerde, R. (2010) 'Vil ha full åpenhet om nye dommere', *Aftenposten*, 10 June.

Glenn, N. D. (2005) *Cohort Analysis*, Thousand Oaks: Sage.

Hanretty, C. (2011) 'Dissent in Iberia: The Ideal Points of Justices on the Spanish and Portuguese Constitutional Tribunals', Mimeo.

Heidar, K. (2000) *Norway: Elites on Trial*, Boulder: Westview Press.

Hjellbrekke, J. and Korsnes, O. (2010) 'Nedturar. Deklassering i det seinmoderne Norge', *Nytt Norsk Tidsskrift* 27 (1/2): 44–57.

Hylland, A. (2009) 'Hva bør gjøres når svært mange høyesterettsdommere er inhabile?', *Lov og Rett* 48 (2): 112–118.

Hönnige, C. (2007) *Verfassungsgericht, Regierung, und Opposition – Die vergleichende Analyse eines Spannungsdreiecks*, Wiesbaden,:VS Verlag.

——— (2009) 'The Electoral Connection: How the Pivotal Judge Affects Oppositional Success at European Constitutional Courts', *West European Politics* 32 (5): 963–984.

Jennings, M. K. and Markus, G. B. (1984) 'Partisan Orientations over the Long Haul: Results from the Three-Wave Political Socialization Panel Study', *American Political Science Review* 78 (4): 1000–1018.

Johnson, T. R. (2003) 'The Supreme Court, the Solicitor General, and the Separation of Powers', *American Politics Research* 31 (4): 426–451.

Kjønstad, A. (1999) 'Er Høyesterett statsvennlig?', *Lov og Rett* 38 (2): 97–122.

Kristjánsson, M. (2010) 'Er gift med staten', *Klassekampen,* 20 February

Lewis-Beck, M., Jacoby, W., Norpoth, H. and Weisberg, H. (2008) *The American Voter Revisited*, Ann Arbor: The University of Michigan Press.

Lund, K. (1987) 'Kontroll av Staten i Statens Egne Domstoler', *Lov og Rett* 48 (4): 211–227.

Magalhaes, P. C. (2003) *The Limits of Judicialization: Legislative Politics and Constitutional Review in the Iberian Democracies*, Colombus: Ohio State University.

Magnussen, A.-M. (2005) 'The Norwegian Supreme Court and Equitable Considerations: Problematic Aspects of Legal Reasoning', *Scandinavian Political Studies* 28 (1): 69–89.

Nylund, A. (2010) 'Mixing Past and Future: The Making of a Nordic Legal Culture 1850–2050' in Sunde, J. Ø. and Skodvin, K. E. (eds) *Rendezvous of European Legal Cultures*, Bergen: Fagbokforlaget, pp. 167–181.

Pedersen, D. (1994) 'Hvor 'blind' er fru Justitia?', *Aftenposten*, 10 May.

Pellegrina, L. D. and Garoupa, N. (2012) 'Choosing Between the Government and the Regions: An Empirical Analysis of the Italian Constitutional Court Decisions', *European Journal of Political Research* 52 (4): 558–580.

Pinello, D. R. (1999) 'Linking Party to Judicial Ideology in American Courts: A Meta-Analysis', *Justice System Journal* 20 (3): 219–254.

Rokkan, S. (1967) 'Geography, Religion, and Social Class: Crosscutting Cleavages in Norwegian Politics' in Lipset, S. M. and Rokkan, S. (eds) *Party Systems and Voter Alignments: Cross-National Perspectives*, New York: Free Press, pp. 367–444.

Rosenthal, H. and Voeten, E. (2007) 'Measuring Legal Systems', *Journal of Comparative Economics* 35 (4): 711–728.

Ryssdal, A. (2006) 'Årstale 2006 - Rettssikkerhet i forvaltningen - hvilke muligheter har du til å vinne frem', *Advokatbladet* 45 (11): 1–11.

Segal, J. A. and Spaeth, H. J. (2002) *The Supreme Court and the Attitudinal Model Revisited*, New York: Cambridge.

Smith, C. (2003) 'Domstolsadministrasjonen - bakgrunn og prinsipper for reformen', *Jussens Venner* 38: 1–7.

Smith, E. (1993) *Høyesterett og Folkestyret: Prøvingsretten Overfor Lover*, Oslo: Universitetsforlaget.

Tate, C. N. (1981) 'Personal Attribute Models of the Voting Behavior of U.S. Supreme Court Justices: Liberalism in Civil Liberties and Economics Cases, 1946–1978', *American Political Science Review* 75 (2): 355–367.

Tate, C. N. and Handberg, R. (1991) 'Time Binding and Theory Building in Personal Attribute Models of Supreme Court Voting Behavior, 1916–1988', *American Journal of Political Science* 35 (2): 460–480.

Tate, C. N. and Sittiwong, P. (1989) 'Decision Making in the Canadian Supreme Court: Extending the Personal Attributes Model Across Nations', *Journal of Politics* 51 (4): 900–916.

Torgersen, U. (1963) 'The Role of the Supreme Court in the Norwegian Political System' in Schubert, G. (ed.) *Judicial Decision-Making*, New York: The Free Press of Glencoe, pp. 221–244.

Vaubel, R. (2009) 'Constitutional Courts as Promoters of Political Centralization: Lessons for the European Court of Justice', *European Journal of Law and Economics* 28 (3): 203–222.

Voeten, E. (2007) 'The Politics of International Judicial Appointments: Evidence for the European Court of Human Rights', *International Organization* 61 (4): 669–701.

— (2008) 'The Impartiality of International Judges: Evidence from the European Court of Human Rights', *American Political Science Review* 102 (4): 417–433.

Wiklund, O. (2008) 'The Reception Process in Sweden and Norway' in Stone Sweet, A. and Keller, H. (eds) *A Europe of Rights: The Impact of the European Convention on Human Rights on National Legal Systems*, Oxford: Oxford University Press, pp. 165–228

Willoch, K. (2002) *Myter og virkelighed:. Om begivenheter frem til våre dager med utgangspunkt i perioden 1965–1981*, Oslo: Cappelen.

Wold, T. (1964) 'Domstolenes deltakelse i justisforvaltningen', *Lov og Rett* 3: 385–400.

Zeisberg, M. (2009) 'Should We Elect the US Supreme Court?', *Perspectives on Politics* 7 (4): 785–803.

Østlid, H. (1988) *Dommeratferd i dissenssaker*, Oslo: Universitetsforlaget.

Chapter Eight

'The Super Legislators': Supreme Court Justices as the Guardians of the Constitution

In this chapter, we focus our attention on that special subset of cases involving issues the Court has identified as especially consequential and salient. These cases are heard and decided in plenary session in order to ensure that the maximum number of justices has a hand in determining the Court's final output. Plenary sessions are convened either to correct previous rulings of the Court, thereby affecting the development of the law, or to address the degree to which laws passed by the legislature are in violation of the Constitution. This latter type of decision – *judicial review* – squarely addresses the relationship between the branches of government. In one sense, the Court moves much closer to the other two branches, becoming – in the words of former law professor and Supreme Court Chief Justice Carsten Smith – 'a super legislature' (Smith 1975: 300). Howard and Steigerwalt succinctly address the importance of judicial behaviour when a Supreme Court moves into the mode of judicial review. Howard and Steigerwalt state that:

> Even within the constraints of the political system, judges make choices and those choices make and change policy. However, few assertions of judicial power have remained as troubling or as controversial as the power of judicial review. The most gripping examples of judicial policymaking are decisions to declare unconstitutional laws of Congress and the state legislatures. The conflict between elected representatives and the appointed judiciary is most pronounced in these situations, and the Court's decision is usually final (Howard and Steigerwalt 2012: 13).

Formally, all Norwegian courts have the authority to review whether a statute or administrative decision complies with the Constitution or with constitutional practice. But as Norway's final judicial authority, any case that has constitutional significance will ultimately land on the doorstep of the Supreme Court.[1]

Here, we explore judicial behaviour in decisions involving Sections 97 and 105 of the Norwegian Constitution. Section 97 prohibits *ex post facto* laws, and Section 105 guarantees that expropriation of private property shall be fully compensated. Since 'the practice of judicial review in Norway falls primarily under Sections 97 and 105 of the Constitution' (Nguyên-Duy 2011: 2n3), the present chapter's analysis of such decisions addresses the lion's share of this consequential form of judicial behaviour.

---

1. Howard and Steigerwalt's assessment is with a few modifications applicable to the Norwegian context of judicial review (*see* Sunde 2012: 60–63).

Figure 8.1 shows the incidence of the 307 such decisions the Supreme Court has handed down between 1841 and 2011 – the period for which data are available. In the 1925 to 2010 period – during which time plenary or Grand Chamber sessions have operated and whose decisions we will specifically examine in this chapter – the Court has addressed Sections 97 and/or 105 a total of 46 times (*see* Figure 8.2). The upper panel of Figure 8.2 shows that the frequency of judicial review was prominent in the post-World War II era. The lower panel of Figure 8.2 shows the 26 plenary decisions in which the justices failed to agree on the outcome of judicial review. In the final part of this chapter, we will analyse the justices' votes in these 26 rulings.

Although the relative infrequency of the Court's exercising its power of judicial review in plenary sessions has contributed to keeping it out of the public eye, two landmark decisions served as public awakenings. The first of these decisions occurred in the 1976 *Kløfta* ruling (Rt-1976–1) when the justices narrowly (9–8) rejected a 1973 act of Parliament as violating Section 105 of the Constitution's prohibition of expropriation without full compensation.[2] Immediately after the

Figure 8.1: Incidents of Decisions on the Constitution's Sections 97 and 105, Norwegian Supreme Court

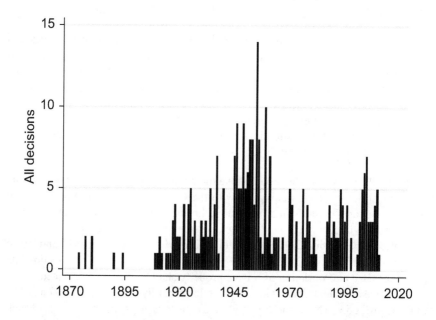

---

2.   The 9–8 vote concerned the constitutional issue of full compensation. In the *Kløfta decision*, the justices also addressed a number of separate issues.

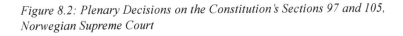

Figure 8.2: Plenary Decisions on the Constitution's Sections 97 and 105, Norwegian Supreme Court

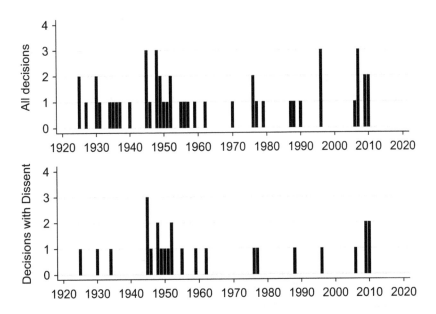

decision, University of Oslo law professor Torstein Eckhoff – the author of the authoritative book on legal method, legal realism and equitable considerations (1971) – was quoted in the Labour Party newspaper *Arbeiderbladet* as saying that the Court's ruling could be characterised as a 'political' decision. When the editorial of the conservative newspaper *Morgenbladet* wrote that Eckhoff's view was 'pure nonsense', Eckhoff retorted that the Court decision was political simply because law and politics are intertwined. He pointed out that the *Kløfta decision* resolved a political issue, and that the justices voted along ideological lines (Eckhoff 1976). As further proof of the justices' political behaviour on the High Court, Eckhoff (1975) cited the many cases in his own historical study of the Court's exercise of judicial review – *The Supreme Court as the Guardian of the Constitution* – published the year preceding the *Kløfta decision*. Whereas Eckhoff's historical study of politicised judicial behaviour in judicial review was prescient, his forecast of the frequency of judicial review decisions was not. In his 1975 study Eckhoff concluded that the Supreme Court's authority of judicial review was unquestionable, but he doubted that this authority would be exercised to any significant extent any time soon (Eckhoff 1975: 202).

The second national awakening involved the 2010 *Ship Owner's Taxation* case (Rt-2010–143). As we noted in Chapter Five, this case has been identified as one of the most important decisions of the Court in modern times (*see* Høgberg 2010b: 735–744). In a 6–5 plenary decision, the Court struck down as unconstitutional a taxation statute passed by the *Storting*. A Court majority found that the statute violated Section 97 of the Constitution, thereby barring the government from collecting a potential tax income of 21 billion NOK (USD 3.547 bn).[3] The public debate that immediately followed the announcement of the Court's decision was less concerned with the Court's power to strike down an act of Parliament than with whether the justices had acted on their policy preferences when deciding the case, since the justices' votes correlated so intimately with the nature of their appointing government (*see* Nguyên-Duy 2011).

Two key Constitutional Sections – 97 and 105

The two constitutional sections we address here are fundamental to a nation's rule of law. The Norwegian Constitution's Section 97 prohibits *ex post facto* laws and succinctly states that no law may be applied retroactively (*Ingen Lov maa gives tilbagevirkende Kraft*). The principles of security under the law, fairness, predictability, and the absence of arbitrariness, justify Section 97's *ex post facto* prohibition. From a court-based point of view, the constitutional provision is one of the Supreme Court's tools for curbing what the justices consider to be parliamentary excesses. If an emboldened parliamentary majority were to attempt to implement legislation that ran roughshod over this right, the Court could intervene with a constitutional mandate. As we shall see later in this chapter, however, the ban is not absolute. Justices have found ways to interpret the ban so that it can be circumvented.

The Norwegian Constitution's Section 105 prohibits expropriation of property without full compensation from the state treasury. (*Fordrer Statens Tarv, at Nogen maa afgive sin rørlige eller urørlige Eiendom til offentlig Brug, saa bør han have fuld Erstatning af Statskassen.*) Here too the principles of security under the rule of law, fairness, predictability, and the absence of arbitrariness justify the section.

Although the two clauses are separate, each containing comprehensible principles in concise language, legal theorists understand them to be closely related. The influential legal scholar Ragnar Knoph (1894–1938), whose legacy has been so strong that the recurrent legal review of Norwegian laws bears his name – *Knophs oversikt over Norges rett* – specifically states that 'no one can be in doubt that sections 97 and 105 are closely related to one another, although that is not directly apparent by the text'. A common 'direction', 'purpose' and 'character' link the sections. The sections have an extensive legal range and, as Knoph puts it, their 'field of action cannot be separated' (Knoph 1939, in Høgberg 2010a: 396–397).

---

3.   Based on the average exchange rate of 5.92 NOK/USD in February 2010. Online. Available http://www.norges-bank.no/Statistikk/Valutakurser/valuta/USD/ (last accessed 15 November 2014).

This notion that Sections 97 and 105 have a common conceptual core is upheld in legal scholarship (e.g. Andenæs and Fliflet 2006: 444–445), and the Supreme Court acknowledges it as well. Take, for example, Justice Liv Gjølstad's majority opinion in the plenary *Thunheim* ruling (Rt-1996–1440: 1448) that the two Sections are closely connected. The legal community reprimands justices when they fail to recognise the sections' common core in their opinions. For instance, the legal scholar Benedikte Moltumyr Høgberg (2010a: 394–401) was critical of Justice Magnus Matningsdal's majority opinion in the *Ullern Terrasse* decision (Rt-2007–1281) for its failure to acknowledge the close association between the sections. To the degree that justices are aware of and respond to their perceived audiences (Baum 2008), this type of criticism may not be without consequence.

Sections 97 and 105 have remained unchanged since the Constitution was adopted in 1814. Hence, the frequency of interpretive readings that justices have given the sections has changed over time. We hypothesise that this change can be linked to two broad sets of forces: the context of the times and the nature of the justices. Historical time, political context, and legislation can be identified as contextual forces that can create opportunities and/or a need for a change in interpretation. On the other hand, the backgrounds, attitudes and values of justices are more immediate forces that might also account for the Supreme Court's changing interpretation of the two sections. The close conceptual relationship of the two constitutional sections makes it appropriate for us to analyse them jointly.

Judicial review

Despite the importance of judicial review in a parliamentary democracy that recognises the principle of separation of powers and the ideal of protections for minority rights, the power of judicial review is nowhere to be found in the Norwegian Constitution.[4] The Norwegian historian Jens Arup Seip boldly argued that judicial review was a conspiracy and was deliberately constructed by the *l'ancien régime* in the 1880s, prior to the dawn of parliamentarism in 1884. True to his stylistic form, Seip argued that judicial review was a reactionary ploy: 'judicial review was a stick deliberately thrown into the wheel of democracy' (1965: 407). Eckhoff (1975: 202f) observed that judicial review actively entered Norwegian politics at the same time as the King's veto waned. According to Eckhoff, judicial review in this sense remains the functional equivalent of the King's veto and serves as a conservative brake on a too populist legislature.

Holmøyvik (2007) points out that Norway was the first country after the United States to develop judicial review, but he rejects Seip's conspiracy thesis and modifies Eckhoff's timing thesis. Holmøyvik establishes that the initial practice of judicial review was a creation of the courts and judicial behaviour alone.

---

4. Here too is the Norwegian Supreme Court similar to its American counterpart. In neither country is this immense judicial power constitutionally spelled out.

Smith (1993) and Slagstad (1990) argue that facts plainly falsify Seip's thesis and weaken Eckhoff's interpretation of the origin of judicial review. Judicial review was established long before 1884 and was not at all linked to the introduction of parliamentarism. Three arguments bear this out (Slagstad 1990). First, case law demonstrates that the Supreme Court introduced judicial review no later than 1854 (Rt-1854–93) and that Chief Justice Peder Carl Lasson explicitly penned the new doctrine of judicial review in an 1866 decision (UfL VI 1866: 165).[5] There is also an argument that judicial review was initiated in a decision as early as 1822 (Smith 1993). Second, the practice of judicial review was theorised in legal scholarship in the 1860s. Third, the position of judicial review was already so strong that opposition to it was also clearly identified, especially through the leadership of Johan Sverdrup – the protagonist of the introduction of parliamentarism – who argued that the power of judicial review was the province of the parliament and executive branches and not that of the judiciary. Today, judicial review is established as a legal practice and considered to have constitutional rank. That is, the institution of judicial review is so legally and politically accepted as to amount to a constitutional practice.[6]

Establishing plenary sessions

In the 1920s the occurrence of a number of non-unanimous seven-justice panel decisions with contradictory outcomes spoke to the fact that decisional outcomes could easily depend on which justices participated on the panel (Eckhoff 1975: 200). They also spoke to the fact that the Court offered poor guidelines for lower courts if its decisions on similar issues changed from case to case, and they spoke to the more limited authority of Supreme Court rulings in which only a panel of justices, rather than the full Court, is involved in decisions raising constitutional issues.

Given the Court's standard decisional format of hearing cases in rotating panels (*see* Chapter Three), plenary decisions would presumably carry more weight. Simply put, that all the justices convene to reach a decision indicates that the case is *not* run-of-the-mill. In 1924 a pair of seven-justice panels reached contradictory decisions on identical cases concerning the constitutionality of tax legislation (Rt-1924–12; Rt-1924–18). Specifically, the second panel narrowly reversed (4–3) the equally narrow majority of the first panel. This 'through the looking glass' result prompted the Court to tread carefully when, in the following year, it confronted a similar situation. In 1925 the Court was again asked to determine the constitutionality of a pair of identical tax laws. This time, however, the Court

---

5. Before Carsten Smith became Chief Justice in 1991, he praised Chief Justice Lasson's stance on judicial review as 'the Norwegian version of Chief Justice Marshall' (1990: 429). But, adds Eivind Smith (1993: 150), this does not mean the 1866 decision (UfL VI 1866) amounts to the Norwegian version of *Marbury v. Madison* (1803), since the practice of judicial review had already been established.

6. The legal underpinning of this constitutional practice can be found in *The Court Act*, Section 5; and *The Dispute Act*, Section 30–13.

availed itself of the rarely used possibility of hearing the cases in plenary session,[7] and, consequently, a pair of consistent decisions was rendered. In 1926 the *Storting* institutionalised this decisional procedure in *The Plenary Act*. It required the Court to hear a case in plenary session when three (in 1939 this was reduced to two) justices questioned the constitutionality of statute.[8]

In 2008, the Grand Chamber was instituted. It consists of 11 justices, including the Chief as the presiding justice. To a large degree Grand Chambers have replaced the need for plenary sessions in the Supreme Court. Since the creation of the Grand Chamber proceedings, plenary sessions have been convened only in extraordinary cases and when at least six justices call for them.

The practice of judicial review is now delineated in *The Dispute Act* Sections 30–12 and 30–13.[9] These sections, together with Section 5 of *The Court Act* (1915 and 2001), also specify that the Supreme Court can exercise its power of judicial review when the justices are convened in either a Grand Chamber or in plenary session. The Court cannot address constitutionality as a separate issue or in an isolated case. The constitutional issue must be addressed as part of a case that has been appealed to the Court and that the Appeals Selection Committee has docketed. If the Court rules a statute to be in violation of the Constitution, the formal and immediate consequence is that the statute is rendered inapplicable and irrelevant to the case at hand. In the longer term, the statute must be changed so the Court does not overrule it in a new case. Of course, the justices can 'save' a statute by narrowly interpreting it so that is not in conflict with the Constitution.

The development and application of legal doctrines in judicial review

A legal doctrine is a principle of law established through earlier decisions. Doctrines are initiated in one or several decisions and may be applied in later decisions in ways that exert a 'gravitational force' on those decisions. A doctrine is never neutral, but serves as a way of ordering a field of reality and limits the range of likely outcomes. It also contributes to a court's stability, legitimacy, and efficiency. Johnson, Spriggs, and Wahlbeck argue that a doctrine can serve 'as a way to legitimize the judiciary and to insulate it from outside political

---

7. Indeed, Eckhoff (1975) notes that these decisions (Rt-1925–588; Rt-1925–769) were the first times a *full* Court exercised the power of judicial review.

8. Presently, in constitutional cases, the Chief Justice may convene the Court in plenary session, and there are several other conditions, related to non-constitutional issues, that can require a plenary session.

9. The 2005 *Dispute Act* Section 30–13 requires that in cases of judicial review the Court shall notify the Ministry of Justice. According to the Act, the government has a right to participate in the case to the extent that it is necessary to attend to the public interests in cases where legal rules may come into conflict. If the government decides to be present during the hearing of the case, the Court can require the government to address in writing its views on the facts and legal questions of the case. This task is performed by the office of the Government Advocate, which is organised directly under the office of the Prime Minister.

attacks' (2012: 168). When a court's institutional legitimacy and independence are sufficiently established, the court gains a more secure position from which it can base its policy-making authority. Also, one can hypothesise that the greater the external threats to the legitimacy of the judiciary, the more the court prefers to 'entrench its decisions' (2012: 178) in precedents and doctrines. This position is consistent with theories on institutional development, change, and outcome. 'Decision-makers create rules in order to structure outcomes in ways they prefer [...] Political decision-makers, in short, recognise that rules can affect outcomes, and they attempt to structure rules to promote their preferences over outcomes' (Johnson *et al.* 2012: 180, 181).[10]

Legal doctrines in the legal literature

In the Norwegian legal literature on the Constitution, the doctrine concerning the Constitution's Section 97 ban on retroactive laws has been more fully explored than the guarantee of full compensation found in Section 105. At its inception in the Constitution of 1814, the ban on *ex post facto* laws was absolute and applied to all areas of legislation (Andenæs and Fliflet 2006). However, a consensus eventually developed that recognised that the development of society required some aspects of legislation to operate retroactively – either as a tool to preempt the ossification of the relationship between laws and society, or to retain legislation as a potent tool for effective intervention in the development of society. One has been concerned that the 'hard core' of criminal law should be especially guarded against *ex post facto* laws. This hard core, however, has become smaller and smaller (Høgberg 2010b: 697, 698).

From the original position that a prohibition of *ex post facto* laws was absolute, three distinct stages in the development of that legal doctrine reducing the extent of that prohibition can be discerned.[11] First, during the nineteenth century, under the influence of European and American law, the *doctrine of acquired rights* emerged. It held that only rights that were possessed by a state's legal subjects were protected against retroactive laws. In its Norwegian version, tensions between the general application of the doctrine and its specific applications resulted in efforts to adapt the doctrine to specific subfields of

---

10. Johnson *et al.* (2012) use *stare decisis* as their foundational concept. In this chapter, doctrines, norms and standards will be used more or less interchangeably since they tap into the same domain, but basically vary in their degree of abstraction. They serve the same purpose when justices of the Court make efforts to establish stability, legitimacy, and efficiency. When studying the Court's decisions, scholars find that these concepts can be sequenced and ordered hierarchically, and sometimes that the ordering of concepts is inconsequential (e.g. Høgberg 2010b: 713, 725; Smith 2010). We remind ourselves of Eckhoff's dictum that one should not take justices seriously when they refer to 'principles' (2001: 21). Justices, Eckhoff writes, are better at arriving at decisions than in arguing for them. We use the concepts interchangeably since we are more interested in the justices' decisions than in the way they are justified.

11. The following paragraphs draw heavily on Høgberg's incisive discussions on the Constitution's Section 97 (2010a: chapter six, 2010b: esp. pp. 702–713).

the law.[12] This contextualised version of the doctrine was referred to as *the doctrine of legal rule* (Andenæs and Fliflet 2006: 446). Ultimately, attempts to fix the doctrine to legal subfields and apply it coherently did not succeed.

Second, during the 1920s and 1930s, legal scholars acknowledged that the fields and subfields to which doctrines could be specifically applied could not be fixed once and for all. Rather, the interpretation of Section 97 needed to be pragmatically adapted to the needs and general developments of society (Augdahl 1938; Knoph 1939). Specifically, interpretations of Section 97 needed to take account of the degree to which the effects of any retroactive laws could be considered fair or unfair. According to Knoph, in order to determine the degree of fairness one would need to assess the consequences of the legislation 'in light of the broader circumstances'.[13] This position was coined the *doctrine of fairness* and later more assertively as *the standard theory*. The doctrine of legal rule and the standard theory should not be considered polar opposites. Rather, they should be understood as two complementing approaches that could be applied by the justices as appropriate (Andenæs and Fliflet 2006: 446).

Third, in the 1970s, the legal scholar Carl August Fleischer (1975) argued that Section 97 could be interpreted to accommodate two legal rules. One rule established a ban on adding a direct *de facto burden* to established acts. The other rule established a protection against indirect interference in established legal practice.[14] Fleischer's two legal rules turned the *doctrine of acquired rights* on its head. Except in special cases, established rights were *not* protected against retroactive laws (Høgberg 2010b: 704). Although Fleischer's two legal rules have found their way into recent Supreme Court rulings, they remain contested because they fail to correspond to the succinct language of Section 97 and they seem to blur the predictability of the law.

Levels of Judicial scrutiny

The landmark *Kløfta decision* (Rt-1976–1) revived judicial review in the post-World War II era. In its decision, the Court narrowly ruled (9–8) against the party claiming a public interest on the constitutional question of full compensation. A central legacy of the *Kløfta decision* was the Court's creation of three categories for the intensity of judicial review.[15] Writing for the majority, Justice Knut Blom stated that if judicial review concerned

12. Across 160 pages, the legal scholar T. H. Aschehoug in 1893 listed in great detail how the ban on retroactive laws was to be understood and applied to, at that time, all conceivable legal subfields (Høgberg 2010b: 702).
13. The term 'in light of the broader circumstances', or 'in light of the bigger picture', stems from our makeshift translation of the Norwegian term *'helhetsvurdering'*. To the best of our knowledge, a precise English term does not exist for this rather vague term that indicates a final weighing and harmonisation of the facts and legal forces of the case.
14. On 'direct' and 'indirect', *see* Andenæs and Fliflet (2006: 444).
15. In the American system, the intensity of judicial review and the hierarchical structure of constitutional norms is known as the 'preferred position principle'.

individuals' personal freedom and safety, the Court has the greatest authority and obligation to rule legislation unconstitutional. As an intermediate standard, the Court has less authority when reviewing economic rights. Finally, on constitutional issues concerning the competence of or operations between the other branches of government, the Court must defer to the views of the *Storting* (Rt-1976–1: 5–6). Later Court rulings have revisited this categorisation over and over again.

Justice Blom's brief discussion of the levels of judicial scrutiny made no references to the bases for these ideas. A likely source, though, is Carsten Smith's speech to the National Conference of Judges in Tromsø on 28 June 1974. Printed in the national legal journal, *Lov og Rett*, Smith (1975) referred to the groundbreaking shift in American law in 1937 when the U.S. Supreme Court gave up its strong protection of economic rights and, under both the New Deal and Warren Courts, became a stalwart advocate for individual civil liberties and civil rights. Smith stated that he was uncertain about the future of judicial review in Norway, but he strongly urged the Norwegian Supreme Court to take the opportunity to establish that personal freedoms are positioned above economic rights in the hierarchy of democratic values, and therefore that personal freedoms should enjoy greater constitutional protections.[16]

Legal doctrines in Supreme Court decisions

In cases dealing with Sections 97 and 105 of the Constitution, the Supreme Court justices neither addressed nor referred to the formal legal doctrines or Fleischer's legal rules when writing their opinions for a long time. Indeed, it was not until the Court's 1996 decisions on social security rights in the *Borthen decision* (Rt-1996–1415) and the *Thunheim decision* (Rt-1996–1440) that the justices made any such explicit references.[17] Accordingly, when writing the Court's majority opinion in the *Borthen decision*, Justice Tore Schei referred to the fairness doctrine and Fleischer's two legal rules.[18] Schei also introduced a new term when he wrote that the case needed to be assessed 'in light of the broader circumstances'.

---

16. Obviously, Smith was familiar with footnote four – 'the most famous footnote in constitutional law' – of the 1938 United States Supreme Court decision in *United States v. Carolene Products Co.* (304 U.S. 144) in which the Court applied a rational basis review to the economic regulation that was decided in the case, but suggested a new level of review in cases that dealt with the rights enshrined in the first ten amendments.

17. Kjønstad (1997: 260) notes that the fairness doctrine was applied to but not mentioned by the justices in the 1962 *Gullklausul decision* (Rt-1962–369). Kjønstad also observes that in the *Borthen decision* (Rt-1996–1415) none of the justices discussed which doctrine should be used when interpreting Section 97 in the case at hand.

18. The 1996 *Borthen decision* had one outcome but three voices: Nine justices agreed with Justice Tore Schei's majority opinion; five justices agreed with Justice Steinar Tjomsland's concurrence, while Justice Finn Backer wrote his own concurrence. Neither Justice Schei nor Justice Backer referred to Fleischer who had coined the legal term they used.

Perhaps the most important consequence of the Court's decision in the *Borthen* case was that the *doctrine of fairness* was to be used when applying Section 97. Only when the effect of a law was 'clearly unreasonable or unfair' would it violate Section 97 of the Constitution. Høgberg (2010b: 705) notes that when Justice Schei phrased the new norm or doctrine '*clearly unreasonable or unfair*', the Court interpreted the older *fairness doctrine* more strictly than was intended by its authors.[19] The new composite norm combined the term of 'unreasonable' from earlier Court decisions, with Knoph and Augdahl's term of 'unfair' and then added the modifier 'clearly'. In so doing, the Court intended to create a norm against which subsequent reviews of Section 97 could be judged, and Schei's new term became one of the Court's new norms, or doctrines, for the next ten years. In arguing for the new norm, Justice Tore Schei (in Rt-1996–1415: 1431) opined that in cases where Section 97 was addressed, the Court should apply the doctrine of 'clearly unreasonable or unfair' and not enter into a trade-off between the interests of parties since that would smack of politics and be less appropriate as a legal norm. Justice Finn Backer, however, when writing his separate concurrence, took issue with Schei's new concept. Backer stated that by applying the term 'clearly unreasonable or unfair' the Court would in fact move into the domain of the law-maker, which eventually would shift the separation of powers between the courts and the legislature to the advantage of the courts. Backer concludes (Rt-1996–1415: 1439): 'Neither of these outlined developments appears to me to be desirable.'

The doctrinal and procedural framework established in the 1996 *Borthen* and *Thunheim* decisions remained unaltered for ten years.[20] But in the significant 2006 plenary taxation case *Arves trafikkskole* (Rt-2006–293), the Court again addressed the ban on retroactive laws. Writing for the 11–4 majority, Justice Toril Øie bypassed Fleischer's two legal rules and introduced the new doctrine of '*compelling societal considerations*'. This doctrine can be understood as occupying a position between an *absolute* ban on retroactive laws and the fairness doctrine (Høgberg 2010b: 708). In effect, the Court applied the new doctrine by stating that taxes cannot be imposed retroactively without *compelling societal considerations*. The majority of the Court decided that this criterion was not met in the present case.

In 2007, the Court addressed the vexatious issue of landlord-to-renter land transfer in three plenary decisions.[21] Writing for a 7–0 majority in *Ullern Terrasse* (Rt-2007–1281), Justice Magnus Matningsdal applied the fairness doctrine,

---

19. Kjønstad (1997: 287) concludes that this version of the fairness doctrine establishes a high threshold before a statute can be deemed to be in violation of the Constitution.

20. The conclusions in the 1996 *Borthen decision* also affected the two unanimous five-justice *Allseas decision* (Rt-2005–855) and *Enkepensjon decision* (Rt-2006–262).

21. In Norway, one can own a house that is on a plot of land owned by someone else – a property owner who collects rent for the land. The Supreme Court cases involved *inter alia* a dispute over a new law that expanded the renter's opportunity to take over the land. Rt-2007–1281, Rt-2007–1306, and Rt-2007–1308.

referred to Fleischer's two rules, and stated that the Court needed to perform a decision 'in light of the broader circumstances'. This conclusion establishes a clear link to the *Borthen decision* (Rt-1996–1415) (Høgberg 2010b: 708). The link was not absolute, however, because the Court also averred that a decision 'in light of the broader circumstances' must be based on a balance of interests of the parties involved. Thus, the doctrine of 'clearly unreasonable or unfair' – stemming from the *Borthen decision* (Rt-1996–1415) – was not to be the basis of interpreting Section 97 in the *Ullern Terrasse decision* (Rt-2007–1281) nor in the parallel case of the *Tomtefeste decision* (Rt-2007–1306).[22] Høgberg notes that the Court reached its conclusion without offering any comments as to why it vacated the 'clearly unreasonable or unfair' doctrine established in the *Borthen decision* (Rt-1996–1415) (Høgberg 2010b: 708).

In 2008, several ship owners sued the government for violating the Constitution's ban on retroactive laws when it demanded the ship owners pay taxes according to new tax legislation (*see* Chapter Five). After contradictory outcomes in two separate trial courts, both the ship owners and the government appealed. Shortly thereafter, the *Ship Owner's Taxation* cases received fast-track status. The Supreme Court's Appeals Selection Committee allowed the appeals to bypass the appeal courts. The cases were then combined, and the Chief Justice decided the Court would hear the case in plenary session (Rt-2010–143: Section 65).

Prior to oral arguments in the *Ship Owner's Taxation* case, Høgberg observed that the status of the legal field of retroactive laws was 'hesitant, inexact, and ambiguous' (2010b: 695). The Supreme Court justices had failed to achieve judicial unity and standardisation, inasmuch as the earlier decisions effectively appeared as 'melting pots of different theories of retroactiveness' (2010b: 709). The 'common denominator' of approaches the justices had taken over the years was to reach decisions 'in light of the broader circumstances' (2010b: 710). To reach a decision using this rule appeared to constitute the justices' 'method for solving issues of retroactiveness' (Høgberg 2010a: 51).

In February 2010, the Supreme Court handed down its decision in the *Ship Owner's Taxation* case (Rt-2010–143). The justices ruled 6–5 that the government's attempt to impose 21 billion NOK in taxes was indeed a violation of Section 97 of the Constitution. As we discussed in greater detail in Chapter Five, what is especially interesting about the *Ship Owner's* case was not that it generated 'a complex interaction between [decisional] norms and different types of facts', but that it seemed that the majority and minority factions had made up their minds as to the outcome of the case '*before* they started to discuss the legal forces of the case, that their disagreement persisted almost consistently throughout their discussion' and that it appears that some of their discussions only were 'a play to the gallery' (Høgberg 2010b: 716, 713, 715).

---

22. *Ullern Terrasse Tomtefeste I* (Rt-2007–1281) addressed people's homes whereas *Tomtefeste II* (Rt-2007–1306) addressed people's vacation homes, both on leased land.

Writing for the six-justice majority, Justice Karl Arne Utgård revisited the three categories of intensity of judicial review established by the Court in the 1976 *Kløfta decision*. Utgård held that 'within each category rights of vastly different types exist' (Rt-2010–143: Section 138). With this redefinition, the majority granted the Court greater discretion in its application of judicial review and moved the economic interests of the ship owners closer to the Constitution's Section 97 protection.

Summary

The Court established the doctrine of 'clearly unreasonable or unfair' in the *Borthen decision* (Rt-1996–1415). A decade later, the Court introduced the doctrine of 'compelling societal considerations' in the *Arves trafikkskole decision* (Rt-2006–293). These two doctrines are 'polar opposites' (Høgberg 2010b: 710f). The former has its roots in the 1930s and was developed to weaken the ban on retroactive laws in order to promote the government's modernisation of society. The latter has more recent origins and appears to have the effect of reining in the government and the promises of governing through legislation. This doctrinal shift corresponds to the changing outcomes of the plenary cases on the ban on retroactive laws that the Court has handed down. Since the turn of the millennium, Justice Jens Edvin Skoghøy (2011: 256) observes, 'one can detect a clear development in the direction of giving the citizens greater protection against retroactive legislation'.

Høgberg, however, concludes that the *Ship Owner's Taxation decision* fails to offer any kind of closure on the Court's development of doctrines. Rather, we are 'witnessing that the Supreme Court once again vacillates in key legal questions' (Høgberg 2010b: 720). This is evidenced by the uncompromising disagreement among the justices in the case and the lack of an indication in the change of the Court's decisional outputs. In fact, a close reading of key decisions indicates that the justices' choice of doctrine is inconsequential for the outcome of cases on retroactiveness (Høgberg 2010b: 724).

On the one hand, the failure to establish a general rule – a doctrine – for the ban on *ex post facto* laws demonstrates the difficulty of deducing one distinct doctrine from a concise constitutional section. This failure on the part of the Court confounds the legislature, which for all practical purposes needs to be able to understand and predict the behaviour of the Court as a veto player in the policy process taking place between the branches of government.

On the other hand, the failure to establish general and predictable doctrines – however little those doctrines may constrain the justices' votes – may also stem from the fact that the values of the justices influence the Court's outputs. Once values enter into negotiations, the likelihood of compromise is immediately reduced. One set of values that justices have advanced, and the legal community has recognised, is the degree to which justices support the government's need to redistribute the resources of society. Put differently, justices may be concerned about the proper role of the government in the economy and scope of the distributive effort on the part of the government. For instance, when writing the 17–0 majority decision in the *Borthen decision* (Rt-1996–1415), Justice Tore Schei agreed that the

> [B]uilding of the welfare state is strongly underlined as an element of importance for judicial review... It is also important to divert public resources where their need is greatest. Strong constraints on the ability to reorder priorities will – at least as a general rule – not take care of the welfare society and its needs (Rt-1996–1415: 1428).

However, when writing for the 6–5 minority in the *Ship Owner's Taxation* case (Rt-2010–143), Justice Matningsdal found that the welfare argument, and the deference to the *Storting*, did not sway a sufficient number of justices to win the case for the government party.

Law professor Asbjørn Kjønstad concluded in his close examination of the *Borthen decision* (Rt-1996–1415) and the *Thunheim decision* (Rt-1996–1440) that the 'common understanding in Norwegian legal literature is that the courts have considerable ... freedom ... concerning both the interpretation of the constitutional sections and the judicial review itself' (Kjønstad 1997: 120f). In the *Thunheim decision* (Rt-1996–1440), Kjønstad pointed out, the justices had the option of defining the collection of social security payments as either taxes or insurance premiums. Both definitions were equally legitimate, but the justices decided 16–1 that social security payments were taxes. In so doing, the justices' decision greatly improved the government's chance of winning the case.[23] Later, in his rebuttal to Justice Jan Skåre's (1997; 1999) indignant replies to the thesis that the Supreme Court was being too government friendly in the *Borthen* and *Thunheim* decisions, Kjønstad simply stated that '[i]n my opinion, from the day of their appointment, all justices have full freedom and independence in legal questions. Here the research question is how this freedom is used' (Kjønstad 1999: 102). We concur.

In the next section we apply the model of judicial behaviour that we have developed earlier in this book to systematically analyse Kjønstad's research question. Specifically, we test the notion that justices with prior employment experience in the government are more apt to vote for the litigant identified with the government's position in cases involving protections afforded in Sections 97 and 105 of the Norwegian Constitution.

---

23. The *Thunheim decision* (Rt-1996–1440) was handed down later the same day as the *Borthen decision* (Rt-1996–1415). The factions in the *Thunheim decision* upheld their same positions as in the *Borthen decision* but with the two changes: Justice Finn Backer turned his concurrence with the majority in the *Borthen decision* into dissent in the *Thunheim decision*; and the author of the main concurrence in the *Borthen decision*, Justice Steinar Tjomsland, vacated his concurrence in the *Borthen decision* and sided fully with the majority in the *Thunheim decision*.

Data

Our data were derived through a search of the *Lovdata.no* database for decisions that contained references to Sections 97 or 105 of the Norwegian Constitution between 1841 and May 2011.[24] This initial search resulted in a total of 480 decisions. Upon closer examination, however, 173 decisions were excluded because their reference to the constitutional sections was not central to the case or decision.[25] The remaining 307 cases contain both unanimous and non-unanimous decisions from plenary sessions as well as panels of three, five, seven, and 11 justices. It is from this pool of 307 decisions that we extracted the 26 plenary cases where (1) either one or both of the two constitutional sections were addressed, (2) one of the parties was a public or governmental body, and (3) the justices failed to agree on the outcome of the case before them (*see also* Figures 8.1 and 8.2).[26] These 26 decisions were handed down between 1925 and 2010 (*see* Table 8.1 for information on the decisions).

As the discussion earlier in this chapter suggests, these 26 decisions are not ordinary run-of-the-mill cases. They are the decisions in which the justices exercise the power of judicial review. There is no circumstance in which judicial decision making is of greater significance than it is in the instance of judicial review. First, these are the cases in which the justices address or tap key provisions in the Constitution, which is Norway's foundational political document. Second, the justices' decisions speak to the other two branches of government, which may readjust a country's political equilibrium. Third, the justices' decisions may well affect legal and political practice for years to come. And finally, the cases have been deemed so important that the entire Court hears them, rather than just a subset of five justices sitting as a panel, as is standard procedure.

Significantly, in the 26 cases we have identified for analysis, the justices failed to reach unanimity, and in so doing the Court failed to send an unambiguous signal to the political and legal communities. Thus, the Court fell short of its ambitions of ensuring 'uniformity, clarity and development of the law'.[27] This prompts the question: why? Indeed, since the wording of these sections has

---

24. Lovdata.no does not as of yet have complete and searchable records of all Supreme Court decisions since its beginning in 1815. Basically, prior to World War II, decisions are included in the searchable database if these decisions have been cited in more recent decisions. This criterion is a sign of them being important, if not, precedential decisions. Consequently, at this stage of our research, we are unable to control for any biases in case selection.

25. On closer inspection, the justices made references to Sections 97 and/or 105 that did not bear upon the case itself, or the references to these sections in the decisions were made in text quoted from lower courts and were not addressed by the justices. A few decisions were rendered prior to September 1864, at which time a newly passed act required that the justices publicise their votes.

26. We define a public or governmental body as an entity with governing authority, including the national government, counties, cities, and townships. Two Grand Chamber decisions are also included among the twenty-six decisions we analyse here: Rt-2009–1412 and Rt-2009–1423.

27. These ambitions were finally established and formalised in the late 1990s (Sunde 2012).

Table 8.1: Twenty-Six Non-Unanimous Plenary Decisions on Sections 97 and 105, Norwegian Supreme Court

Reference	Name (if any)	Type	Votes	97[ca]	105[cb]	Gov't/Publc
Rt-2010–1445	Mirsad Repak*	Criminal	11–6	5	0	Lost
Rt-2010–143	Rederibeskatning	Civil	6–5	5	1	Lost
Rt-2009–1423[d]		Criminal	10–1	0	0	Lost
Rt-2009–1412[d]		Criminal	10–1	4	0	Lost
Rt-2006–293	Arves Trafikkskole	Civil	11–4	5	0	Lost
Rt-1996–1440	Thunheim decision	Civil	16–1	4	5	Won
Rt-1988–276	Røstad decision	Civil	11–6	5	0	Lost
Rt-1977–24	Østensjø decision	Civil	12–5	0	4	Won
Rt-1976–1	Kløfta decision[e]	Civil	9–8	0	4	Lost
Rt-1962–369	Gullklausul decision II	Civil	12–5	4	0	Won
Rt-1959–306		Civil	13–4	2	0	Won
Rt-1955–525	Jeppesen II	Civil	14–1	2	3	Won
Rt-1952–1089	Hvalavgift decision	Civil	13–2	5	2	Won
Rt-1952–932	Meyer	Civil	9–4	3	0	Lost
Rt-1951–87	Opdahl	Civil	9–5	0	3	Won
Rt-1950–831	Nørve decision	Civil	10–5	0	3	Won
Rt-1949–224		Criminal	13–2	4	0	Won
Rt-1948–928		Civil	10–9	3	0	Won
Rt-1948–89	Morgenposten	Criminal	10–7	2	0	Won
Rt-1946–198	Klinge decision	Criminal	9–4	5	0	Won
Rt-1945–52	Stephanson decision II	Criminal	8–3	2	0	Won
Rt-1945–43		Criminal	7–2	4	0	Won
Rt-1945–26	Stephanson decision I	Criminal	6–4	5	0	Won
Rt-1934–997	Ellen Larsen*	Civil	14–7	0	4	Lost

Table 8.1 (*continued*)

Reference	Name (if any)	Type	Votes	97[ca]	105[cb]	Gov't/Publc
Rt-1930–381	Tveraamo Hansen*	Criminal	16–5	2	0	Won
Rt-1925–588	Odegaard*	Civil	13–7	2	0	Won

Notes: Popular names are not always given to Supreme Court decisions.

* = tentative names only.
[a] Number of parties mentioning constitutional Section 97 in the decision.
[b] Number of parties mentioning constitutional Section 105 in the decision.
[c] Government/other public party lost/won on the constitutional issue.
[d] Justice Jens Edvin Skoghøy voted in solitary minority twice. In the second decision (Rt-2009–1423) he reiterated his views from the first decision (Rt-2009–1412) handed down earlier the same day.
[e] In the *Kløfta decision*, the official vote is held to be 10–7, while others argue that the vote was 9–8 (Nadim 2013). Law professor Opsahl (1976) argues that Justice Sigurd Lorentzen cast an intermediate vote giving a 9–1–7 outcome. Speaking for the minority, Justice Lilly Bølviken stated, with reference to Section 97 (p. 26) that no retroactive effect was present in the case.

remained unchanged, what other forces might account for the differences in the justices' opinions? Specifically, we examine the political contexts surrounding the cases and the matrix of forces that we have shown to affect judicial behaviour in earlier chapters.

The analyses presented below examine 398 votes distributed across the 26 non-unanimous plenary decisions the Court made between 1925 and 2010. A total of 115 justices participated in the 26 plenary sessions under analysis. It must be noted, however, that there is substantial variation in the number of votes made by any individual justice.[28] Thus, there are sufficient votes to establish a voting profile for only a handful of justices.

Dependent Variable

Our dependent variable measures the individual justice's support for the public interest claim. It is scored as 1 if the justice votes for the governmental entity (*see* footnote 26, supra), 0 otherwise. Since our objective is to take soundings on the effects of an array of legal and non-legal forces on the individual justice's exercise of the power of judicial review, we include the standard set of independent variables that we have developed throughout the book. Given the nature of our data, we estimated our models using logit regression, and clustered our observations on both the case and the justice.

---

28. At one extreme is Sverre Grette, who voted in all 12 plenary sessions convened between the conclusion of World War II and 1955. At the other end are 25 justices who participated in only one plenary session each.

Analysis and findings

The Pre-World War II Period

The Court handed down three plenary non-unanimous decisions before the outbreak of the Second World War. Due to the dearth of biographical and legal career information on many of the 27 justices who participated in these early decisions, a full regression model including all of the independent variables cannot be applied to the 62 votes in these three decisions.[29] Accordingly, we specified a reduced model that includes four independent variables and estimated it on 61 of the 62 votes cast by the individual justices.

The results of the model estimation are displayed in Table 8.2. They indicate that older justices are significantly more likely than their younger counterparts to vote in favour of the private party ($p < .05$). The results also show that neither geography nor the nature of the justice (i.e. whether the justice is a permanent appointee, an interim appointee, or the Chief) has a systematic effect on the vote.

It is interesting that age is the one force that has some traction on the voting patterns in these decisions. Since the three decisions take place in the politically turbulent years between the First and Second World Wars, the effect of age indicates either a generational or an ageing effect. In the case of a generational effect, older justices bring to the Court values from a time when the government was expected to play a smaller role in society. In the case of an ageing effect, as the adage goes, justices may simply grow more conservative as they get older.

Table 8.2: Clustered Logit Estimates of Forces of Public Support in Sections 97 and 105 Non-Unanimous Plenary Decisions 1926–1934

	Coef.	T-stat	P > |t|
Oslo-Born	-0.951	-1.15	0.25
Interim Justice	0.534	0.59	0.55
Chief	0.589	0.37	0.71
Age	-0.126	-1.95*	0.05
Constant	7.862	2.43*	0.02

Notes: *$p < 0.05$. DV = Support for Government or Public Party. Dummy independent variables are coded 1 for quality indicated. Age and seniority are metric variables. Log Pseudo likelihood = -36.33. Wald Chi^2 = 9.37; Prob > Chi^2 = 0.05. Pseudo R^2 = .13. N = 61. Decisions = 3. Justices = 26.

---

29. Three justices – Ludvig Chr. A. Bade; Marius Cathrinius Backer; and Ditlef Hvistendahl Christiansen – were 68 years or older in the last of the three pre-war decisions, in 1934. In addition to the transition of justices in the 1920s and 1930s, five justices had passed away during World War II, leaving many vacancies to be filled by the Labour government in the immediate post-war period (Sandmo 2005: 321).

The post-World War II period

Table 8.3 displays the coefficient estimates of the fully specified model for the plenary session votes in the post-war era. Although a number of forces fail to meet conventional levels of statistical security, three independent variables stand out as significant.

First, justices with a background in the Office of the Government Advocate are more likely to vote in favour of the private party. In our data set 17 justices had served in this office prior to taking a seat on the High Bench. In total, these 17 justices cast 48 votes, 65 per cent of which were in support of the private party. Except for his single vote as associate justice in favour of the public party in the *Thunheim decision* (Rt-1996–1440), in non-unanimous decisions Chief Justice Schei voted for the private party at every other opportunity (n = 5).

Second, the effect of experience in the Legislation Department falls just short of the conventional .05 significance threshold. Its slightly weaker effect (p = 0.07) suggests – with the appropriate caveats – that justices with this background also tend to favour the private party. Thirty-three justices had a background in the Legislation Department; they cast a total of 101 votes in the 23 decisions. However, as might be expected, given the moderate significance level, there is no clear pattern in their voting behaviour. For those 16 justices who participated in at least three decisions, only five had a consistent voting history. Justices Vera Louise Holmøy and Helge Klæstad always voted for the public party, while Justices Karin Maria Bruzelius, Einar Hanssen, and Elisabeth Schweigaard Selmer unfailingly found for the private party.[30]

Third, the analysis also demonstrates the effect of appointing government. Socialist government appointees are – as we would expect, given the results of the model estimates from earlier chapters – significantly more likely to vote in favour of the public party. These justices cast a total of 215 votes, 64 per cent of which were for the litigant claiming a public interest. Non-socialist appointees, however, do not evince as clear a pattern. To be sure, they are substantially *less* supportive of public claims than their socialist appointed counterparts; yet, even so, 50 per cent of the time (in 60 out of 121 votes) they ruled against the private party.

Sub-period

For the post-World War II period, judicial review decisions can be cut in different ways. Several scholars hold that the famous *Kløfta decision* (Rt-1976–1) changed the judicial climate and augured a new era of judicial review (Smith, 1993). Prior to 1976, the Supreme Court had not fully realised its judicial review potential. But in the *Kløfta decision*, the justices declared a statute unconstitutional for

---

30. Justice Jørgen Berner Thrap participated in ten decisions and voted eight times in favour of the public party. He is an influential justice in this analysis: were we to control for Thrap's votes, the effect of the Legislation Department would remain negative and turn significant (b = -2.19; p < 0.03).

Table 8.3: Clustered Logit Estimates of Forces of Public Support in Sections 97 and 105 Non-Unanimous Plenary Decisions 1945–2010

	Coef.	T-stat	P > |t|
Sex	-0.802	-1.40	.16
Oslo-Born	0.244	0.74	.46
Bergen Law Degree	-1.723	-1.26	.21
Private Practice	-0.287	-0.80	.42
Law Professor	0.337	0.81	.42
Earlier Judge	-0.299	-1.01	.31
Government Advocate	-1.123	-2.79**	.01
Legislation Department	-0.686	-1.83*	.07
Public Prosecutor	-0.010	-0.02	.99
Socialist Appointee	0.796	2.63**	.01
Interim Justice	0.713	0.48	.63
Chief	-0.236	-0.34	.74
Age	-0.021	-0.71	.48
Seniority	0.023	0.73	.47
Constant	1.564	0.89	.38

Notes: *$p < 0.10$; **$p < 0.01$. DV = Support for Government or Public Party. Dummy independent variables are coded 1 for quality indicated. Age and seniority are non-dummy variables. Log Pseudolikelihood = -197.52. Wald Chi^2 = 25.34; Prob> Chi^2= 0.001. Pseudo R^2 = .09. N = 320; Decisions = 23; Justices = 90.

the first time in 50 years (Smith 1993). And since 1976 – writes Justice Jens Edvin Skoghøy – judicial review has both increased and become more intense, especially for the review of retroactive laws. Skoghøy concludes that the most recent development of judicial review has strengthened the citizens' protection against retroactive legislation (Skoghøy 2011).

In the pre-*Kløfta decision* period, the Court handed down 14 non-unanimous decisions, many of which were war crimes cases.[31] When we estimate the logit model on only the pre-*Kløfta decisions* and then compare the results to the estimates derived for the analysis of the full post-War era, we see that significant effects are lost (analysis not shown), although prior experience in the Office of the

---

31. One issue of the war crime cases was whether the lack of public proclamation of new ordinances passed by the London-based Norwegian government in exile toward the end of the Second World War could prevent war crime prosecutions to be based on these ordinances. Another issue was the degree to which the justices ruled that Section 97 of the Constitution applied to Norwegian citizens only, and not to German occupants. And a final issue was whether failure to apply a statute retroactively would not only violate the public's conception of justice but also be an affront to the 'the noble conception of justice which is the foundation of section 97 and the demand for justice which it upholds' (Justice Reidar Skau in majority Rt-1946–198: 202, the *Klinge decision*).

Government Advocate and the Legislation Department do retain the direction of their effects. Only the force of the nature of the appointing government continues to find some statistical traction: justices appointed by socialist governments still favour the public party (p < 0.06).[32]

On the expectation that a new era of judicial review started with the 1976 *Kløfta decision*, the analysis of the nine decisions for that era does suggest that new forces are at play (analysis not shown). In seven of the nine post-*Kløfta decisions* in this period, the public party lost the case. The effect of socialist government appointment no longer exists. Although the effect is still positive, it is not even within shouting range of statistical significance (b = 0.93; p = 0.35). On the other hand, the negative impact of a background in the Legislation Department has become more pronounced and highly significant (b = -2.68; p < 0.01). In addition, two other forces achieve significance. Justices with backgrounds as private lawyers, and justices who have previously worked as lower court judges are more likely to vote for the private party (b = -3.79; p < 0.01; b = -3.59; p < 0.01, respectively). It also bears mentioning that former law professors seem to be more supportive of the public party, all other things being equal. Although the coefficient estimate fails to meet conventional levels of significance, it is too close to dismiss out of hand (b = 1.84; p < 0.07). As to the post-1976 *Kløfta decision* era, it appears that the effect of government appointee with respect to judicial review decisions has vanished. The tide against the government and the public's position on constitutional cases are advanced by other groups of justices.

Fields of judicial review

Although the legal literature tends to see the constitutional sections dealing with retroactive laws and full compensation of expropriation as more or less intimately linked (Knoph 1939; Andenæs and Fliflet 2006), we must analytically study the degree to which that common core is manifest in the justices' decisional behaviour.

When compared to the overall analysis presented in Table 8.3, the pattern of coefficient estimates on cases dealing with each constitutional section separately evinces hardly any difference at all.[33] The forces of Government Advocate and Government appointment are similar (negative and positive, respectively) and still significant. The force of Legislation Department is negative and significant for Section 97 cases, but it fails to achieve significance for Section 105 cases. In other words, justices with a background from the Legislation Department vote against the public party in judicial review of retroactive laws, but take no distinct position on full compensation cases. Given the very close similarity in the coefficient estimates, it appears the legal community's perception that the

---

32. Analyses not shown can be provided.
33. Note that some of the judicial review cases can be classified as concerning both Sections 97 and 105. Five post-World War II decisions address both clauses. *See* Table 8.1.

two constitutional provisions share a common core is echoed in the Court's behaviour. And this makes good sense, given the nature of the justices' legal training and the likely effect of the legal community as an audience on their behaviour (Baum 2008).

Types of decisions

Finally, we analyse the justices' voting patterns across civil versus criminal law.[34] For the 14 civil law cases, justices with a background in the Legislation Department and justices appointed by a socialist government vote in manners similar to the overall model displayed in Table 8.3 (significantly negative and positive, respectively). Justices with a background in the Office of the Government Advocate, however, do not appear to vote in any systematic way.

There are greater differences in the model estimates on the criminal law cases. First, of the three forces that were significant at 0.07 or better in the model estimates on the full data set, only a background in the Office of the Government Advocate achieves significance for the subset of criminal cases ($b = -2.83$; $p < 0.01$). Second, two other forces bob at or near the surface of statistical security. In criminal cases women are less supportive of the public party than are their male counterparts ($b = -1.71$; $p < 0.10$), and justices born in Oslo are significantly more supportive of the public party ($b = 2.36$; $p < 0.02$).

The consistency and power of judging

When it comes to judicial review cases, justices participate in decisions across a number of important political issues. This permits us to study the degree to which their voting is ideologically consistent. On the issue of ideological voting after World War II, we first look at the voting pattern of justices with previous stints as members of Parliament and Ministers of Justice. Then we look at the voting consistency of associate justices and Chief Justices.

Does party background influence voting?

There were 14 votes cast on the Court by justices who had previously served as Ministers of Justice. We look primarily at the traditional left–right distinction as established in Norwegian politics with the 1927 election of the first socialist government (Rokkan 1966; Valen 1992; Aardal 2011). We disregard the three votes of Chief Justice Paal Berg, who served as Minister of Justice for the Liberal Party, because the Liberal Party's ideological direction cannot be clearly placed on the left–right dimension we are examining here. (We do note, however, that Berg voted for the public party in all three decisions where he participated as Chief Justice.) Ninety-one per cent – 10 of the remaining 11 votes – of former Ministers of Justice were in the ideological direction of the party for which they served

---

34. This analysis was suggested to us by Ulrik Sverdrup-Thygeson, Jr.

in government.[35] Eighteen votes were cast by justices who had previously been elected members to the *Storting*, and all but one of these votes (Egil Endresen) were cast by justices who had represented the Labour Party. Thus, if these ex-parliamentarians followed their party inclinations on the High Bench, we would expect them to overwhelmingly favour the public interest claimant. They did so 67 per cent of the time. In the end, then, it seems that service as Minister of Justice strongly supports the expectation that justices who were former politicians vote in a direction that is consistent with their party's ideology, whereas service as a member of Parliament seems to offer less support for this hypothesis.

Chief Justices

The Chief Justice always presides over any panel in which he is a member, both during oral arguments and during the justices' deliberation in chambers. This rule applies to the rotation of justices in the five-justice panels. And since all justices participate in plenary decisions, the Chief necessarily serves as presiding justice here too (*see* Chapter Three).[36] Since the Chief is the presiding officer during oral arguments, he also has the task of summarising and laying out the case for the other justices when these meet for deliberation. Recall that cases that are placed before the full Court are definitely not run-of-the-mill cases. Since the case is significant and the Chief has the important task of summarising the case and offering his views and recommendations on it, the Chief occupies a highly influential position.

How have the nine Chief Justices voted in the 26 non-unanimous constitutional cases we analyse here? Five Chief Justices have consistently voted in favour of the public party: Paal Berg, Sverre Grette, Terje Wold, Rolv Ryssdal, and Carsten Smith. But we must necessarily temper the conclusion for Carsten Smith, who only voted once (the *Thunheim decision*, Rt-1996–1440), with the overwhelming 16–1 majority of the Court. Two other Chiefs cast only one vote and both times for the private party: Herman Scheel (Rt-1925–588) and Erling Sandene (Rt-1988–276). As associate justice, Emil Stang voted all four times for the public party, but

---

35. These votes of the ex-ministers were cast by O.C. Gundersen (two votes) and Terje Wold (four votes) of the Labour Party, and Herman Scheel (one vote) and Elisabeth Schweigaard Selmer (three votes) of the Conservative Party. The only exception was Egil Endresen of the Conservative Party, who was appointed to the Court by a Labour government in 1977. Endresen had in fact succeeded Schweigaard Selmer as the Conservative Party's Minister of Justice when Schweigaard Selmer was appointed to the Supreme Court. Endresen's single vote in the 1988 judicial review case (Rt-1988–276) was cast in favour of the public party. In this decision, Schweigaard Selmer voted with the 11–6 majority.

36. In plenary cases, all justices participate except those who recuse themselves due to conflict of interest or those who are deemed to have conflicts of interest. For instance, in the *Ship Owner's Taxation decision* (Rt-2010–143), five justices were deemed to have conflict of interest (Rt-2009–1617), and two justices had leaves of absence (Rt-2010–143, Section 67). Since this procedure left the nineteen-justice court with an even number of justices, the junior justice Arnfinn Bårdsen also had to be excused (*The Court Act*, Section five, fifth clause, second period). Thus, 11 justices participated in this important decision. Of course, the Chief is also the presiding justice in the eleven-justice Grand Chamber. The practice of Grand Chamber commenced in 2008.

after elevation to Chief Justice, he voted in favour of the private party four out of six times. Finally, as an associate justice Tore Schei voted with the public party in the 1996 *Thunheim decision*, but as Chief Justice he has voted consistently with the private party in all five subsequent decisions in which he has been the presiding justice.

If there is ideological voting among the Chief Justices, it may be most evident in the cases of Sverre Grette and Terje Wold, both of whom were appointed as Chief Justice by Labour Party governments. Grette was first appointed to associate justice by the Labour Party government in 1936, whereas Wold was appointed associate justice by the 'maximum coalition government' in 1945.[37] The complete voting consistency of Grette and Wold refer both to their time as associate and Chief Justices. In this respect, Emil Stang is an interesting, but inconsistent, case. Stang was appointed as associate justice in 1938 by a Labour government and appointed to Chief Justice in 1946 by the majority Labour government. For Stang's votes that we analyse here, Stang cast all four votes for the public party as associate justice, but four out of a total of six votes for the private party as Chief Justice. Finally, Tore Schei was appointed as associate justice by the non-socialist Willoch government in 1986 and elevated to Chief Justice by the non-socialist Bondevik government in 2002.

Can Chiefs sway the Court and avoid ending up on the losing side?

Given that the Supreme Court's exercise of judicial review places it at the center of the national political stage of policy making; that when the justices make these decisions they are 'super-legislators' (Smith 1975: 300); and that the Chief Justice presides over the oral arguments and speaks first during the Court's deliberations, an interesting question is whether the Chief Justice is able to sway the Court to his preferred outcome. In other words, does it ever happen that the Chief loses? After all, at these essential moments of policy making, the Chief Justice is, more than ever, a super-politician.[38]

Of the 26 non-unanimous decisions we study here, the Chief found himself in the minority only six times.[39] The first two instances of the Chief losing his Court were handed down before 1940. Chief Herman Scheel voted for the private party and lost. Chief Paal Berg voted for the public party and lost. Chief Emil Stang – the deradicalised justice who veered from supporting the public party before he was elevated to predominantly supporting the private party in the decisions we study here – lost three votes when he voted for the private party and the Court supported the public party. The final case was Chief Rolv Ryssdal's vote in the

---

37. In 1945 Terje Wold decided to suspend his Supreme Court appointment and serve out his four years in the *Storting* after having been elected as a Labour Party politician from the county of Finnmark.

38. We thank Jørn Øyrehagen Sunde for discussing this question with us.

39. Herman Scheel (Rt-1925–588), Paal Berg (Rt-1934–997), Emil Stang (Rt-1948–928, Rt-1950–831, and Rt-1951–87), and Rolv Ryssdal (Rt-1976–1).

Kløfta decision (Rt-1976–1) where he failed to have his Court defer to the *Storting* on the interpretation of the Constitution's full compensation clause.

On the other hand, in 20 instances the Chief did not lose the vote, including the three times that Associate Justice Thomas Bonnevie in 1945 sat in for Chief Justice Paal Berg during his brief leaves of absence.[40] Chief Justices Sverre Grette and Terje Wold did not lose the two non-unanimous judicial review decisions over which they presided. Significantly, Chief Justice Tore Schei has won all five non-unanimous judicial review decisions over which he has presided.

Of the 20 decisions that were won by the Chiefs, in what ideological direction did the Chief take the Court? Prior to 1976, the Chief took the Court in favour of the public party in 11 out of 12 decisions. In the twelfth decision, Chief Justice Emil Stang succeeded in handing the decision to the private party. After 1975, Chief Justices Rolf Einar Ryssdal and Carsten Smith succeeded in letting the Court decide for the public party (Rt-1977–24 and Rt-1996–1440), while Erling Sandene in one case (Rt-1988–276) took the Court in the other direction. Interestingly, in the last five decisions in our data, not only has Chief Justice Schei been on the winning side, but he has also led the non-unanimous Court in deciding for the private party against the public party.[41] The consistency of outcomes in favour of the private party for the Court's five latest non-unanimous decisions may be testament to Schei's commanding control of his Court. But as we saw in the regression analyses above, his position was, more often than not, supported by justices with backgrounds in private practice, lower judgeships, and even justices with stints at the Legislation Department.

The Legislation Department – Same justices, different context, different voting?

In Chapter Seven we studied the justices' votes in civil cases where the government was a party. The chapter investigated the hypothesis that Supreme Court justices were government friendly. The hypothesis has been made of the Supreme Court for many years, but was perhaps most strongly advocated by law professor Asbjørn Kjønstad (1997; 1999) in his two articles on government friendliness following the plenary *Borthen* and *Thunheim* decisions (Rt-1996–1415; Rt-1996–1440). The

---

40. Chief Justice Paal Berg had turned 70 during the war in 1943 and had reached the mandatory retirement age. But along with several other ageing justices, he willingly served longer in order to help with the transition from war to peacetime and the corresponding war-trial cases. Berg retired in June 1946 and died in 1968 at the age of 95.

41. Two of the decisions included here are the two Grand Chamber cases of Rt-2009–1412 and Rt-2009–1423 in which both were decided 10–1 in favour of the private party. In Rt-2009–1412, Justice Jens Edvin Skoghøy forcefully argued that he, in contrast to the other justices, held a principled different view of the role of the lawmakers' intentions. In the absence of other criteria, he argued, the Court should defer to the lawmakers' intentions and in the cases before the Court comply with those intentions (Section 46). Even though Justice Skoghøy lost the first decision, he refused to budge in the second decision and reiterated his solitary dissent from the first case that was decided earlier the same day.

analysis in Chapter Seven found that justices with a background in the Legislation Department of the Ministry of Justice tended to support the government party at significantly higher rates than justices who did not share that background attribute.

By contrast, in this chapter we discovered that justices with a background in the Legislation Department voted *against* the public party in these more extraordinary plenary decisions addressing constitutional issues. A closer examination of this discrepancy lies outside the framework of this book, but we do offer some simple speculation. Upon reflection it seems that this discrepancy may have at least three explanations.[42] First, since our study covers many cases across many decades, with justices coming and going (permanent and interim), the Legislation Department justices who cast these votes may not be the same across the different set of decisions we study. Second, as we have noted throughout this chapter, cases concerning judicial review are by no means regular or run-of-the-mill. These cases may, then, activate a different field of forces and result in a somewhat different decisional behaviour than standard cases. To put it simply, deciding constitutional issues in plenary sessions may be of a different nature than run-of-the-mill civil cases in five-justice panels. Finally, there may also be panel effects in that the constellation of justices and forces among the group of justices themselves are different in plenary versus five-justice panels. These hypotheses await testing in more focused analyses.

Conclusion

After the *Storting* passed the 1925 *Plenary Act* that established that the Supreme Court's judicial review should be addressed by the Court *en banc*, judicial review became a less heated political topic. True, judicial review decisions followed, but both unanimous and non-unanimous decisions tended to be less controversial and were less likely to be perceived as political confrontations between the branches of government. During the three decades following World War II, the government and public parties won 13 of the 14 non-unanimous decisions that we have studied here. In the 1976 *Kløfta decision* (Rt-1976–1) – for the first time in the post-war era – the Court explicitly ruled a parliamentary act unconstitutional and explicitly applied the dormant doctrine of judicial review. In the famous *Ship Owner's Taxation decision* (Rt-2010–143) the Court again not only invoked the judicial review doctrine, it also asserted a greater independence vis-à-vis the *Storting* by *de facto* stating that the Court will rule a statute unconstitutional if it does not agree with the views of the *Storting* (Sunde 2011). The careful deference to the views of the *Storting* that Chief Justice Rolv Ryssdal opined in his dissenting concurrence in the *Kløfta decision* (Rt-1976–1: 36) has now been replaced with a more vigorous self-confidence of the Court under the leadership of Chief Justice Tore Schei.

---

42. In our data of the non-unanimous decisions in the post-war period, the Legislation Department justices cast a total of 517 votes in five-justice panel decisions and a total of 69 votes in plenary decisions.

Following the Supreme Court's *Borthen decision* (Rt-1996–1415) and *Thunheim decision* (Rt-1996–1440), law professor Kjønstad (1997) initiated a debate that examined the government friendliness of the Supreme Court. One of the most vehement critics of Kjønstad's position was Justice Jan Skåre (1997; 1999) who failed to see any substance in Kjønstad's claims (*see* our discussion in Chapter Seven). Kjønstad did not exclude the possibility that the debate contributed to a slight change of direction in the views of the Court (1999). Justice Jens Edvin Skoghøy (2011) claims that the increased intensity of the Court's judicial review concerning the Constitution's ban on retroactive laws has strengthened the protection of citizens vis-à-vis the government.

In this chapter we have shown that one of the significant causes for the views that the Court holds and the decisions that it makes can be attributed to the background and values of the justices who have been appointed to the Bench. In general, justices appointed by socialist governments tend to support the public position in judicial review cases. The recent change in the direction of the Court, identified by legal scholars like Kjønstad and Sunde, as well as Justice Skoghøy, has been that the public party loses more and the citizens receive greater protection. These changes can be attributed, we argue, to justices who have been recruited from private practice, earlier judgeships, and – somewhat surprisingly – the Legislation Department.

References

Aardal, B. (ed.) (2011) *Det politiske landskap. En studie av stortingsvalget 2009*, Oslo: Cappelen Damm.

Andenæs, J. and Fliflet, A. (2006) *Statsforfatningen i Norge*, Oslo: Universitetsforalget.

Augdahl, P. (1938) 'Ingen lov må gis tilbakevirkende kraft' (Grunnlovens § 97), *Tidsskrift for Rettsvitenskap* 51: 379–407.

Baum, L. (2008) *Judges and Their Audiences: A Perspective on Judicial Behavior*, Princeton: Princeton University Press.

Eckhoff, T. (1971) *Rettskildelære*, Oslo: Tanum.

—   (1975) 'Høyesterett som Grunnlovens vokter' in Dahl, O., Bull, E., Hølmebakk, G., Maurseth, P. and Mykland, K. (eds) *Makt og motiv. Et festskrift til Jens Arup Seip 1905–11. Oktober 1975*, Oslo: Gyldendal, pp. 182–207.

—   (1976) 'Høyesterett og politikk', *Morgenbladet, 5 February.*

Eckhoff, T. and Helgesen, J. (2001) *Rettskildelære*, Oslo: Universitetsforlaget.

Fleischer, C. A. (1975) 'Grunnlovens § 97', *Jussens Venner* 10: 183–251.

Holmøyvik, E. (2007) 'Årsaker til utviklinga av prøvingsretten i Norge og Danmark', *Tidsskrift for Rettsvitenskap* 120 (5): 718–779.

Howard, R. M. and Steigerwalt, A. (2012) *Judging Law and Policy: Courts and Policymaking in the American Political System*, New York: Routledge.

Høgberg, B. M. (2010a) *Forbud mot tilbakevirkende lover*, Oslo: Universitetsforlaget.

—   (2010b) 'Grunnloven § 97 etter plenumsdommen i Rt. 2010 s. 143 (Rederiskattesaken)', *Tidsskrift for Rettsvitenskap* 123 (4–5): 694–744.

Johnson, T., Spriggs II, J. F. and Wahlbeck, P. J. (2012) 'The Origin and Development of Stare Decisis at the U.S. Supreme Court' in McGuire, K. T. (ed.) *New Directions in Judicial Politics*, New York: Routledge, pp. 167–185.

Kjønstad, A. (1997) 'Trygderettigheter, Grunnloven og Høyesterett', *Lov og Rett* 33: 243–292.

—   (1999) 'Er Høyesterett statsvennlig?', *Lov og Rett* 35: 97–122.

Knoph, R. (1939) *Rettslige standarder. Særlig Grunnlovens § 97*, Oslo: Grøndahl.

Nadim, M. (2013) 'Er Høyesterettsdommere politisk farget? En undersøkelse av 17 dommeres votum i dissenssaker', *Lov og Rett* 52 (10): 655–671.

Nguyên-Duy, I. (2011) 'From Parliamentary Sovereignty to Constitutional Democracy? [What is the scope of constitutional judicial review of legislation in Norway in the light of the Shipping Tax case and the OVF case of 2010?]', Paper presented at the 2nd International Conference on Democracy as Idea and Practice, Oslo, 13–14 January 2011.

Opsahl, T. (1976) 'Kløfta-dommen, dommerkunsten og dens tolkning', *Lov og Rett* 12: 49–50.

Rokkan, S. (1966) 'Norway: Numerical Democracy and Corporate Pluralism', in Dahl, R. A. (ed.) *Political Oppositions in Western Democracies*, New Haven: Yale University Press, pp. 70–115.

Sandmo, E. (2005) *Siste ord: Høyesterett i norsk historie. 1905–1965*, Oslo: Cappelen.

Seip, J. A. (1965) 'Jus og politikk', *Lov og Rett* 1: 396–423.

Skoghøy, J. E. A. (2011) 'Forbud mot tilbakevirkende lovgivning', *Lov og Rett* 50 (5): 255–282.

Skåre, J. (1997) 'Høyesteretts sammensetning', *Lov og Rett* 33: 499–504.

—   (1999) 'Betydningen av Høyesteretts sammensetning', *Lov og Rett* 11: 67–77.

Slagstad, R. (1990) 'Den norske Høyesteretts prøvingsrett i perioden 1850–1920' in Nygren, R. (ed.) *Högsta domsmakten i Sverige under 200 år: Rättshistoriska studier, bd. 16*, Lund: Institutet för rättshistorisk forskning, pp. 149–174.

Smith, C. (1975) 'Domstolene og rettsutviklingen', *Lov og Rett* 11: 292–319.

—   (1990) 'Jus og politikk. Samspill og konflikt', *Lov og Rett* 26: 425–429.

Smith, E. (1993) *Høyesterett og folkestyret. Prøvingsretten overfor lover*, Oslo: Universitetsforlaget.

—   (2010) 'Rederiskatt og rettsstat', *Lov og Rett* 49 (4): 177–178.

Sunde, J. Ø. (2011) 'Dissenting votes in the Norwegian Supreme Court 1965–2009. A legal cultural analysis', Paper.

—   (2012) 'Dissenting votes in the Norwegian Supreme Court 1965–2009: A legal cultural analysis', *Rechtskultur* 1: 59–73.

Valen, H. (1992) *Valg og politikk. Et samfunn i endring*, Oslo: NKS-Forlaget.

Chapter Nine

Conclusion: Reflections on the Attitudinal Model

The principal aim of this book has been a systematic exploration of the decisional behaviour of Norwegian Supreme Court justices. A collateral, although not unintended, effect has been to demonstrate the transportability of a model of judicial politics developed and most fully tested in the context of the American judicial system. In Chapter One we made the case for the application of the attitudinal model to judges generally. We averred that the effect of the preferences of individual judges on a court's outputs is a function of *means*, *motives*, and *opportunities*. Now, judges in the American judicial system – and not just those sitting on its highest bench – have these in spades, but so too do the judges of many other countries. Certainly, these phenomena are not alien to Norway's justices. Indeed, in Chapters Two, Three and Four we described the *Høyesterett*'s institutional structure; jurisdictional authority; appointment system; decisional process; and the key social-political trends present in its composition from 1945 to 2009. The foundation provided in these chapters suggests that the conditions facilitating attitudinal decision making are present in Norway.

The *Høyesterett* has appellate jurisdiction and sits atop a hierarchical judicial system. Armed with discretionary authority, its members can cherry-pick the most complex cases – i.e. those cases that *are not* controlled by obvious legal rules and precedent, in other words those cases that allow the greatest chance for the individual justice's policy preferences to come to the fore. Moreover, the Supreme Court has the power to interpret the law and to determine whether an act of the legislature is consistent with the Constitution. To state the matter bluntly, then, Norway's justices have the opportunity to act on their preferences, and they have the means to have those preferences enshrined in the law.

Thus, two of the three conceptual legs of the attitudinal model are extant in the Norwegian context, but what of motives? In its purest form, the attitudinal model presumes that judges overtly pursue their own policy goals. While we acknowledge that law school graduates seek to ascertain the plain meaning of the law, and predicate their behaviour upon such an understanding, we also realise that they are not devoid of policy and political preferences that are products of early political socialisation and ongoing social and political experiences. The notion that experienced and highly educated Supreme Court justices are political blank slates, both unaware of and without clear policy preferences is, to us, incomprehensible. On the contrary, justices

Figure 9.1: Summary Attitudinal Model

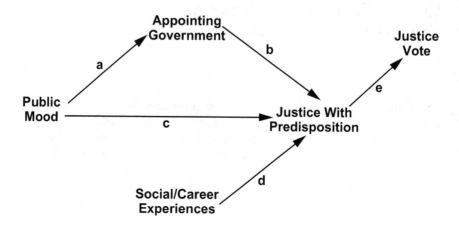

do have political values that help them reach their own interpretations of the plain meaning of the law, legislative intent, and the proper application of constitutional principles. It strains credulity to suggest that the third component is missing.

A theoretical summary

Given the appropriateness of the attitudinal model and in an effort to build on the findings reported in the previous chapters, we offer a purely theoretical summary of a modified attitudinal model as it could apply to decision making in the Norwegian Supreme Court (*see* Figure 9.1).[1] While we have sought to explain the justices' votes – a goal that could be pursued by the application of a variety of models – the primary object of our attention is the policy views of those occupying a seat on the High Bench. Whatever else bears on an individual justice's vote must be mediated through his or her attitudes. What exactly are these predispositions? The answer to this question largely rests upon the nature of the public policy under consideration. For example, in a social democracy, litigation involving public versus private economic interests might tap into justices' opinions about the proper economic role of the government. The location of a judge along this continuum is hypothesised to influence his or her decisional behaviour, which would be cloaked in legal reasoning.

---

1. We use the term 'modified attitudinal model' consciously because it is important to emphasise that ideological motivation, which we have drawn upon in this initial effort to approach the Norwegian Supreme Court, is just one of several kind of motivations that researchers should include in their analyses of judicial behaviour (*see* Epstein and Knight 2013).

Social/career experiences

In Figure 9.1, one set of conditions shaping judicial attitudes is subsumed under our rubric of 'Social/Career Experiences'. One major influence on *political values* is the party identification internalised by Norwegian citizens, who – like those in other democratic societies – internalise party loyalty through the process of political socialisation that can be traced to early childhood. Since even the most casually engaged citizens sympathise with a party, we can only assume that highly educated justices with considerable political knowledge and attentiveness to policy matters harbour partisan affinities, and the policy preferences with which these affinities are associated. Given the broad policy outlines of party manifestos, justices with sympathies for, say, the Labour Party, or the Conservative Party, or the Christian People's Party, would not be indifferent to policy concerns that cases arriving at the bar stimulate, and – as far as the constraints of the institution in which they are acting allow – they would respond to those stimuli in a manner consistent with their partisan predispositions.

A judge's policy predispositions may also, in part, be a product of *region of origin*. Many nations exhibit a tension between the centre and the periphery and Norway is no exception. We have noted that the Supreme Court was disproportionately populated from the Oslo region. Inasmuch as, for most of the time period under examination here, the bulk of the eligible applicant pool was located in the nation's capital and studied at the University of Oslo Law School, it is quite natural that the Court would reflect that reality. As other universities created law schools and legal curricula, an increased number of potential appointees resided in the nation's periphery, and found their way onto the High Bench. Perhaps more importantly, a commitment to create a more diverse judiciary resulted in an increase in the number of justices recruited from the periphery. Some evidence has emerged that illustrates an occasional centre–periphery effect on economic policy questions (Grendstad *et al.* 2011). However, the more complete model specifications we presented in Chapters Five, Seven, and Eight fail to reveal any centre–periphery effects, at least with respect to place of birth.

A major thrust in the push to diversify the Supreme Court has been the concern for appointing *women* to the Bench. Of course, gender differences are undeniable, and would serve as *prima facie* evidence for including women on the Court. Certainly gender diversity in governmental institutions should ensure better representation of societal interests. However, as we showed in Chapter Six, gender has no impact on judicial votes over family and estate law, and a barely noticeable effect on sentencing adjustments – issue areas in which gender based voting would seem most likely to occur. Nevertheless, gender may influence litigation, and we suggested ways in which it may have relevance for the judicial process apart from recorded votes.

During the course of our research project we have repeatedly heard that *government insiders* were advantaged in the selection process for seats on the Supreme Court. More specifically, those serving in the Legislation Department seemed to be on an inside track to the Court, and they do account for a major proportion of Supreme Court justices serving in the post-World War II period. This executive department drafts legislation and offers constitutional interpretations of laws. Accordingly, we would be surprised if such a career pattern held no relevance for subsequent decisional behaviour of High Court justices. Indeed, we find that on litigation in which the government is a party, Legislative Department employment appears to predispose a justice to side with the government, an outcome that may well be expected (*see* Chapter Seven). Interestingly, Legislative Department employment appears to have an opposite effect in judicial review cases (*see* Chapter Eight).

Since we the authors are university faculty members, we understand that the rarified atmosphere of academia is likely to provide future justices with a set of experiences not obviously shared by those who have pursued 'normal' careers. Given the academic proclivity to discuss *ad nauseam* even the most inconsequential fragment of thought, we are not surprised by the increased levels of dissent exhibited since the advent of the appointment of professors to the High Court in 1991 (*see* Chapter Three: Figures 3.2 and 3.3). Generally speaking, however, we have not unearthed differential voting patterns, at least in terms of favouring some outcomes over others, between academics and non-academics, perhaps because for most of the post-war era no professor occupied a seat on the Supreme Court.

The reader will note that we do not specify a link between 'Social/Career Experiences' and 'Appointing Government' in Figure 9.1. While left and right bloc governments might be inclined to appoint justices with different social backgrounds and career choices, we find little evidence for such a pattern. Socialist and non-socialist led governments appointed roughly the same proportions of justices who were born in Oslo; women; law school professors; Legislation Department employees; government advocates; and prosecutors (*see* Table 9.1). The greatest disparity during the entire period under analysis (and the only one that attains conventional levels of statistical security) is the .3 difference in the appointment of individuals with some background in private practice. Interestingly, the greater tendency for non-socialist governments to appoint lawyers with private practice experience is intuitively consistent with the nature of each party bloc.

Public mood

In a democratic society, even the most invisible and insular group of political decision-makers is not impervious to popular influence. We specify two possible paths of influence in Figure 9.1. An indirect effect (Norpoth and Sega 1994) may be in force, starting with the self-evident outcome that the party or parties in government are likely to respond directly to public mood and public opinion – the principal reason for elections in the first place. This outcome, in turn, could influence the pool of applicants and inform the actions of those responsible for the appointment process.

Table 9.1: Social and Career Background Factors by Appointing Government 1945–2009

Background Factor	Nature of Appointing Government		Significance
	Non-Socialist	Socialist	
Oslo-Born	.458	.389	ns
Female	.036	.143	.09
Private Practice	.400	.100	.01
Professor	.236	.150	ns
Legislation Department	.200	.300	ns
Government Advocate	.015	.100	ns
Government Prosecutor	.073	.100	ns

Note: Of course, the columns do not sum to 1.0 since, for example, appointees can be Oslo-born women with a stint in the Legislation Department.

Alternatively, public opinion may directly influence the predispositions and votes of Supreme Court justices. Mishler and Sheehan (1993) suggest two explanations for a direct impact of public opinion on the positions staked out by the judiciary. First, mindful of the importance of their legitimacy, justices are reluctant to stray 'too far or too long from strongly held public views on fundamental issues' (Mishler and Sheehan 1993: 174). Second, as is the case with the citizenry at large, judges too are affected by long-term changes in social, economic, and political trends. Indeed, if the Supreme Court is becoming more diverse, it may reflect public opinion more faithfully than it has in the past. To these, we add a third explanation, namely that Supreme Court justices have 'audiences' from whom they seek approval (Baum 2008). Public opinion could influence the justices if these audiences tap into facets of broader public opinion. Interestingly, the fairly recent efforts to make the Supreme Court more open, accessible, and transparent could transform the Court into an institution that is a bit more directly accountable to the Norwegian citizenry.

Appointing government

Finally, the analyses we have reported here underscore the important impact on Supreme Court decisional behaviour exhibited by the nature of the appointing government. Nowhere is the colour of the government more consequential than on litigation that raises questions about the proper role of government in directing the economy. Should the Court embrace a robust collective management of the economy, or should greater latitude be extended to private economic interests? While the nature of the appointing government is not uniform across all cases analysed, in most instances its influence simply will not go away, even under a range of statistical controls. Indeed, as a proxy for the attitudinal preferences of the justices with respect to the role of government in the economy, the nature of the appointing government attains significance in a series of multivariate tests presented in Chapters Five, Seven, and Eight.

That the nature of the appointing government has a statistically secure effect on judicial decisional behaviour is by far the most controversial finding to date. Associate Justice Jens Edvin Skoghøy (2010: 723) flatly dismisses our argument as 'clearly invalid', while Chief Justice Tore Schei (2011: 334) emphatically rejects our claim as 'meaningless'. They hold that the appointment of justices and their subsequent positions on cases adjudicated are not about party politics, pure and simple. They have a point, and we agree: Norway's Supreme Court justices are not party functionaries. The justices, however, do have legal philosophies and attitudinal preferences that broadly reflect the partisan cleavages giving order to the political system.

Still, more than one caveat is in order. Like others that ground their research on the attitudinal model, we need to take into account the fact that if we want to describe 'how much politics matters in judicial decision making, it is inappropriate to isolate solely on the subclass of cases that are most likely show political influences' (Tamanaha 2009: 146). Yet, given our emphasis on non-unanimous, economic rights cases, we are guilty of this transgression. Furthermore, as Judge Richard Posner properly notes,

> [J]udging is not *just* personal and political. It is also impersonal and nonpolitical in the sense that many, indeed *most*, judicial decisions really are the product of a neutral application of rules not made up for the occasion to facts fairly found (Posner 2008: 370, our italics).

Clearly, we must be ever mindful of the fact that Norway's Supreme Court justices act in an institution that is qualitatively different than other policy-making arenas. The law and courts have norms, rules, and institutional constraints, and in a large majority of cases, these rules and constraints effectively muzzle the effect of the justices' preferences.[2] The law matters. We do not dispute that. But because of its place in the nation's constitutional system, the Norwegian Supreme Court hears and decides cases that are legally ambiguous and that therefore allow individual preferences to guide decisional behaviour.

Future research: Going forward

To test more fully models of decisional behaviour of Norway's Supreme Court justices a number of steps are required that would push beyond the limitations of our current research. Specifically, (1) we need to develop more direct measures of judicial ideological preferences, (2) monitor the continuing impact of appointing government, (3) generate indicators of public mood at discrete time intervals,

---

2. For a recent and well-founded discussion on law versus politics and their unequal influences on unanimous versus non-unanimous decisions, *see* Epstein, Landes and Posner (2013).

(4) more directly incorporate seemingly perfunctory rule application, (5) consider other manifestations of decisional behaviour, (6) incorporate the role of 'audiences', (7) explore collegial and case effects, and (8) explore the potential link between parliament and Supreme Court decisional behaviour.

Judicial ideology

More direct, and ostensibly valid, measures of judicial ideology are highly desirable. Creating such indicators, however, becomes more and more difficult as one goes back in time, most obviously if the measures rely upon the justices reporting their views. Even those very much with us these days are reluctant to stake out attitudinal beliefs either publicly or in surveys, where anonymity and confidentiality are assured. So, we fell back on the default strategy employed in many earlier studies, namely, utilising the appointing government party as a crude proxy for value preferences.

Producing more satisfying measures of political philosophy poses a number of issues one needs to address. For example, do we assume that ideology is unidimensional – which may find some support (Grofman and Brazill 2002) – or do we specify a multidimensional ideological construct? However, even if a general left–right axis accounts for the lion's share of ideological orientation, some policy domains may not be easily subsumed by one dimension. Our inclination is to develop somewhat more narrowly construed indicators that focus more exclusively on a variety of policy questions – e.g. economic regulation, family law, environmental law, and so on.

Regardless of whether we conceive of ideology as unidimensional or multidimensional, constructing indicators is no mean task. We have used a proxy measure, socialist/non-socialist appointing governments – a common practice in much of the literature. Crude as this approach seems, the party proxy has been quite robust in most research. Indeed, if anything, party probably understates the impact of ideology (Fischman and Law 2009). There are of course other proxies that might be adopted, including gender, region, or government employment. However, we prefer to treat these factors as social background variables that, in turn, help to shape political ideology.

A second methodological strategy to measure ideology relies on constructing such a scale on the basis of votes cast by justices. The sophisticated Martin-Quinn scores (Martin and Quinn 2002) and the refined Bailey measure (Bailey 2007) are based upon votes cast in a current session and those preceding the one under scrutiny. Presumably, with most votes used to construct the ideological measure not treated as dependent variables, the problem of endogeneity might be circumvented. We are dubious and offer the caveat that if justices are ideologically consistent over time, then how they vote is explained by how they vote (Epstein and Mershon 1996). Or, ideology is statistically associated with ideology. Furthermore, if we wish to treat political ideology as multidimensional, the Martin-Quinn and Bailey scales may not be helpful. After all, since a median voter can be identified, the scores are by necessity unidimensional.

Appointing government

Unless and until we can unearth variables that wash out the effects of the appointing government, we will continue to include it in our empirical analyses. Notwithstanding opinions to the contrary, the ideological location of a governing party or coalition may affect the judicial selection process, if not overtly, by shaping the applicant pool. However, developing measures that would allow us to evaluate the expanded model presented in Figure 9.1 might eliminate the relationship between appointing government and voting on the High Court. Only further research can address this matter.

Further insight into the role of appointing government as an explanatory variable could be revealed by a 'natural experiment' that should be undertaken within the next few years. In 2002 the Supreme Court appointment process underwent significant reform when the selection committee was taken out of the Ministry of Justice in Oslo (centre) and moved to Trondheim (periphery). Does this reform alter the link between the colour of the appointing government and decisional behaviour? Future research should address this question.

Public mood

In addition to expanding our efforts to tap into judicial value preferences, our fuller model of decisional behaviour assigns a role to broad public opinion. Judges may well be influenced or constrained by the general tenor or mass policy preferences, and may do so because they feel some obligation to be attentive to societal values, or may consider public views in an effort to maintain political legitimacy. As we noted in an earlier chapter, judicial policy making can track the opinions of the citizenry.

Devising a proper measure of public opinion is not an easy task. Surely, citizen attitudes on specific issues of public policy probably are not of any real utility here. Instead, we think that basic predispositions may be most salient for our purposes. Specific survey items might include general left–right ideology and basic orientations regarding entire domains of public policy. For example, how do voters sort themselves on the question of the role of government in managing the nation's economy? At present we propose to make use of readily available survey items to map the trends in public mood at discrete time intervals. This research strategy may enable us to assess the degree to which Supreme Court votes track public opinion.

Perfunctory rule application

Almost by definition, perfunctory rule application would most likely be observed in unanimous rulings handed down by the Court. Most cases before the Court are non-controversial, with justices invoking widely accepted precedents. (Indeed, 85 per cent of the post-war cases heard in five-justice panels were decided unanimously.) However, even if such rulings seem almost matter of fact, this does not mean that political value preferences are absent. We suggest that a careful review of unanimous decisions may further elucidate the Court's role as a political organ.

We have followed the conventional practice of thoroughly analysing non-unanimous decisions on the premise that one can best assess the role of policy preferences when justices split their votes in cases heard by the Court. Nevertheless, we have not forfeited the remaining decisions just because justices have followed precedent: the fallback position. We share the view of jurisprudential scholars that precedent should not be dismissed lightly. On the contrary, precedent provides a measure of stability and predictability in legal matters. However, *stare decisis* is not politically neutral. In staking out a position, a justice may invoke precedent because he or she agrees with the underlying value premise, and may seek to overturn a precedent when it does not accord with the justice's philosophy (Hansford and Spriggs 2006). Statistical analyses of Supreme Court votes may initially not offer much traction in understanding seemingly perfunctory rule application, and that brings us to another line for future research.

Other manifestations of judicial behaviour

Of course, votes cast by justices in unanimous cases cannot be subjected to the kind of simple single-level statistical models we have used in this volume, and so, systematic evaluation of alternative forms of judicial behaviour must be considered.[3] Perhaps the most obvious place to start is to explore the justices' decisions as texts. Justices take great care in drafting their decisions, and these drafts are circulated among the other justices on the panel. In cases of non-unanimous decisions, more than one voice will influence the message that the Court hands down. These texts can be analysed for clarity, complexity, latent structures, as well as for developing more advanced text mining techniques (e.g. Baye and Wright 2011; Owens and Wedeking 2011).

Another obvious place to start is to explore the statements (written and otherwise) made by justices off the bench. Here the notion is that justices may in these statements offer a glimpse into their value preferences. For example, some members of the Court publish books or articles on a variety of issues that find their way into the judicial system. Of course, not all justices are actively engaged in penning their views for public consumption, and we suspect that the practice is dominated by the academics on the Supreme Court. Insight into the attitudes and behaviour of the justices could be gleaned from their written opinions addressing cases heard by the Court. Be forewarned that justices are likely to express themselves in the legal vernacular, perhaps clouding underlying value preferences. Nevertheless, we may be able to tease out politically relevant content that might elucidate decisional behaviour.

---

3. With adequate information on unanimous and non-unanimous decisions on both justice and case levels, multilevel modelling is appropriate.

Audience effects

As Baum (2008) has persuasively argued, judges – like most other social creatures – care what relevant others think of them and, as a consequence, they may stake out positions that will be favourably received by valued audiences. Such groups will vary by justice, most likely determined by the nature of an individual's social network. Those drawn from the ivory tower may wish to demonstrate to academic colleagues that just because they moved out of the cloistered university environment, they still have the intellectual chops to maintain the respect of those they left behind. Or a sitting justice may perhaps enjoy a reputation for having been identified with a cause, such as a firm stance on law and order, or a commitment to feminism, or a support for the society's underdogs, or a support for free enterprise. Or maybe justices recruited from the Legislation Department would hope to gain the approval of former colleagues in that division of the Ministry of Justice. From Baum's theoretical perspective, such justices may well write and act in such a way as to maintain the adulation or respect of these various audiences. Future research could pursue this line of inquiry.

Collegial and case effects

We also know that justices as decision-makers are constrained by their social environment. Collegial effects are covered in American studies and hypothesised in the emerging European literature on judicial behaviour. Specifically, we need to develop robust measures and test the effects of panel composition depending on what majorities of justices – in terms of their social and career experiences – may or may not generate a critical-mass effect that sways the other justices toward specific case outcomes. Similarly, we know that justices as decision-makers are constrained by the nature of the case before them. As political scientists, we need to better understand the legal nature of the case. And for our models of judicial behaviour, we need to develop concepts and instruments that permit us to hew out from the mountain of jurisprudence boulders of data.

Parliament–Supreme Court connection

Careful observers of the Norwegian court system do not ascribe any role to Parliament in judicial actions, and for good reason. After all, the *Storting* plays no part in nominating jurists, scrutinising Supreme Court applicants, or in confirming future justices. However, Parliament approves legislation that, from time to time, results in laws that may not withstand judicial scrutiny. In this strategic environment, for example, legislation could be challenged on grounds that it contains an unconstitutional provision, is bad public policy, or is in some fashion unfair (*see* e.g. Dyevre 2010). No one argues that these laws are devoid of ideological or policy preferences. From all appearances, socialist governments and MPs promote a set of policies that will not reflect the priorities of non-socialist governments and their *Storting* supporters. The first research effort to examine the *Storting–Høyestrett* connection finds both a general link between voting in Parliament and voting in the Supreme Court, and an *ideological* connection between individual Court justices' and Parliamentary voting in particular (Kisen 2014). The *Storting–Høyesterett* connection needs to be more fully examined and developed.

Some concluding thoughts

We close with some general thoughts about the implications of our research in a broader institutional and cross-national context. Simply put, does our present treatment of the Norwegian Supreme Court have any relevance beyond the Court itself? We began our study by noting the Court's limited visibility and transparency, but anticipate that this state of affairs will change, in part due to the Court's commitment to improving transparency. In addition, the media has focused increased attention on the Supreme Court, and this will continue as rulings are handed down on important and potentially controversial matters of public policy. If the judiciary becomes more politicised, what will be the response of other actors, perhaps most notably the *Storting*? If a more visible Supreme Court renders decisions on controversial political questions, will the perceived legitimacy of the Court decline in the eyes of the public? As a political organ, the Supreme Court may address a variety of 'audiences' beyond the cloistered halls of the judiciary.

Looking beyond the Norwegian borders, our research should have relevance for judicial behaviour in other countries, most notably the Scandinavian nations. The Supreme Courts of Denmark, Finland, and Sweden have nearly the same number of justices (eighteen to nineteen). Only Iceland has a relatively small number (nine). All four employ an appointment procedure similar to the one Norway used for nearly the entire post-World War II years included in our data set – namely, selection housed in an executive agency, such as the Ministry of Justice or, in the case of Finland, presidential appointment with the advice of a commission. The Scandinavian high courts are constitutional courts with appellate jurisdiction that typically hear cases in non-plenary panels. As in Norway, the Supreme Courts of Denmark, Finland, Iceland, and Sweden are not highly visible, but may become so in the years to come. At a minimum, we expect that our findings can travel throughout Scandinavia and perhaps beyond the European northern periphery where the justices' individual voices can be identified. Indeed, the empirical results we have presented here could well serve as points of departure for genuinely comparative studies of judicial behaviour.

References

Bailey, M. A. (2007) 'Comparable Preference Estimates across Time and Institutions for the Court, Congress, and Presidency', *American Journal of Political Science* 51 (3): 433–448.

Baum, L. (2008) *Judges and Their Audiences: A Perspective on Judicial Behavior*, Princeton: Princeton University Press.

Baye, M. R. and Wright, J. D. (2011) 'Is Antitrust Too Complicated for Generalist Judges? The Impact of Economic Complexity and Judicial Training on Appeals', *Journal of Law and Economics* 54 (1): 1–14.

Dyevre, A. (2010) 'Unifying the Field of Comparative Judicial Politics. Towards a General Theory of Judicial Behaviour', *European Political Science Review* 2 (2): 297–227.

Epstein, L. and Knight, J. (2013) 'Reconsidering Judicial Preferences', *Annual Review of Political Science* 16: 11–31.

Epstein, L., Landes, W. M. and Posner, R. A. (2013) *The Behavior of Federal Judges: A Theoretical and Empirical Study of Rational Choice*, Cambridge, Mass.: Harvard University Press.

Epstein, L. and Mershon, C. (1996) 'Measuring Political Preferences', *American Journal of Political Science* 40 (1): 261–294.

Fischman, J. B. and Law, D. S. (2009) 'What is Judicial Ideology and How Should We Measure It?' *Washington University Journal of Law and Policy* 29: 133–214.

Grendstad, G., Shaffer, W. R. and Waltenburg, E. N. (2011) 'When Justices Disagree: The Influence of Ideology and Geography on Economic Voting on the Norwegian Supreme Court', *Retfærd* 34 (2): 3–22.

Grofman, B. and Brazill, T. J. (2002) 'Identifying the Median Justice through Multidimensional Scaling: Analysis of "Natural Courts" 1953–1991', *Public Choice* 112 (1–2): 55–79.

Hansford, T. G. and Spriggs, J. F. I. (2006) *The Politics of Precedent on the U.S. Supreme Court*, Princeton: Princeton University Press.

Kisen, R. (2014) 'Felles makt – felles ideologi? En sammenlikning av lovgivning i Stortinget og rettsutvikling i Høyesterett mellom 1976 og 2013', Department of Comparative Politics, University of Bergen.

Martin, A. D. and Quinn, K. M. (2002) 'Dynamic Ideal Point Estimation via Markov Chain Monte Carlo for the U.S. Supreme Court', *Political Analysis*, 10 (2): 134–153.

Mishler, W. and Sheehan, R. S. (1996) 'Public Opinion, the Attitudinal Model, and Supreme Court Decision Making: A Micro-Analytic Perspective', *Journal of Politics* 58 (1): 169–200.

Norpoth, H. and Segal, J. A. (1994) 'Comment: Popular Influence on Supreme Court Decisions', *American Political Science Review* 88 (3): 711–716.

Owens, R. J. and Wedeking, J. P. (2011) 'Justices and Legal Clarity: Analyzing the Complexity of U.S. Supreme Court Opinions', *Law* and *Society Review* 45 (4): 1027–1061.

Posner, R. A. (2008) *How Judges Think*, Cambridge, Mass.: Harvard University Press.

Schei, T. (2011) 'Har Høyesterett en politisk funksjon?', *Lov og Rett* 50 (6): 319–335.

Skoghøy, J. E. A. (2010) 'Dommeratferd og dommerbakgrunn. Særlig om yrkesbakgrunnens betydning for utfallet av tvister mellom private og det offentlige' in Lambertz, G., Lindskog, S. and Möller, M. (eds) *Festskrift till Torgny Håstad*, Uppsala: Iustus, pp. 711–726.

Tamanaha, B. Z. (2009) *Beyond the Formalist-Realist Divide: The Role of Politics in Judging*, Princeton: Princeton University Press.

Appendices

Appendix A: Norwegian Supreme Court Justices 1945–2014, by Appointing Government

On the following pages we list all appointments to the Norwegian Supreme Court for the 1945–2014 period. The list includes the appointments of both permanent justices and interim justices. An individual justice will appear more than once on the list if that justice was appointed more than one time. The list totals 240 appointments.

The list of appointments is organised as follows. First, we organise the justices by appointing government. This includes the name of the government's prime minister, whether the government was socialist/social democratic or non-socialist, and the time this government was in office. Next, we list the appointed justice's name; gender (woman = 1); birthplace; whether the justice served as Chief (= 1); years of birth and death; year of appointment; as well as years of start and end of service on the Court. For each section of government appointments, we first list the group of justices who were appointed to a permanent position on the Court and then the group of justices who were appointed as interim justices. The latter distinction is relevant only for the post-1945 years.

The list of the 240 appointments to the Supreme Court is as complete as possible, and far more comprehensive than any other compilation of justices. The list was generated by going through every non-unanimous Court decision for the 1945–1959 period and all Court decisions since 1960. The list of voting justices was matched with comprehensive searches in libraries and government archives to add information on the individual justices. As is evident from a closer look at the list, information on interim justices is sometimes missing. The authors are grateful for any information that can be added the information that we present here.

Supreme Court Justices 1945–2014, by Appointing Government

Blehr II — Non-Socialist — In government (from–to): 22.06.1921–05.03.1923

Justice's name	Birthplace	Woman = 1	Chief = 1	Born – Died (Year)	Appointed, started, ended (Year)
Henry Ludvig Larssen	Drammen	0		1871 – 1956	–, 1922, 1947

Mowinckel II — Non-Socialist — In government (from–to): 15.02.1928–11.05.1931

Justice's name	Birthplace	Woman = 1	Chief = 1	Born – Died (Year)	Appointed, started, ended (Year)
Einar Hanssen	Nesodden	0	0	1874 – 1952	1928, 1928, 1946
Thomas Bonnevie	Trondheim	0	0	1879 – 1960	1928, 1928, 1950
Paal Olav Berg	Hammerfest	0	1	1873 – 1968	1929, 1929, 1946
Edvin Albion Jarl Alten	Tønsberg	0	0	1876 – 1967	1929, 1929, 1948
Axel Theodor Næss	Mandal	0	0	1874 – 1945	1930, 1930, 1945

Kolstad — Non-Socialist — In government (from–to): 12.05.1931–13.03.1932

Justice's name	Birthplace	Woman = 1	Chief = 1	Born – Died (Year)	Appointed, started, ended (Year)
Thorleif Ferdinand Schjelderup	Kristiania	0		1886 – 1955	1932, 1932, 1952

Mowinckel III — Non-Socialist — In government (from–to): 03.03.1933–19.03.1935

Justice's name	Birthplace	Woman = 1	Chief = 1	Born – Died (Year)	Appointed, started, ended (Year)
Svend Josef Einar Evensen	Vestby	0		1880 – 1948	1933, 1933, 1948

Supreme Court Justices 1945–2014, by Appointing Government (*continued*)

Nygaardsvold I — Socialist — In government (from–to): 20.03.1935–21.04.1940

Justice's name	Woman = 1	Birthplace	Chief = 1	Born – Died	Appointed, started, ended
Helge Klæstad	0	Levanger	0	1885 – 1965	1935, 1935, 1946
Sverre Grette	0	Kristiania	0	1888 – 1959	1936, 1936, 1952
Emil Stang	0	Kristiania	0	1882 – 1964	1937, 1938, 1946
Sigurd Fougner	0	Ø. Gausdal	0	1879 – 1959	1938, 1938, 1950
Erik Toralf Solem	0	Kristiania	0	1877 – 1949	1939, 1939, 1947

Gerhardsen I — Non-Socialist — In government (from–to): 25.06.1945–04.11.1945

Justice's name	Woman = 1	Birthplace	Chief = 1	Born – Died	Appointed, started, ended
Asmund Eirik Soelseth	0	Vadsø	0	1886 – 1975	1945, 1945, 1956
Anton Cathinko Stub Holmboe	0	Kristiania	0	1892 – 1980	1945, 1945, 1962
Reidar Skau	0	Kristiania	0	1893 – 1975	1945, 1945, 1963
Bent Berger	0	Kristiania	0	1898 – 1985	1945, 1945, 1968
Terje Wold	0	Evenes	0	1899 – 1972	1945, 1949, 1958
Thomas Bonnevie (interim)	0	Trondheim	1	1879 – 1960	1945, 1945, 1945
Henrik Eiler Stoeren Bahr (interim)	0	Kristiania	0	1902 – 1982	1945, 1945, 1946

Supreme Court Justices 1945–2014, by Appointing Government (*continued*)

Gerhardsen II	Socialist		In government (from–to): 05.11.1945–18.11.1951		
Justice's name	Woman = 1	Birthplace	Chief = 1	Year Born – Died	Year Appointed, started, ended
Emil Stang	0	Kristiania	1	1882 – 1964	1946, 1946, 1952
Carl Kruse-Jensen	0	Kristiania	0	1889 – 1981	1946, 1946, 1959
Jørgen Berner Thrap	0	Kristiania	0	1898 – 1990	1946, 1946, 1968
Karsten Gaarder	0	V.Toten	0	1902 – 1979	1946, 1946, 1972
Henrik Eiler Støren Bahr	0	Kristiania	0	1902 – 1982	1946, 1946, 1972
Andreas Olai Schei	0	Førde	0	1902 – 1989	1946, 1946, 1972
Ernst Fredrik Eckhoff	0	Kristiansand	0	1905 – 1997	1946, 1946, 1975
Sverre Dæhli	0	Oslo	0	1896 – 1968	1949, 1949, 1954
Marius Nygaard	0	Kristiania	0	1902 – 1978	1949, 1950, 1972
Otto Helgesen	0	Fredrikstad	0	1898 – 1973	1950, 1950, 1968
Trygve Bendiksby	0	Modum	0	1907 – 1992	1951, 1952, 1977
Thomas Bonnevie (interim)	0	Trondheim	1	1879 – 1960	1945, 1945, 1945
Adolf Fridtjof Lindvik (interim)	0	Dypvåg	0	1886 – 1946	1946, –
Johannes Bratt Andenæs (interim)	0	Innvik	0	1912 – 2003	1946, –
Fredrik Christian S. Sejersted (interim)	0	Kristiania	0	1901	1946, 1946, 1947
Johannes Bratt Andenæs (interim)	0	Innvik	0	1912 – 2003	1946, 1946, 1946
Johannes Bratt Andenæs (interim)	0	Innvik	0	1912 – 2003	1946, 1946, 1946
Aksel Colbjørn Johannessen (interim)	0		0	1880	1947, –, 1948
Fin Krog (interim)	0		0	1881 – 1950	1947, –, 1948

Supreme Court Justices 1945–2014, by Appointing Government (*continued*)

| Gerhardsen II | Socialist | | In government (from–to): 05.11.1945–18.11.1951 | | |
| | | | | Year | Year |
Justice's name	Woman = 1	Birthplace	Chief = 1	Born – Died	Appointed, started, ended
Johannes Stenersen (interim)	0		0	1881	1947, ?, 1948
Bjarne Torstenson (interim)	0		0	1882 – 1949	1947, ?, 1948
Gulbrand Jensen (interim)	0	Hamar	0	1885	1947, 1947, 1948
Sverre Berg (interim)	0		0	1897	1947, 1947, 1948
Bjarne Randers Rognlien (interim)	0	Eidanger	0	1891	1948, 1948, 1948
Fin Krog (interim)	0		0	1881 – 1950	1948, ?, 1949
Johannes Stenersen (interim)	0		0	1881	1948, ?, 1949
Bjarne Torstenson (interim)	0		0	1882 – 1949	1948, ?, 1949
Bjarne Randers Rognlien (interim)	0	Eidanger	0	1891	1948, 1948, 1949
Aksel Colbjørn Johannessen (interim)	0		0	1880	1948, ?, 1949
Johannes Stenersen (interim)	0		0	1881	1949, ?, 1950
Bjarne Randers Rognlien (interim)	0	Eidanger	0	1891	1949, 1949, 1949
Johannes Stenersen (interim)	0		0	1881	1949, ?, 1950
Johannes Stenersen (interim)	0		0	1881	1949, 1950, 1950
Johannes Bratt Andenæs (interim)	0	Innvik	0	1912 – 2003	1951, 1951, 1952
Johannes Stenersen (interim)	0		0	1881	1951, 1951, –

Supreme Court Justices 1945–2014, by Appointing Government (continued)

Torp	Socialist			In government (from–to): 19.11.1951–21.01.1955	
					Year
Justice's name	Woman = 1	Birthplace	Chief = 1	Born – Died	Appointed, started, ended
Sverre Grette	0	Kristiania	1	1888 – 1959	1952, 1952, 1958
Axel Heiberg	0	Kristiania	0	1908 – 1988	1952, 1953, 1978
Oscar Christian Gundersen	0	Kristiania	0	1908 – 1991	1953, 1953, 1958
Kristian Qvigstad (interim)	0	Tromsø	0	1890	1952, 1952, 1953
Kristian Qvigstad (interim)	0	Tromsø	0	1890	1952, 1953, 1953
Johannes Bratt Andenæs (interim)	0	Innvik	0	1912 – 2003	1952, 1953, 1953
Kristian Qvigstad (interim)	0	Tromsø	0	1890	1953, 1953, 1953
Knut Ingebrikt Robberstad (interim)	0	Askøy	0	1899 – 1981	1953, 1953, 1953
Gulbrand Jensen (interim)	0	Hamar	0	1885	1954, 1954, 1954
Kristian Qvigstad (interim)	0	Tromsø	0	1890	1954, 1954, 1955
Carl Fridtjof Hassel Rode (interim)	0	Kristiania	0	1897 – 1984	1954, 1954, 1954

Gerhardsen III	Socialist			In government (from–to): 22.01.1955–27.08.1963	
					Year
Justice's name	Woman = 1	Birthplace	Chief = 1	Born – Died	Appointed, started, ended
Finn Hiorthøy	0	Kristiania	0	1903 – 1991	1955, 1955, 1973
Carl Fridtjof Hassel Rode	0	Kristiania	0	1897 – 1984	1956, 1956, 1967
Terje Wold	0	Evenes	1	1899 – 1972	1958, 1958, 1969
Trygve Leivestad	0	Tromsø	0	1907 – 1994	1958, 1958, 1977
Atle Roll-Matthiesen	0	Aurland	0	1906 – 1989	1958, 1958, 1976
Andreas Endresen	0	Stavanger	0	1908 – 1985	1959, 1959, 1978
Per Lykke Anker	0	Kristiania	0	1900 – 1983	–, 1962, 1970

Supreme Court Justices 1945–2014, by Appointing Government (*continued*)

Gerhardsen III	Socialist		In government (from–to): 22.01.1955–27.08.1963		
				Year	Year
Justice's name	Woman = 1	Birthplace	Chief = 1	Born – Died	Appointed, started, ended
Carl Fridtjof Hassel Rode (interim)	0	Kristiania	0	1897 – 1984	1955, 1955, 1955
Carl Fridtjof Hassel Rode (interim)	0	Kristiania	0	1897 – 1984	1955, 1955, 1956
Carl Fridtjof Hassel Rode (interim)	0	Kristiania	0	1897 – 1984	1956, 1956, 1956
Gunnar Brun Nissen (interim)	0	Trondheim	0	1897 – 1991	1957, 1957, 1957
Thor A.H. Breien (interim)	0	Kristiana	0	1899	1957, 1957, 1957
Kristian P. F. A. Lunde (interim)	0		0	1900	1958, 1958, 1958
Per Lykke Anker (interim)	0	Kristiania	0	1900 – 1983	1958, 1958, 1958
Kristian P. F. A. Lunde (interim)	0		0	1900	1958, 1958, 1958
Per Lykke Anker (interim)	0	Kristiania	0	1900 – 1983	1958, 1958, 1958
Per Lykke Anker (interim)	0	Kristiania	0	1900 – 1983	1958, 1958, 1958
Eivind Torp Eftestøl (interim)	0	Bergen	0	1899	1959, 1959, 1959
Gunnar Brun Nissen (interim)	0	Trondheim	0	1897 – 1991	1959, 1960, 1960
Gunnar Brun Nissen (interim)	0	Trondheim	0	1897 – 1991	1960, 1960, 1960
Erling Lind (interim)	0		0		1960, –, –
Rolf Semmingsen (interim)	0	Stor-Elvdal	0	1908 – 1979	1960, –, –
Per Lykke Anker (interim)	0	Kristiania	0	1900 – 1983	1960, 1961, 1961
Carl Ludovico Stabel (interim)	0	Kristiania	0	1912 – 1988	1963, 1963, 1963
Erling Lind (interim)	0		0		1963, –, –
Knut Moe (interim)	0		0		–, 1963, 1963
Edv. Raastad (interim)	0		0		1963, –, –
Kristian P. F. A. Lunde (interim)	0		0	1900	1963, 1963, 1963

Supreme Court Justices 1945–2014, by Appointing Government (*continued*)

Gerhardsen IV	Socialist			In government (from–to): 25.09.1963–11.10.1965	
Justice's name	Birthplace	Woman = 1	Chief = 1	Born – Died	Year Appointed, started, ended
Carl Ludovico Stabel	Kristiania	0	0	1912 – 1988	1963, 1964, 1982
Rolv Einar Ryssdal	Laksevåg	0	0	1914 – 1998	1964, 1964, 1969
Arne Z. Trosdahl (interim)		0	0		–, 1965, 1965
Gunnar Brun Nissen (interim)	Trondheim	0	0	1897 – 1991	1964, 1964, 1964
Knut Moe (interim)		0	0		–, 1965, 1965
Kristen Andersen (interim)	Kristiansand	0	0	1907 – 1986	1965, 1965, 1965

Borten	Non-Socialist			In government (from–to): 12.10.1965–16.03.1971	
Justice's name	Birthplace	Woman = 1	Chief = 1	Born – Died	Year Appointed, started, ended
Oscar Christian Gundersen	Kristiania	0	0	1908 – 1991	–, 1967, 1977
Lilly Helena Bolviken	Arendal	1	0	1914 – 2011	1968, 1968, 1984
Jens Christian Mellbye	Kristiania	0	0	1914 – 1993	1968, 1968, 1982
Knut Blom	Kristiania	0	0	1916 – 1996	1968, 1968, 1986
Rolv Einar Ryssdal	Laksevåg	0	1	1914 – 1998	1969, 1969, 1984
Per Tonseth	Arendal	0	0	1914 – 1993	1969, 1969, 1984
Elisabeth Schweigaard Selmer	Kristiania	1	0	1923 – 2009	1970, 1971, 1990
Edv. Raastad (interim)		0	0		1965, –, –
Erling Lind (interim)		0	0		1965, –, –
Arne Z. Trosdahl (interim)		0	0		–, 1967, 1965
Knut Moe (interim)		0	0		–, 1967, 1967

Supreme Court Justices 1945–2014, by Appointing Government (*continued*)

Borten — Non-Socialist — In government (from–to): 12.10.1965–16.03.1971

Justice's name	Woman = 1	Birthplace	Chief = 1	Born – Died	Appointed, started, ended		
					Year		
Mats Stensrud (interim)	0	Trondheim	0	1913	1968,	1968,	1968
Gunnar Brun Nissen (interim)	0	Trondheim	0	1897 – 1991	1969,	1969,	1969
Carl Jacob Arnholm (interim)	0		0	1899 – 1976	1969,	1969,	1969
Eiliv Fougner (interim)	0		0		1969,	1969,	–
Johannes Bratt Andenæs (interim)	0	Innvik	0	1912 – 2003	1969,	1969,	1969
Gustav M. Sverdrup-Thygeson (interim)	0	Kristiania	0	1903 – 2000	1969,	1969,	1969
Jens Fagereng (interim)	0	Lillestrom	0	1908 – 1997	1970,	1970,	1970
Jens Fagereng (interim)	0	Lillestrom	0	1908 – 1997	1970,	1971,	1971

Bratteli I — Socialist — In government (from – to): 17.03.1971–17.10.1972

Justice's name	Woman = 1	Birthplace	Chief = 1	Born – Died	Appointed, started, ended		
					Year		
Sigurd Juell Lorentzen	0	Sunndal	0	1916 – 1979	1972,	1972,	1979
Hans Methlie Michelsen	0	Bergen	0	1920 – 2014	1972,	1972,	1990
Erling Sandene	0	Bærum	0	1921	1972,	1972,	1984

Korvald — Non-Socialist — In government (from–to): 18.10.1972–15.10.1973

Justice's name	Woman = 1	Birthplace	Chief = 1	Born – Died	Appointed, started, ended		
					Year		
Reidar Dick Henriksen (interim)	0	Skien	0	1904	1973,	1973,	1973

Supreme Court Justices 1945–2014, by Appointing Government (*continued*)

Bratteli II	Socialist		In government (from–to): 16.10.1973–14.01.1976		
				Year	Year
Justice's name	Woman = 1	Birthplace	Chief = 1	Born – Died	Appointed, started, ended
Harald Magne Elstad	0	Kristiania	0	1913 – 2003	1973, 1974, 1983
Arne Christiansen	0	Oslo	0	1926 – 2012	1974, 1974, 1996
Helge Rostad	0	Kristiansand S	0	1923 – 1994	1974, 1975, 1993
Reidar Dick Henriksen (interim)	0	Skien	0	1904	1973, 1973, 1973
Reidar Dick Henriksen (interim)	0	Skien	0	1904	1973, 1974, 1974

Nordli	Socialist		In government (from–to): 15.01.1976–03.02.1981		
				Year	Year
Justice's name	Woman = 1	Birthplace	Chief = 1	Born – Died	Appointed, started, ended
Vera Louise Holmøy	1	Oslo	0	1931	1976, 1976, 2001
Einar Løchen	0	Bærum	0	1918 – 2008	1977, 1977, 1985
Egil Endresen	0	Stavanger	0	1920 – 1992	1977, 1977, 1988
Tore Sinding-Larsen	0	Bergen	0	1929	1977, 1977, 1997
Jan Rasmus Skåre	0	Forde	0	1929	1978, 1978, 1998
Gunnar Aasland	0	Bærum	0	1936	1978, 1979, 2006
Rolv Hellesylt	0	Synnylven	0	1927	1979, 1979, 1997
Kristen Syvertsen (interim)	0		0	1913 – 2003	1976, 1976, 1976
Kristen Syvertsen (interim)	0		0	1913 – 2003	1976, 1976, 1976
Erling Haugen (interim)	0		0	1913 – 1980	1978, 1979, 1979

Supreme Court Justices 1945–2014, by Appointing Government (*continued*)

Nordli	Socialist		In government (from–to): 15.01.1976–03.02.1981		
				Year	Year
Justice's name	Woman = 1	Birthplace	Chief = 1	Born – Died	Appointed, started, ended
Kristen Syvertsen (interim)	0		0	1913 – 2003	1979, 1979, 1979
Kristen Syvertsen (interim)	0		0	1913 – 2003	1976, 1980, 1980

Brundtland I	Socialist		In government (from–to): 04.02.1981–13.10.1981		
				Year	Year
Justice's name	Woman = 1	Birthplace	Chief = 1	Born – Died	Appointed, started, ended
Astri Sverdrup Rynning (interim)	1	Sandefjord	0	1915 – 2006	1981, 1981, 1981

Willoch I	Non-Socialist		In government (from–to): 14.10.1981–07.06.1983		
				Year	Year
Justice's name	Woman = 1	Birthplace	Chief = 1	Born – Died	Appointed, started, ended
Jens Bugge	0	Oslo	0	1930	1982, 1982, 2000
Jan Frøystein Halvorsen	0	Oslo	0	1928	1983, 1983, 1995
Kristen Syvertsen (interim)	0		0	1913 – 2003	1982, 1982, 1982
Kristen Syvertsen (interim)	0		0	1913 – 2003	1982, 1982, 1982

Willoch II	Non-Socialist		In government (from–to): 08.06.1983–08.05.1986		
				Year	Year
Justice's name	Woman = 1	Birthplace	Chief = 1	Born – Died	Appointed, started, ended
Charles Philipson	0	Oslo	0	1928 – 1990	1984, 1984, 1990
Nils Peder Langvand	0	Volda	0	1929 – 2002	1984, 1984, 1996
Erling Sandene	0	Bærum	1	1921	1984, 1984, 1991
Trond Dolva	0	Kongsberg	0	1934	1984, 1984, 2004
Finn Backer	0	Oslo	0	1927	1985, 1986, 1997

Supreme Court Justices 1945–2014, by Appointing Government (*continued*)

Willoch II — Non-Socialist — In government (from–to): 08.06.1983–08.05.1986

Justice's name	Woman = 1	Birthplace	Chief = 1	Born – Died	Year Appointed, started, ended
Tore Schei	0	Oslo	0	1946	1985, 1986, 2002
Finn Backer (interim)	0	Oslo	0	1927	1984, 1984, 1984
Finn Backer (interim)	0	Oslo	0	1927	1985, 1984, 1985
Arne Christiansen (interim)	0		0	1938	1985, 1985, 1985
Arne Christiansen (interim)	0		0	1938	1985, 1985, 1986

Brundtland II — Socialist — In government (from–to): 09.05.1986–15.10.1989

Justice's name	Woman = 1	Birthplace	Chief = 1	Born – Died	Year Appointed, started, ended
Liv Gjølstad	1	Tønsberg	0	1945	1988, 1988, 2015
Arne Christiansen (interim)	0		0	1938	1986, 1986, 1987
Carsten Smith (interim)	0	Oslo	0	1932	1987, 1987, 1987
Christian Borchsenius (interim)	0	Oslo	0	1927 – 2006	1989, 1989, 1990
Carsten Smith (interim)	0	Oslo	0	1932	1989, 1989, 1989

Syse — Non-Socialist — In government (from–to): 16.10.1989–02.11.1990

Justice's name	Woman = 1	Birthplace	Chief = 1	Born – Died	Year Appointed, started, ended
Ketil Lund	0	Oslo	0	1939	1990, 1990, 2009
Karenanne Gussgard	1	Sandefjord	0	1940	1990, 1990, 2010
Christian Borchsenius (interim)	0	Oslo	0	1927 – 2006	1990, 1990, 1990
Carsten Smith (interim)	0	Oslo	0	1932	1990, 1990, 1990

Supreme Court Justices 1945–2014, by Appointing Government (*continued*)

Syse	Non-Socialist		In government (from–to): 16.10.1989–02.11.1990			
						Year
Justice's name	Woman = 1	Birthplace	Chief = 1	Born – Died		Appointed, started, ended
Christian Borchsenius (interim)	0	Oslo	0	1927 – 2006		1990, 1990, 1990
Birger Stuevold Lassen (interim)	0	Molde	0	1927 – 2011		1990, 1990, 1990
Magnus Aarbakke (interim)	0	Tysnes	0	1934		1990, 1990, 1990
Birger Stuevold Lassen (interim)	0	Molde	0	1927 – 2011		1990, 1990, 1990
Sverre Dragsten (interim)	0	Selbu	0	1931		1990, 1990, 1990
Ola Rygg (interim)	0		0	1935		1990, 1990, 1991
Brundtland III	**Socialist**		**In government (from–to): 03.11.1990–24.10.1996**			
						Year
Justice's name	Woman = 1	Birthplace	Chief = 1	Born – Died		Appointed, started, ended
Steinar Tjomsland	0	Kristiansand	0	1948		1991, 1991, 2015
Carsten Smith	0	Oslo	1	1932		1991, 1991, 2002
Leif Thomas Eldring	0	Vardø	0	1933 – 1994		1993, 1994, 1994
Kirsti Coward	1	Kristiansand	0	1940		1994, 1994, 2010
Magnus Aarbakke	0	Tysnes	0	1934		1994, 1994, 2002
Johan Eilert Stang Lund	0	Tønsberg	0	1939		1994, 1995, 2009
Lars Oftedal Broch	0	Oslo	0	1939		1996, 1996, 2009
Hans Flock	0	Melhus	0	1940		1996, 1996, 2010
Ola Rygg (interim)	0		0	1935		1991, 1991, 1991
Peter Lødrup (interim)	0	Bærum	0	1932 – 2010		1991, 1991, –
Birger Stuevold Lassen (interim)	0	Molde	0	1927 – 2011		–, 1992, 1992

Supreme Court Justices 1945–2014, by Appointing Government (*continued*)

Brundtland III	Socialist			In government (from–to): 03.11.1990–24.10.1996	
				Year	Year
Justice's name	Woman = 1	Birthplace	Chief = 1	Born – Died	Appointed, started, ended
Birger Stuevold Lassen (interim)	0	Molde	0	1927 – 2011	1992, 1992, 1992
Sverre Dragsten (interim)	0	Selbu	0	1931	1992, 1992, 1992
Peter Lødrup (interim)	0	Bærum	0	1932 – 2010	?, ?, 1992
Christian Borchsenius (interim)	0	Oslo	0	1927 – 2006	1994, 1994, 1994
Peter Lødrup (interim)	0	Bærum	0	1932 – 2010	1994, 1994, 1994
Agnes Nygaard Haug (interim)	1	Oslo	0	1933	1994, 1994, 1995
Erik Arnt Foss (interim)	0	Bergen	0	1926	1994, 1994, 1994
Agnes Nygaard Haug (interim)	1	Oslo	0	1933	1995, 1995, 1995

Jagland	Socialist			In government (from – to): 25.10.1996–16.10.1997	
				Year	Year
Justice's name	Woman = 1	Birthplace	Chief = 1	Born – Died	Appointed, started, ended
Magnus Matningsdal	0	Hå	0	1951	1997, 1997, –
Georg Fredrik Rieber-Mohn	0	Lillehammer	0	1945	1997, 1997, 2007
Karin Maria Bruzelius	1	Lund	0	1941	1997, 1997, 2011
Peter Lødrup (interim)	0	Bærum	0	1932 – 2010	1997, 1997, 1997

Supreme Court Justices 1945–2014, by Appointing Government (*continued*)

Bondevik I	Non-Socialist			In government (from–to): 17.10.1997–16.03.2000	
				Year	Year
Justice's name	Woman = 1	Birthplace	Chief = 1	Born – Died	Appointed, started, ended
Jens Edvin A. Skoghøy	0	Tromsø	0	1955	1998, 1998, –
Karl Arne Utgård	0	Sykkylven	0	1951	1999, 1999, –
Nina Frisak	1	Oslo	0	1950	1999, 2000, 2001
Peter Lødrup (interim)	0	Bærum	0	1932 – 2010	1997, 1998, 1998
Odd Jarl Pedersen (interim)	0	Kristiansand	0	1944 – 2011	1998, 1998, 1998
Odd Jarl Pedersen (interim)	0	Kristiansand	0	1944 – 2011	1998, 1998, 1998
Kai Krüger (interim)	0	København	0	1940	1999, 1999, 1999

Stoltenberg I	Socialist			In government (from–to): 17.03.2000–18.10.2001	
				Year	Year
Justice's name	Woman = 1	Birthplace	Chief = 1	Born – Died	Appointed, started, ended
Ingse Stabel	1	Oslo	0	1946	2001, 2001, –

Bondevik II	Non-Socialist			In government (from–to): 19.10.2001–16.10.2005	
				Year	Year
Justice's name	Woman = 1	Birthplace	Chief = 1	Born – Died	Appointed, started, ended
Ole Bjørn Støle	0	Bergen	0	1950 – 2010	2002, 2002, 2010
Tore Schei	0	Oslo	1	1946	2002, 2002, –
Sverre Mitsem	0	Oslo	0	1944 – 2005	2002, 2002, 2005
Toril Marie Øie	1	Oslo	0	1960	2004, 2004, –

Supreme Court Justices 1945–2014, by Appointing Government (*continued*)

Bondevik II — Non-Socialist

In government (from–to): 19.10.2001–16.10.2005

Justice's name	Woman = 1	Birthplace	Chief = 1	Born – Died (Year)	Appointed, started, ended (Year)		
Henry John Mæland (interim)	0		0	1949	2001,	2001,	2002
Federik Zimmer (interim)	0	Oslo	0	1944	2002,	2002,	2002
Federik Zimmer (interim)	0	Oslo	0	1944	2003,	2003,	2003
Knut Kaasen (interim)	0	Harstad	0	1951	2005,	2005,	2005

Stoltenberg II — Socialist

In government (from–to): 17.10.2005–16.10.2013

Justice's name	Woman = 1	Birthplace	Chief = 1	Born – Died (Year)	Appointed, started, ended (Year)		
Bård Tønder	0	Sjøvegan	0	1948	2006,	2006,	–
Clement Endresen	0	Stavanger	0	1949	2006,	2006,	–
Hilde Indreberg	1	Oslo	0	1957	2007,	2007,	–
Arnfinn Bårdsen	0	Stavanger	0	1966	2007,	2008,	–
Bergljot Webster	1	Oslo	0	1966	2008,	2009,	–
Erik Møse	0	Oslo	0	1950	2008,	2009,	2011
Wilhelm Matheson	0	Oslo	0	1955	2008,	2009,	–
Aage Thor Falkanger	0	Bærum	0	1965	2010,	2010,	2014
Kristin Normann	1	Oslo	0	1954	2010,	2010,	–
Ragnhild Noer	1	Oslo	0	1959	2010,	2010,	–
Henrik Bull	0	Oslo	0	1957	2010,	2011,	–
Knut Herbrand Kallerud	0	Kongsberg	0	1956	2011,	2011,	–
Per Erik Bergsjø	0	Levanger	0	1958	2011,	2012,	–
Knut Kaasen (interim)	0	Harstad	0	1951	2005,	2006,	2006

Supreme Court Justices 1945–2014, by Appointing Government (*continued*)

Stoltenberg II	Socialist			In government (from–to): 17.10.2005–16.10.2013	
				Year	Year
Justice's name	Woman = 1	Birthplace	Chief = 1	Born – Died	Appointed, started, ended
Tone Sverdrup (interim)	1	Oslo	0	1951	2006, 2006, 2006
Tone Sverdrup (interim)	1	Oslo	0	1951	2006, 2007, 2007
Federik Zimmer (interim)	0	Oslo	0	1944	2007, 2007, 2007
Aage Thor Falkanger (interim)	0	Bærum	0	1965	2007, 2007, 2007
Aage Thor Falkanger (interim)	0	Bærum	0	1965	2007, 2007, 2007
Tone Sverdrup (interim)	1	Oslo	0	1951	2007, 2007, 2008
Knut Kaasen (interim)	0	Harstad	0	1951	2007, 2008, 2008
Aage Thor Falkanger (interim)	0	Bærum	0	1965	2008, 2009, 2009
Tone Sverdrup (interim)	1	Oslo	0	1951	2009, 2009, 2009
Kirsten Sandberg (interim)	1	Oslo	0	1954	2010, 2010, 2011
Eirik Akerlie (interim)	0	Nes, Hallingdal	0	1958	2011, 2011, 2011
Finn Arnesen (interim)	0	Oslo	0	1962	2011, 2011, 2011
Finn Arnesen (interim)	0	Oslo	0	1962	2011, 2012, 2012
Solberg	**Non-Socialist**			**In government (from–to): 16.10.2013 – …**	
				Year	Year
Justice's name	Woman = 1	Birthplace	Chief = 1	Born – Died	Appointed, started, ended
Arne Ringnes	0		0	1955	2014, 2014, –
Wenche Elizabeth Arntzen	1	Oslo	0	1959	2014, 2014, –
Rune Sæbø (interim)	0		0	1960	2013, 2014, 2014
Knut Kaasen (interim)	0	Harstad	0	1951	2013, 2014, 2014

Appendix B: The Ideology of Norwegian Supreme Court Justices

In 2011 we mapped the ideological position of the most recent Supreme Court justices. The effort was motivated by the public debate that followed our earliest publications on judicial behaviour. Among the participants in the debate, there was agreement that justices did hold ideological positions and that these positions were likely to influence the justices' decision making. The research questions that remained unanswered were in what ways these positions influence the justices' decisions and in which legal fields or on which issues these ideological positions were activated. A first effort was to establish a measure of ideological position that could complement the common measure – i.e. our use of the government that had appointed the justice as a proxy for ideology (Grendstad, Shaffer, and Waltenburg 2011; Pinello 1999).

Expert surveys are considered efficient and valid ways of measuring allegedly elusive concepts (Mair 2001; Steenbergen and Marks 2007). From lists of Supreme Court bar lawyers[1] published in the December 2010 issue of *Advokatbladet* (*'Lawyers Monthly'*), we compiled a list of 310 lawyers with verifiable email addresses. We emailed these lawyers a very short questionnaire where they were asked to rate the 24 most recent justices and two interim justices on a seven-point, left–right (radical–conservative, or liberal–conservative) ideological scale. The response rate was 34.5 per cent.

The left–right positions of the 26 justices are shown in Figure B.1. Five groups can be identified. Justices Matheson and Normann are clearly seen as conservative, whereas Justices Coward and Stabel are clearly seen as radical. Justice Noer and Interim Justice Sandberg constitute a third group as moderate radicals. The final two groups are separated by the mean position of all justices. Immediate analyses of the expert survey showed that female justices were more radical than male justices, and that justices who previously had served at the Legislation Department in the Ministry of Justice were more radical than justices without such service. The measure of perceived left–right ideological position does not correlate with the cruder measure of government appointment.

The expert survey was published by the authors in 2012 in *Lov og Rett* vol 50 (4), and is reprinted here with the publisher's permission.

---

1. I.e. *'Høyesterettsadvokater'* or *'Advokater med møterett for Høyesterett'*.

Figure B.1: Ideological Positions of Norwegian Supreme Court Justices 2011

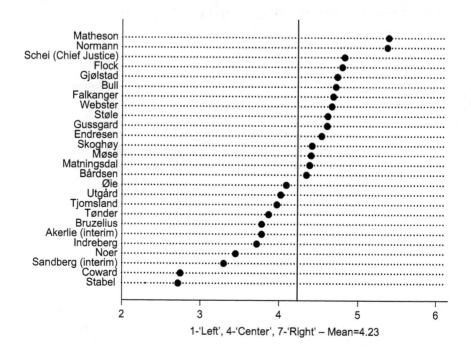

1-'Left', 4-'Center', 7-'Right' – Mean=4.23

References

Grendstad, Gunnar, William R. Shaffer, and Eric N. Waltenburg (2011) 'Ikke til verden av politisk hvite storker', *Lov og Rett* 50 (7): 432–442.

— (2012) 'Ideologi og grunnholdninger hos dommerne i Norges Høyesterett', *Lov og Rett* 51 (4): 240–253.

Mair, Peter (2001) 'Searching for the Positions of Political Actors. A Review of Approaches and a Critical Evaluation of Expert Surveys', in M. Laver (ed.) *Estimating the Policy Positions of Political Actors*, London: Routledge.

Pinello, Daniel R. (1999) 'Linking party to judicial ideology in American courts: A meta-analysis', *Justice System Journal* 20 (3): 219–254.

Steenbergen, Marco R., and Gary Marks (2007) 'Evaluating expert judgments', *European Journal of Political Research* 46 (3): 347–366.

Index

Numbers in italics refer to material in Figures and Tables